A Programmed Course in Self-Discipline

Joseph M. Strayhorn, Jr., M.D.

Psychological Skills Press
Wexford, Pennsylvania

Published by:
Psychological Skills Press
263 Seasons Drive
Wexford, Pennsylvania 15090
 www.psyskills.com

Author's email: joestrayhorn@juno.com

ISBN: 1-931773-10-6

Contents

Introduction

Self-discipline is one of the most important skills that a human being can possess. It can make the difference between success and failure as a student. It can determine whether or not a person is successful in a career. It can make the difference between a happy relationship and a failed relationship. It can make the difference between peaceful conflict resolution and violence.

It is the ability to work for long-term goals, and to avoid getting sidetracked onto whatever is most pleasant at a given moment. Thus possessing this skill lets a person accomplish any long-term goal more readily.

It goes by various names, in addition to self-discipline, most notably self-control and skill in delay of gratification.

There are millions of people who suffer greatly from shortage of self-discipline skills. Yet if my clinical experience may be extrapolated, the fraction of these who have taken a course in self-discipline, or who have read one book about how to gain it, is approximately zero. Those who have visited doctors or therapists have often received little or no instruction in how to promote their own self-discipline.

If this skill is so important, why is it not more often systematically taught? Surely learning how to increase self-discipline is more important than memorizing state capitals. And even though I love teaching math, I must admit that many students will never have to solve a quadratic equation after they finish studying algebra. But approximately every day of their lives they will be called upon to exercise self-discipline in some way or another. Why is the skill of self-discipline not widely taught, while vastly larger amounts of time are spent on less crucial skills?

Part of the answer to this question is that until recently, we had not done sufficient research on self-discipline to know exactly what to tell the student of this subject. And even now, our research knowledge is still rapidly accumulating. I've had the privilege of reviewing this research in great detail. I feel that we now know enough to teach students very useful ideas about how to cultivate this essential skill.

Another reason that self-discipline is not taught like other school subjects is that time is in short supply, and time must be spent on "basic" subjects. The most basic of subjects are reading and writing. I thoroughly agree with principals' and teachers' putting a high priority on reading and writing. For that reason, I have tried to make this book conducive to practice in both reading comprehension and writing.

To improve reading comprehension, a central exercise is for the student to read a bit of information and to answer a question on it. Indeed, answering questions on material one has just read is the main way in which reading comprehension is tested, on individual tests of reading comprehension and group standardized tests from first grade level up. This book is written in the format where one question follows each small chunk of information. The student who reads it can get much practice in reading comprehension.

One format that is particularly useful is one in which a learner and a preceptor take turns reading sections to each other. The learner answers the question on each section, and the preceptor enthusiastically reinforces the learner for correct answers.

Another format that gives even more practice in reading comprehension is one in which the preceptor and the tutor take turns reading the sections aloud; the learner answers the question; and the one who did not read the section aloud does a "reflection" of it, or paraphrases it in his or her own words. This is an even more rigorous and demanding exercise in reading comprehension and language expression. While it is possible to guess the answer to a two-choice question half the time without comprehending the section, it is not possible to do reflections of sections without comprehending.

For writing, practice is crucial to increasing skill. One of the exercises this book stresses is the "fantasy rehearsal." A fantasy rehearsal of self-discipline is a narrative of a successful use of this skill, which includes the thoughts, emotions, and behaviors of the person who is handling the self-discipline challenge well. Fantasy rehearsals can be written as well as spoken. For a student to accumulate a large portfolio of written fantasy rehearsals of responses to self-discipline choice points is a major practice in the subject of writing, as well as in the subject of self-discipline.

Another way of practicing writing within this course is for the student to write essays on the "Topics for Writing or Discussion" at the end of each chapter. These should be a sufficient challenge that almost almost all learners will not find the course "too easy."

If the learner has "tuned in" to the information presented, answering the question at the end of each section should not be very difficult. The questions help keep the learner actively engaged, give the learner challenges, and make the learner more than a passive recipient of the information. The questions give a teacher an idea of whether the student is taking in the information.

Some people, upon seeing that the learner gets almost all the questions right, infer that the material is too easy or that the learner already knows it.

This is a mistake. Getting questions correct means that the learner is paying attention and doing what should be done. It doesn't mean "Do something else"; it means "Keep up the good work."

I am very interested in hearing about your experiences in using this book. Any teacher or learner is invited to email me at joestrayhorn@juno.com.

Checklist of Techniques for Meeting Goals

How much do you use each of these, for each particular goal?

1. Careful goal selection. Did you select the goal carefully, thinking about what is most ethical and worthy of your effort?
2. Goal written, specifically. Have you written the goal, describing specifically what achieving it would be like? Do you read those words often?
3. Internal sales pitch. Have you written an internal sales pitch, and do you read those words often?
4. Plans. Do you write overall plans and daily plans for how you will achieve your goals?
5. Hierarchy of difficulty. Do you make resolutions that are neither too hard nor too easy for your current skill?
6. List of choice points. Have you listed the most important self-discipline choice points?
7. Decisions. Have you decided clearly what you would like to do, think, and feel in those choice point situations?
8. Rehearsals. Do you often do fantasy rehearsals of triumphing in those choice points? Do you frequently practice the skills you need?
9. Self-reinforcement. Do you use self-reinforcement for bits of progress toward your goal, immediately after such successes?
10. Celebrations exercise. Do you think back and recall your triumphs, and feel good about them?
11. External reinforcement. Do you use external rewards for your triumphs?
12. Self-monitoring. Do you frequently monitor your progress toward your goal, using numbers?
13. Advanced self-discipline. Do you use techniques such as selective attention to learn to enjoy work toward the goal?
14. Work capacity. Do you use "exposure" and "habituation" to increase your work capacity? Do you believe in the effort-payoff connection?
15. Stimulus control. Do you avoid tempting situations?
16. Routines and momentum. Do you try to keep habits and precedents on your side?
17. Organization. Are you using organization techniques?
18. Twelve thoughts. Do you choose consciously among twelve types of thoughts?
19. Modeling. Do you collect positive models, and avoid negative ones?
20. Frequently reading instructions. Do you keep reading about how to accomplish this goal?
21. Time on task. Are you devoting enough time to get the job done?
22. Restoring persistence power. Do you use techniques to restore your persistence power?

Chapter 1: The Meaning and Worth of Self-Discipline

What Is Self-Discipline?

1. This course is meant to teach you one of the most important skills that anyone can have: self-discipline. Having this skill means that you do well in a certain type of situation, called a "self-discipline choice point" or a "self-discipline challenge."

In these situations, there is something that you can do that you think will make things come out better in the long run. There is something different that you could do, that would feel better in the short run. Self-discipline means doing what you think will make things better in the long run, even though it is less pleasant at the moment.

Self-discipline involves

A. doing what feels best now,
or
B. doing what makes things turn out best in the long run?

2. There are many different situations where you have to do something less pleasant now if you want to get something more pleasant in the future. Here are some examples of those self-discipline choice points:

If you want to do well on a test, you have to study instead of spending all the study time watching TV or playing with friends.

If you want to keep from getting cavities, you have to spend time brushing your teeth, even though it might be more pleasant to skip that job.

If you want to be more rested in the morning when it's time to get up, you have to go to bed earlier than you might feel like going to bed.

If you want to have money to use for something important, you have to pass up the urge to spend all your money as soon as you get it.

What do these four situations have in common?

A. They all are self-discipline choice points,
or
B. some are for health and some are for achievement?

3. Here are some more examples of self-discipline choice points.

If you want to keep a friend, you keep yourself from saying mean things to that friend, even though you may feel like it sometimes.

If you want to win a mile run in a track meet, you will have to run and work out lots of times when it would be more pleasant to lie around and relax.

For these two examples, what would you call keeping a friend and winning a track race?

A. goals that you use self-discipline to get,
or
B. things that are pleasant now, but get in the way of your goals?

4.   Here are more self-discipline choice points.

   If you want to have good judgment and live your life well, you will have to stay away from a bunch of illegal drugs that might make you feel good for a while after taking them.

   If you want to get your work done well, you will probably have to spend time organizing your time and tasks and papers, even though it would feel more pleasant to do lots of other things than to get things organized.

The short-term good feeling a drug addict gets from drugs can be called a *temptation* that gets in the way of long-term goals. The fun of playing when you should be getting organized is another temptation. What are the long-term goals those two temptations can mess up?

A. Having the good sense that you get from being off addictive drugs, and the work you get done by being organized,
or

B. the short-term bad taste of a drug and the short-term fun of putting things away?

5.   All these examples have something in common. In all of them, if you want some really good thing in the future, you have to give up some pleasure or put up with some discomfort right now. The good thing in the future is called the long-term goal. The more fun thing you have to give up is called the temptation. In self-discipline choice points, choosing the temptation would get in the way of the long-term goal.

   A person has a goal of doing well on a test. Watching TV or playing with friends can be a temptation that gets in the way of that goal.

Another person has a goal of losing some weight. If that person gets the urge to eat a whole apple pie all at once, that urge would be

A. a temptation,
or
B. a long-term goal?

6. Someone really wants to feel rested in the morning, and to be wide awake for school during the day. But she knows it will be fun to stay up really late the night before school. She decides that the pleasure of feeling rested and awake the next day is greater than the pleasure of staying up late.

Which of these is the temptation?

A. the fun of staying up late,
or
B. feeling rested and wide awake the next day?

7. We have been focusing so far on the meaning of self-discipline.

What does self-discipline mean?

A. Avoiding things that are fun,
or
B. passing up temptations, to meet goals?

8. In self-discipline choice points, there is a contest between the temptation and the long-term goal. The temptation is to get the most enjoyment and avoid the most discomfort right now. The long-term goal is to make things come out well in the future.

Sometimes it's fun to think of the wish for the temptation and the wish for the long-term goal as two parts of yourself, and to make up a dialogue between them. For example:

Temptation: Oh boy. Here comes a good television show. Of course I'll watch it! It will be fun!
Long-term goal: Not so fast! Aren't you forgetting about me? I'm the one who'll be taking that test tomorrow. I hate it when you don't prepare me enough, and I have to guess answers. And I'm the one who'll be getting back the grade

three days from now! I'll be embarrassed if it's a bad grade.
Temptation: Oh. But this show will be so interesting! It will be so much more fun than studying. Come on, just this time?

The part of the self who is arguing for a self-disciplined choice is

A. the temptation
or
B. the long-term goal?

9. There is a lot more of the future than there is of the present. For that reason, it's often very wise to use self-discipline. But the pleasure from the temptation is available right now! For that reason, temptations are often hard to pass up.

Suppose that someone really wants to win a mile run in a track meet. He is thinking about whether to run and work out or lie around and listen to music. He's in the mood to lie around and listen to music at this time, but if he does so he'll not have time to run today.

The wish to lie around and listen to music is

A. the temptation,
or
B. the long-term goal?

Self-Discipline and Success

10. How successful do you want your life to be? Do you want to enjoy life, have good friends, have a happy family, do well in your job, have lots of money, and make the world a better place? There are lots of smart and talented people who fail at these things, because they don't have enough self-discipline. If you make very strong your skill of working toward long-term goals, and not getting sidetracked by temptations, you have a much higher chance of success in life.

The last section said that
A. Very few people have excellent self-discipline,
or
B. self-discipline makes success more likely?

11. A man named Walter Mischel did experiments with preschool aged children. Here's an experiment that is like one of Mischel's. Suppose you show the child one little marshmallow, and say, "You can eat this now if you want. But if you wait, and keep yourself from eating it, you can have five marshmallows when I come back into the room. I'm leaving now." Then you leave the room and leave the child alone with the marshmallow. But you watch the child through a one-way mirror or videotape. You record what the child does. You time how long the child lasts before eating the marshmallow.

In the type of experiment Mischel made famous, the long-term goal for the child is

A. five marshmallows,
or
B. one marshmallow?

12. Remember that self-discipline means passing up temptations so that you can be more likely to achieve a long-term goal.

In the type of experiment just described, the one marshmallow right now would be called the

A. temptation,
or
B. long-term goal?

13. Some of the children in this experiment could keep from eating the marshmallow for 15 or 20 minutes until the experimenter came back into the room. Others ate it right away. Others lasted for a while before eating it.

This is a self-discipline challenge or choice point. The five marshmallows in fifteen or twenty minutes is the long-term goal, and the one marshmallow now is the temptation. The task measured how much self-discipline the children had for that particular challenge.

Why are five marshmallows in 15 minutes called a long-term goal here?

A. Because they were the payoff that the child had to pass up a temptation to get, in this experiment,

or

B. because marshmallows are typical of the types of payoffs people usually use self-discipline to get in life?

14. Years later, Walter Mischel managed to find most of these children when they had gotten to be high school kids. He asked their parents to rate how good they were at making decisions. He also looked at their SAT standardized test scores. The children who had been able to wait longer for the bigger reward, the ones who were more self-disciplined, were rated as better decision-makers by their parents, and they also did better on the SAT test.

Which explanation for why these kids did better on the SAT test fits better with the point of this experiment?

A. They were just smarter,

or

B. they had the self-discipline to study more, to check their answers more carefully, or to concentrate instead of daydreaming?

15. Doing well on the SAT test can be very important for someone's career. But it's certainly not the highest and most important goal of living. Do you think it is likely that the Mischel's more self-disciplined children will eventually go on to achieve more important goals,

such as more improvement of the world, greater happiness in their own lives, and greater contribution to others' happiness? If they choose worthy goals, I believe it's likely. When you define self-discipline as the ability to work toward goals without getting sidetracked by the temptations, it's much more likely that more self-disciplined people will meet their goals.

The above paragraph implies that of all the goals that are fostered by greater self-discipline,

A. nothing is more important than SAT scores,

or

B. making a contribution to others' happiness, and to your own, is more important than test scores.

16. What if the preschool children who couldn't wait for the five marshmallows in Mischel's experiment had been able to study and practice the ideas in this book, very carefully? Could they have improved their ability to wait for marshmallows? Could they have gotten better SAT scores? Could they contribute more to the world and be happier?

The idea of this book is that you don't have to stick with the same degree of self-discipline that you had as a preschooler. You can improve the skill of self-discipline just as you improve any other skill such as typing or dancing or playing the piano or doing math. One of the most important ways to improve any of these skills is to practice it.

The author of this book believes that

A. self-discipline is a skill in which you can improve,
or
B. self-discipline stays the same whatever you do?

Self-Discipline Is Not A Fear of Pleasure or a Wish for Pain

17. Someone says, "I don't want to be self-disciplined. I want to have fun!" This person probably doesn't remember that self-discipline is not just passing up something pleasurable. It's passing up something pleasurable in order to get something even better later. People with very low self-discipline tend to be very unhappy, and those with high self-discipline tend to be much happier. Self-discipline is giving up a marshmallow to get five of them later; it's not just throwing the marshmallow away!

The idea you've just read is that

A. using self-discipline makes you much happier than failing to use it,
or
B. the people with no self-discipline are very happy but they don't get much work done?

18. In a movie, *Lawrence of Arabia*, the main character did an exercise where he closed his fingertips upon the head of a burning match. In this course in self-discipline, do we recommend that you get some matches and light them, and train yourself to put them out in this way, even though it will blister your fingertips? Would this be a good example of self-discipline?

This certainly would represent choosing an option that is not pleasant in the short run, wouldn't it? But something is missing. Where is the long-term payoff? What is the goal that is accomplished? Maybe the man wanted to prove to himself that he could put up with pain. Sometimes it's very useful to prove this to yourself. But couldn't he have picked a way to do it that wouldn't hurt his body? Self-discipline does not mean hurting yourself for no good reason.

If you agree with the last paragraph, which of the following ways to practice self-discipline will you think is better?

A. sticking needles through your skin,
or
B. passing up junk food for a while?

19. Passing up something pleasant or doing something unpleasant makes sense when it helps you work toward a worthy goal. There are lots of worthy things that need to be done in this world, that require lots of self-

discipline. It's not necessary to do useless things to practice self-discipline.

Which of the following two activities do you think the author likes better as a way of practicing self-discipline?

A. Working very long and very carefully to help build a house for someone who couldn't otherwise afford one,
or
B. taking a long hike out into the woods and back again, while putting up with lots of biting insects and thorny brambles?

20. Some people (not very many) try to pass up pleasure, even when the pleasure does not get in the way of a long-term goal. A word that describes this philosophy is *ascetic*. This course teaches something very different: that pleasure is good, but we often have to pass it up in order to accomplish a worthy goal in the future.

If you agree that the point of self-discipline is to accomplish a worthy goal, not just to prove you can take pain, which of the following two ways of practicing self-discipline will you like better?

A. seeing how long you can stand in freezing weather without a jacket,
or
B. seeing how long you can do math problems with speed and accuracy?

21. Some people, especially teenaged females, have a problem called anorexia nervosa. They pass up the pleasure of fattening food. They also pass up the pleasure of nourishing food. They get skinnier and skinnier. They would look lots better if they gained weight. Some of them actually die from not eating enough. It is very hard to pass up food and stay hungry all the time. But the goal if thinness gets pushed so far that it isn't useful, and in fact is harmful.

Is it a great example of self-discipline when someone with anorexia nervosa passes up food?

A. Yes, because you have to be very tough and strong to do this,
or
B. No, because extreme thinness that's dangerous to health is not a worthy goal?

22. Anorexia nervosa is not a good example of self-discipline, for the same reason we talked about earlier. When using self-discipline, you pass up present rewards to get better rewards in the future. You don't pass up present rewards to get results that harm you or possibly even kill you.

Fear of pleasure and wish for pain are NOT good things to have. Self-discipline is a very good thing to have. It's very important for people to be able to know the difference.

The person with self-discipline usually

A. puts off pleasure now so as to be lots happier later,
or
B. puts off pleasure now so as to be very miserable later?

23. Suppose you see someone goofing off with a friend. She and her friend are laughing, saying silly things, and having a great time. The result of this is that they feel friendlier to each other than they did before. Now would someone more self-disciplined have sat looking stone-faced and serious instead? The person in this little story could have been one of the most self-disciplined people in the world. She was not in a self-discipline choice point. She didn't have to delay gratification. It was perfectly fine for her to have fun in this way. Self-discipline means making good choices. Choosing to have fun when it's a good idea is something that truly self-disciplined people do well.

When you get the opportunity to do something pleasurable right now, do you always have to put it off till later, if you want to be a self-disciplined person?

A. Yes, because that's what self-discipline is,
or
B. No, because not all situations are self-discipline choice points.

24. In the situations where you don't have to choose between present fun and future fun, it's good to be able to enjoy the present. I once saw a video of a man named Richard Feynman, having fun with his friends. He was banging upon a bongo drum, and chanting, over and over, "Oh, I like my orange juice! Oh, I like my orange juice!" He was having a great time acting silly. When he wasn't banging on bongo drums, he did some of the most productive and brilliant work in physics that the world has seen. His chanting party was not a failure to use self-discipline. His gleefulness probably made it easier for him to use self-discipline later on.

Productive people know how to "recharge their batteries." They know that self-discipline is easier to do when you also get some present enjoyment. Having fun is not in competition with being self-disciplined. The two cooperate with each other. It's easier to use self-discipline if you can have fun, and it's easier to enjoy yourself if you can use self-discipline.

The author believes that self-discipline is

A. easier if you have good skills of gleefulness,
or
B. harder if you have good skills of gleefulness?

Three More Concepts

25. A very close relative of self-discipline is called *work capacity*. How much work of a certain sort can you get done in a day, week, or year? How long can you keep working at one time without needing to stop? How quickly do you get a burning desire to stop working and entertain yourself by goofing off for a while, versus how much can you entertain yourself while working toward your goals? The ability to keep working toward a goal, of course, helps very much in achieving that goal.

A different way of saying the previous sentence is

A. greater work capacity increases your chance of success,
or
B. you should not take breaks from your work?

26. Part of the way people increase their work capacity and their self-discipline is by *habituation*. Habituation means "getting used to it." Someone at first can't stand to do homework for more than fifteen minutes without stopping, but he pushes himself do work for longer and longer. The more experience he gets with working for longer times, the more he gets used to it. It isn't so unpleasant as it was before. As he habituates to working, he becomes able to work for a couple of hours without stopping.

Another example of habituation is

A. getting used to swimming in cool water, once you've been in it a few seconds,
or
B. deciding which goals are most important?

27. I made up the phrase *advanced self-discipline* to refer to a very important accomplishment. When you use advanced self-discipline, you gradually train yourself to *enjoy* the activities and choices that accomplish your long-term goals. For example, someone starts on an exercise program. At first, it is very unpleasant to exercise. The person uses ordinary self-discipline to make himself keep running. But gradually, something changes. The person trains himself to take pleasure from running. He looks forward to his runs. Now his long-term motive and his short-term motive are less in conflict with each other. He can use some of his self-discipline energy on something else.

Advanced self-discipline means

A. being so tough that you can put up with any amount of pain to reach your goal,
or
B. training yourself to enjoy doing what helps reach your goal?

28. A student doesn't like math. The student starts devoting lots of effort

toward getting better at math. At first, this effort is unpleasant, and it takes lots of ordinary self-discipline for the student to make herself keep going. But after working very hard for many days, the student gets skilled enough that she can see the beauty and the fun in math. She starts to enjoy it. She looks forward to it. Now she doesn't have to use up so much energy to make herself do it, and she can use that energy somewhere else. She is now using advanced self-discipline.

Another example of advanced self-discipline occurs when

A. a person makes himself organize his papers, although he doesn't enjoy doing this,
or
B. a piano student gradually starts enjoying piano practice?

29. Let's review some of the important ideas you've read so far.

Dierdre gets a note from Sally. The note says, "Dierdre Ill see you in 2 howers." Dierdre thinks it's funny how Sally has misspelled the word *hours*. Dierdre gets the urge to show the note to another friend, so that they can laugh together at the misspelling. This would be lots of fun for a little while. But Dierdre thinks it's likely that Sally would find out, and she would feel very bad about being laughed at. Dierdre's relationship with Sally would be harmed.

The situation Dierdre finds herself in is called

A. work capacity
or
B. a self-discipline choice point?

30. In this situation, as in all other self-discipline choice points, there is a temptation that competes with a long-term goal.

In this situation, what do we call the wish to have fun laughing at Sally and the wish to have a good relationship with Sally?

A. the first is the temptation and the second is the long-term goal,
or
B. the first is advanced self-discipline and the second is habituation?

31. Jeffrey goes to a party where other people are drinking alcohol. Someone offers him a beer, and Jeffrey says "No, thanks." The other kid says, "Aw, come on!" Jeffrey ignores him and moves on to talk with someone else.

Jeffrey recalls that the first time this ever happened to him, he felt self-conscious and uneasy about not doing what the other person wanted him to do. But by now, he has had so much experience with turning down booze that he does it automatically and doesn't feel bad in the slightest.

Jeffrey's change is probably due to

A. habituation,
or
B. a short-term motive?

32. Another important idea is that you work on self-discipline in order to enjoy life more. It is not about being glum and grim all the time.

Jane is having some fun and enjoyment that lasts only a short time. Is Jane failing to use self-discipline when she should be using it?

A. Yes, because she is not working for a long-term goal,
or
B. We can't tell, because we don't know whether she's in a self-discipline choice point, "recharging her batteries," or just using an opportunity to enjoy life.

33. Ralph is taking a test. He has taught himself to look at the test as he would an athletic contest. He has trained and prepared for the test with eager effort. He thinks that he has gotten all the questions right so far, and as he approaches the last few questions his heart pounds with excitement at the thought that he might get a perfect score. He concentrates with all he's got, and as he turns in the test he feels very much like he does when he has won a tennis match. He has actually had a really good time.

His enjoyment of seeking his goal is an example of

A. low work capacity,
or
B. advanced self-discipline?

34. Steve has his first meeting with a tutor. Five minutes after they have gotten started, Steve takes a bathroom break. After they have worked for five minutes more, Steve wants to stop working and just chat for a while. After they work five minutes more, Steve wants to go outside and walk around to take a break.

The tutor might correctly think,

A. "He has a fear of pleasure,"
or
B. "He needs more work capacity"?

35. Let's tie some of these ideas together. It takes self-discipline to work for long-term goals and to pass up the temptations that would distract you from them. The more you work on long-term goals, the more you get used to working on them. Through habituation, you increase your work capacity. And if you make a lot of good choices, you may learn to use advanced self-discipline, so that you actually enjoy working toward your goals. If you have chosen worthy long-term goals, achieving them makes you successful and happy.

What does this course aim to help you get, by self-discipline?

A. habituation and temptations,
or
B. success and happiness?

Topics for Writing and Discussion

You can use the following questions as topics for written essays, or for discussion with your preceptor or classmates.

1. Please visualize someone who is a "self-discipline hero." What sort of person do you bring to mind? In what sorts of self-discipline choice points does this person triumph?
Is there such a thing as a stereotype of self-discipline?

2. In your life, how much have you ever read, spoken, or heard about the idea of self-discipline, or any other phrase that means the same thing? Do you think that in our culture, the idea gets more attention than it deserves, or less attention than it deserves?

3. What do you think about the author's belief that people can learn to improve their self-discipline skills? Do you think that this is true, or that people are born with a certain amount of self-discipline that can't be changed? Or do you want to wait until you've heard more about exactly how people can work on this skill?

4. Do you think it's possible to have too much self-discipline? Or do you think that the more you have, the better?

5. Please imagine two classes in a school. In the first class, all the kids have lots of self-discipline. In the second, all the kids have almost no self-discipline. Which class would you like to be a part of? What do you think these classes would be like?

6. How important is it for you that someone have self-discipline, if that person is your favorite model, taxi driver, spouse, parent, child, president of your country, or favorite musician?

Chapter 2: Types of Self-Discipline Choice Points

36. If you develop good self-discipline skills, you can use these skills millions of times during your lifetime, in all sorts of seemingly different situations. In this chapter we will think about some of the different types of self-discipline choice points. If you develop good skills in one type of self-discipline choice point, it is probably a lot easier to transfer those skills to a different type of self-discipline choice point. For example, someone who learns to stick to a very healthy diet may find it easier to stick to a healthy sleep schedule.

Another example of transferring self-discipline skills from one type of choice point to another is

A. taking the self-discipline skills you use for sports training and using those same skills for anger control,
or
B. taking the self-discipline skills you use for anger control and teaching them to someone else.

37. Before reading the following list, you may find it useful or fun to make your own list. How many types of self-discipline choice points can you think of? Can you think of an important type that I didn't list?

You are being asked to think of types of choice points such as:

A. not putting off work, controlling your temper, and getting out of bed on time,
or
B. being able to remember lots of things, being able to react quickly, and being able to run fast?

38. Here is the list of ways to use self-discipline. You'll notice that there are three main areas: productivity, relations with people, and self-care.

Types of Self-Discipline Choice Points

Productivity and achievement:
1. Concentrating versus attending to whatever's most interesting at the moment.
2. Working versus goofing off
3. Choosing when to work versus procrastinating
4. Planning ahead versus failing to plan
5. Organizing and putting things away

Human Relations:
6. Kindness versus selfishness
7. Honesty versus deception
8. Keeping commitments versus being a no-show
9. Frustration-tolerance versus tantrums
10. Calm nonviolence, controlling your temper, versus verbal or physical aggression

11. Complying with reasonable authority versus ignoring or defying authority

Taking Care of Yourself:
12. Saving versus spending
13. Gambling versus taking only wise risks.
14. Healthy diet versus eating whatever is pleasurable
15. Exercising versus inactivity
16. Safety-consciousness versus not worrying about safety
17. Medical self-care versus not bothering with self-care
18. Keeping regular sleep cycles
19. Avoiding addictive drugs versus using addictive drugs
20. Making wise choices about sexual activity
21. Tolerating low stimulation versus stimulus-seeking
22. Courage skills versus unrealistic fear

What were the headings for the three groups of self-discipline choice points?

A. dedication, commitment, and integrity
or
B. productivity and achievement, human relations, and self-care?

39. Now let's think about each of these in a little more detail.

Concentration

Suppose that you have a homework assignment to do. Let's say you are doing some math problems. Halfway into the first problem, it occurs to you that it would be more pleasant to have a daydream about what you are going to do over the weekend than it would be to think about math. What type of situation is this? It's a self-discipline choice point. There is one option that gets the math homework accomplished more quickly, more efficiently, and with more time to daydream afterwards. There's another option that is more pleasant at this particular instant.

In the example you just read, daydreaming is the

A. temptation,
or
B. the long-term goal?

40. Self-discipline choice points having to do with directing your attention occur very frequently. Suppose someone is driving a car. The person is very interested in something his friend in the car is saying, and he wants to look at the person while talking to him. It is much more interesting to look at and talk with the friend than to watch the road and other cars. Looking at the friend and forgetting about the road is the temptation.

The long-term goal for this self-discipline choice point is

A. not getting killed in a car accident, or
B. not missing anything the friend has to say?

41. Being able to turn your attention where you want it to go appears to be very useful for all sorts of other self-discipline challenges. If you want to make something more pleasant or less unpleasant, you can turn your attention toward the pleasant parts of it and away from the unpleasant parts.

Someone who is using "advanced self-discipline" for doing lots of schoolwork should

A. pay close attention to how much progress she is making in the work, or
B. pay close attention to the nice weather, and all the things she can't do outside because she is studying?

Working Versus Goofing Off

42. A boy has an important test in school tomorrow. Instead of studying, he is surfing the Internet.

A man is out of money. He owes money to people who are getting mad at him because he isn't paying it back. Instead increasing his work and making more money, he spends more time playing pool with friends, to take his mind off his troubles.

A man is really ashamed of how his apartment looks really trashed. He doesn't feel like having friends over. But instead of cleaning it up, he gets away from his troubles by watching a TV movie.

A society is troubled by problems of violence, poverty, ignorance, pollution, and disease. But instead of devoting most of human effort to solving these problems, the people in this society work for large amounts of time in sports, gambling casinos, movies, rock concerts, television shows, and electronic entertainment. The whole society has a self-discipline problem!

In all the examples you just read, it would have been better for people to

A. do more useful work, or
B. entertain themselves more?

43. What is work, anyway? It's effort that you do to accomplish a certain goal. The people who work are much more likely to accomplish goals than those who are addicted to goofing off.

This paragraph defines the word "work" as

A. something that someone makes you do that is not fun, or

B. putting out effort to try to accomplish a goal?

44. Sometimes, some people can't get much work done, even when other people are spending lots of energy trying to get them to do so. At other times, people can do work, but only immediately after other people command or request or remind them to work. But at other times, some people can figure out what needs to be done, assign tasks to themselves, and get to work on these tasks without needing someone else to nag or remind them. Getting going on what needs to be done, without having to be commanded or reminded, is called *self-starting*, or taking *initiative*.

What's an advantage of having lots of self-starting go on in your family?

A. Your family members will share the same goals,
or
B. people don't have to keep nagging each other to get things done?

Choosing When to Work, Versus Procrastinating

45. Sometimes people cannot possibly fool themselves into thinking that certain work should not be done. They just fool themselves about whether it should be done now or later. They keep putting off the job until tomorrow. Sometimes they put it off so long that it never gets done. This pattern is procrastination.

Procrastination can be very painful. The thought, "I know I resolved to do this at this time, but I just can't make myself do it," is very unpleasant. If people can "gut it out" and get started working on unpleasant tasks, usually they habituate fairly quickly to the unpleasantness of the work. In other words, once you get started, you get used to the work and it isn't so bad.

Procrastination usually results in

A. less total happiness than doing the job at the time someone has resolved to do it,
or
B. more total happiness than doing the job at the time someone has resolved to do it?

Planning Ahead, Versus Failing to Plan

46. A man starts a business. He buys some of the things he needs to start the business. Then, when he needs several more important things that would really make the business possible, he runs out of money. He finds that he can't continue the business. Suppose he had sat down at a desk, before buying anything. Suppose he had figured out how much everything would cost. He would have realized that he didn't have enough money for the business, before he spent any money. But sitting down at a desk and making calculations is a

boring activity. It's lots more fun to go out and buy things. The man gave in to the temptation and failed to achieve the long-term goal.

The long-term goal was

A. making the business successful,
or
B. getting pleasure from buying things the business can use?

47. A person goes to work. He pulls out of his pocket a special notebook that he uses to keep track of his plans. He writes down the most important things to do today. He numbers those things in order of how important they are. He starts working on the task that is the most important one. When he finishes it, he checks it off, feels good about it, and starts on the second task.

This way of using a written to do list sounds simple, but a small fraction of people use it. The people who use it are more likely to be successful than those who don't. Those who don't use a to do list get sidetracked more easily onto things that aren't important to do; goals don't get accomplished as fast.

The point of this section is that

A. you need an overall plan for what you will do over a course of months,
or
B. one important way to plan ahead is to use a daily to do list?

Putting Things Away

48. Where do you do your most important mind-work? Is it at a desk, at a table, in a chair? How cluttered up is your work area? Is there junk all over the place? Is it so cluttered that you have a hard time even getting to it? Is it hard to find an empty space to put anything?

It's possible to be very productive while living in a mess. But if your work area is neat and in order, with empty space to put things, you have a real advantage in getting work done. You can concentrate on what you're doing without having to be distracted by other things. You can find the things you need more easily. You are more likely to sit down at your work place rather than to avoid it.

But deciding where to put things and putting them away is for almost all of us, not the world's most exciting and fun activity. We do it to accomplish a goal, not for pleasure. For this reason it is a self-discipline activity, and for many people it's a very hard one.

You can conclude from this section that

A. organizing your things is a way of practicing self-discipline,
or
B. no one who has a cluttered work area ever accomplishes anything?

Kindness Versus Selfishness

49. Two girls are sitting with each other at lunch, having a fun but somewhat private conversation. Another girl who is new in school, very shy, and not very attractive, says, "May I join you?" What the friends might feel like doing is to say, "We'd rather talk with each other," or to frown and sigh and say, "Oh, I guess so," giving the message that they are being imposed upon. But the right and good thing to do is to put off the conversation until later, smile at the new kid, and say, "Sure, we'd love for you to join us," and to turn the attention to getting to know this child better. What's the future payoff? Maybe it's a good and loyal new friend. Maybe it's just the satisfaction of knowing they have done the right thing. Maybe it's that there's just a little bit more kindness in how the whole class acts toward one another. Maybe it's that their own habit of kindness versus selfishness gets strengthened.

The temptation in this situation is

A. the pleasure from continuing the private conversation,
or
B. the pleasure of eating lunch?

50. The people who have used "advanced self-discipline" to enjoy greatly their acts of kindness to other people, even when they get no obvious payoffs, are some of the luckiest people in the world. These are the people who have trained themselves to take pleasure in making a positive difference to someone else.

An example of this type of person is

A. one who helps a lost child, but is mad when he doesn't get a reward,
or
B. one who helps a lost child, and feels great despite no reward?

Honesty Versus Deception

51. A senator is trying to persuade his fellow lawmakers to pass a certain bill. In a speech, he tells all sorts of facts and figures. These are very persuasive, and people vote his way. He gets an immediate payoff. But it turns out that some of the facts and figures he quoted in his speech were lies. Very careful reporters investigate these. They show that the senator himself knew these things were untrue. As a result, the other senators get very mad at the senator. The people who voted for him are very mad. He gets voted out in the next election.

In this example, the short-term benefit of votes for the bill didn't outweigh the defeat of the long-term goals, which were to

A. please the voters, stay in office, and be an honest person,
or

B. be famous and get his picture in the paper?

52. The choice of whether to lie or tell the truth is often a self-discipline challenge. One long-term goal is keeping people's trust. This goal gets a big setback when you get caught in a lie.

Another long-term goal is keeping up your own habit of honesty. That is: each lie that you tell, gets you a little more out of the habit of telling the truth. You get into the habit of lying easily, especially when you tell a lie and *don't* get caught!

Why might it be worse not to get caught in a lie than to get caught? Because when you are not caught,

A. your punishment will be greater, or
B. you will be more likely to stay in the habit of lying?

Keeping Commitments Versus Being a No-Show

53. "I'll meet you at this place at this time on this date." This is making an appointment. But what happens when on the appointed date and time, you don't feel like showing up, or you're too busy, or you have other things on your mind and it's too much work to remind yourself of the appointment? It's another self-discipline challenge, isn't it?

It has been said that "Eighty per cent of life consists in showing up." If you want to get hired, get the part in the play, ace the test, get your cancer removed before it spreads too far, or have someone fall in love with you, the first step is showing up when and where you promise to.

Imagine that someone who lacks the self-discipline to show up for appointments wants to get therapy for this problem. The therapist says, "I'll see you at 4:45 p.m. next Wednesday."

For the person just mentioned, what is likely to be a problem in the therapy?

A. that the person is too hostile to the therapist, or
B. that the person doesn't show up?

54. In addition to appointments, people make all sorts of other promises and commitments to each other. In the business world, a very important commitment is a promise of the sort that says, "I can do this job, by this certain time, for this amount of money." The people who can keep these sorts of commitments get more business; the people who can't do what they promise tend to go out of business.

It is often difficult not to promise too much to people – the temptation is to promise whatever will make people happy at the moment. It is also difficult to deliver on promises once they have been made – the temptation is to let deadlines pass and hope that no one will be too upset.

Making yourself not promise too much, and making yourself keep promises once they're made, are

A. two types of self-discipline challenges,
or
B. two types of unrealistic fears?

Frustration-Tolerance Versus Tantrums

55. Two boys ask a parent to be able to buy something; both parents say no. One child throws a screaming fit. The other accepts his fate and remains pleasant. One has made a self-disciplined choice, and the other hasn't. What are the long-term payoffs for self-disciplined choice? They include having a better relationship with the parent, looking more mature to anyone else who's around, causing a better mood for the parent, and not losing friends quickly.

When you don't get your way, the first priority is to

A. figure out something reasonable and useful to do,
or
B. to "let your feelings out?"

Nonviolence Versus Aggression

56. Often when we are very angry at someone else, there is a certain pleasure or satisfaction in punishing or hurting the person we're angry at. But if we give in to the temptation to hurt and punish, often the result is that the other person becomes angry and hurts us back. This then makes us more angry. These circles of hurting and more hurting can keep going until someone is badly injured or killed; they often do.

One of the problems with giving in to the temptation of hurting the other person when we are angry is that

A. the other person is tempted to do the same thing, and hurt us in response,
or
B. the other person will always learn from the punishment and act right from then on?

57. Suppose that Mr. Smith is a legislator. The people in his district are very much in favor of fighting a war. Mr. Smith believes that this war is a very bad idea and will cause needless deaths. But he also predicts that if he does not support the war, the voters in his district will elect someone else and he will lose his job as a lawmaker.

Mr. Smith votes against the war anyway, and as he predicts, he gets voted out of office.

Some people define self-discipline as giving up a small reward now for a bigger reward later on. But in Mr. Smith's situation, he passes up the reward of getting voted back into office even though he expects no bigger reward later, other than the satisfaction of knowing that he did what was right.

This is why I define self-discipline as choosing an option that you predict will make things come out better in the long run. Sometimes the person for whom it comes out better is someone other than yourself. Sometimes you use self-discipline because you are an ethical person and care about someone else's welfare as well as your own, not because you are looking for a payoff.

The point of this example is that

A. if you don't have much of a conscience, you won't mind hurting people,
or
B. self-discipline includes behavior you do because it is ethical and right, as well as behavior you do to get a long-term payoff for yourself.

58. Choosing nonviolent, rational ways of handling disagreements, even when it would feel better to hurt or punish or kill the opponent, is a very important form of self-discipline. It may turn out to save humanity from destroying itself. There now exist enough nuclear bombs for the human race to end its own existence. Let's hope that the self-discipline of nonviolence grows!

Each year, citizens of the U.S. murder about 20,000 other U.S. citizens. We kill each other in far larger numbers than terrorists from other countries have ever killed us.

If you read the reports of these murders, you sometimes find that they were prompted by very trivial conflicts. One person gets into another person's parking space. One person gets in front of another person in a line. One person gives a too-friendly look to another's girlfriend.

What you have just read suggests that if everyone learned really good self-discipline in the area of anger control and nonviolence,

A. thousands of lives would be saved each year,
or
B. maybe one or two lives would be saved?

59. There are rational, calm ways of dealing with disagreements. It takes great self-discipline to use these methods, especially when you are very angry and the only pleasurable thing at the moment is to hurt the other person, not to solve the problem.

When two people are mad at each other, sometimes other people make anger control and nonviolence even harder for these two. Sometimes people want to see a fight, and may urge the two people to fight. At other times, other people are angry at someone, and will want to see someone else punish him violently. Sometimes they will be very angry with the person who uses nonviolence. Then nonviolence requires great self-discipline, for the person must overcome not only his own anger, but that of other people as well.

This section suggests that in certain situations, the challenges of anger control and nonviolence are

A. very easy,
or
B. super hard?

Complying with Authority

60. A girl is visiting a friend. The friend's parent says, "It's time to go home now." The visitor ignores this. The parent says, "Come on, I need to take you back home now. Your mom is expecting you." But the visitor is having fun. She ignores the command and does not comply. This continues. The result is that the girl does not get invited back to that friend's house. Future fun gets sacrificed for a few seconds of present fun.

Ignoring the parent's command is called

A. noncompliance,
or
B. self-discipline?

61. A teenager doesn't feel like stopping his car completely at a stop sign. It's more pleasurable, at that moment, to keep rolling on. But the teenager gets a ticket. He does not enjoy having to pay a fine, having his insurance rate increased, and getting "points" toward losing his driver's license.

The long-term goal would have been accomplished by

A. obeying a rule given by authority,
or
B. disobeying a rule, because it is unreasonable?

62. Compliance with the rules and commands of reasonable authority is one of the first training grounds where people learn self-discipline. From earliest childhood, people do things they don't feel like doing, because their parents make them do these things. A toddler may think something like, "My parent wants to change my diaper, but I want to keep on playing!" But the child who has to comply with rules and commands that go against what is most pleasurable at the moment is getting very valuable practice in self-discipline.

Compliance provides practice in something necessary for self-discipline, which is

A. doing only what you feel like doing,
or
B. doing what you don't feel like doing?

63. Not all compliance with authority is good. Sometimes the most self-disciplined thing to do is to say "No" to authority. In a famous experiment, Stanley Milgram asked people to turn dials and push buttons that they thought would deliver electric shock to other people. He found that most people were willing to give other people very painful shocks, just because someone who seemed to be an authority asked them to! A very few people were willing to say, "No, I refuse to do it." These people took a principled stand against doing violent things.

If some people chose to work for their long-term goal of nonviolence by disobeying authority, then

A. noncompliance was the more self-disciplined way to act in this case,
or
B. compliance would have been the more self-disciplined way to act.

64. In deciding whether the self-disciplined response is to comply with or disobey authority, you have to figure out whether the authority is right or wrong. You have to figure out whether compliance serves your long-term goal, or interferes with it.
    Some people think they are taking a principled stand, when they are just being lazy.
    A boy looks at his homework assignment and thinks, "It is unjust for a teacher to assign so much homework! I'm going to take a principled stand, and refuse to do it." He gets to school and discovers that his classmates have been able to complete the assignment fairly quickly. The assignment just looked long.

    In this case it would have been more self-disciplined to

A. comply,
or
B. refuse to comply?

Saving Versus Spending

65. For many people, a "shopping addiction" is a big problem. Some people run up huge credit card debts and pay huge amounts of interest to credit card companies, because they don't have the self-discipline to buy only what they need. The choice point, "Should I buy this, or save my money," is often a very important self-discipline challenge.

With saving versus spending, the long-term goal is increasing savings and using money for worthwhile goals. The temptation is

A. the pleasure of getting something new,
or
B. the pleasure of making money?

Gambling

66. Many people, all over the world, are addicted to gambling. They go to big casinos. They know that the money used to build the lavish buildings and make the casino owners rich did not come from charity. They know it came from people like themselves who throw money into slot machines or card games or roulette. The gamblers with the worst problems take the money that their families need for the necessities of life and gamble it away. Some of these get help through Gamblers Anonymous, a group run very much like Alcoholics Anonymous.

What is the long-term pleasure involved in gambling, particularly when someone loses fairly consistently? Part of what makes gambling a big temptation is excitement: the thrill of thinking, "I may hit it big." Lots of addicted gamblers find that thrill and excitement too tempting to pass up.

The long-term goal that the temptation of gambling interferes with is

A. using money on something really worthwhile,
or
B. supporting horse-racing and other useful sports?

Healthy Diet

67. By some counts, over half of U.S. adults are overweight. That's a lot of unhealthy eating! If you've ever tried to lose weight, you know that this goal makes nearly every moment a self-discipline challenge! "What would really feel best to me at this moment would be to have a big piece of pie with a milk shake; what would make things better in the long run would be to have some vegetable soup and carrots." For almost all people, foods with lots of sugar and fat in them are more pleasurable. Many lucky people are able do "advanced self-discipline" and cultivate in themselves the feeling that veggie burgers and peas and fresh fruit smoothies are more appealing than bacon cheeseburgers and fries and milk shakes.

If you want to be most healthy, the pleasure of eating large quantities of junk food is a

A. temptation,
or
B. long-term goal?

Exercise Versus Inactivity

68. The health benefits of exercise are so large that if they could be put into a pill, everyone would be taking this pill. But many people miss out on the health benefits of exercise. Why? Exercise requires self-discipline, especially when you are not used to it. Some people use advanced self-discipline to get "hooked" on exercise; they would not want to miss their daily run or walk or weightlifting session.

Why is it correct to say that people who enjoy daily exercise use advanced self-discipline?

A. Because they have taught themselves to enjoy the option that is best for the long-term goal of health,
or
B. because they do what they really don't feel like doing?

Safety Consciousness

69. Someone gets in a car and doesn't put his seat belt on. Why? He just "doesn't feel like it." In the short term, he enjoys his time more by not bothering with buckling up. But if he's unlucky, he could be killed by this decision.

Someone goes bicycling or ice skating without a helmet. Someone climbs the side of a cliff without expert help with the ropes. Someone allows a toddler or preschooler in a house without checking to see if there are things the preschooler can pull over onto himself. Here's the biggest killer of all: someone is in a hurry, and drives very fast.

In all of these examples, the "temptation" is not bothering with safety. The long-term goal is

A. avoiding accidental injury or death,
or

B. spending extra time on safety precautions?

70. Two people find a cave. They are so joyous at their discovery that they bound down the halls of the cave, turning first one way and then the other. At any given moment, it is more pleasurable to explore the cave than to plan ahead. But the "planning ahead" questions are very important: How are we going to remember how to get out of here? And how long will our flashlight last? A few seconds of interrupting the fun and planning ahead may make the difference between a fun outing and a tragedy.

The point of this is that if the two people want to explore the cave, they should

A. stay out of all caves anyway,
or
B. plan how they could explore the cave safely?

71. A kid finds a lighter, gets the urge to start a fire, and burns some paper. The paper catches some leaves on fire, and a big forest fire starts.

In this example the kid did not "plan ahead" or "think before acting." What should he have done instead? He should have predicted the consequences of his action. He should have thought, "If I light the paper, what could happen as a result? It is possible that I could start a forest fire. I'd better try out this lighter in a safer place."

In this example, like the one just before it, the biggest barrier to carefulness is

A. not caring about the consequences of the action,
or
B. not bothering to think about the consequences of the action?

Medical Self-Care

72. Medical self-care is very similar to safety consciousness. It involves doing the things that prevent illnesses.

Getting lots of sun exposure without protection may be fun in the present but cause skin cancer in the future.

Hearing rock concerts without ear protection can be fun in the present but create deafness in the future.

Using pesticides can be convenient in the present but produce Parkinson's Disease in the future.

Eating lots of fat tastes good in the present but may create a heart attack in the future.

In the examples you just read, something

A. is fun or convenient now, and makes your health better too,
or
B. is fun or convenient now but causes long-term health problems?

Sleep Cycles

73. Did you know that there is a part of your brain (it's called the suprachiasmatic nucleus, and it's part of the hypothalamus) that contains the "clock" for the body? This part of the brain keeps up with when your body is supposed to be awake and supposed to be asleep. The more you keep a steady rhythm of sleep and wakefulness, the more your body "knows" whether it is "supposed" to be awake or asleep. When you are trying to be awake when your body clock is telling you to be asleep, you don't feel as good or perform as well. When you are trying to sleep when your body clock is telling you to be awake, you tend to lie in bed without falling asleep. If you go to bed and get up at about the same time each night and morning, your body clock gets clear on what time to put you to sleep and what time to wake you up. It's easier to sleep, and you wake up refreshed.

What you just read leads to the conclusion that you should

A. go to bed and get up at lots of different times, so you won't get into a rut,
or
B. go to bed and get up at close to the same time, so you'll sleep better and stay alert more?

74. There's only one problem with the advice to go to bed and get up at the same time each night and morning. It takes a lot of self-discipline. You may not feel like stopping whatever you are doing at night to go to bed, and you may not feel like getting out of bed in the morning.

All over the country, in probably every college, some students fail because they don't use self-discipline to set their sleep rhythms. They stay up with friends too late at night and can't get up in the morning early enough to catch even the 10 o'clock class. As a result, thousands of dollars of tuition money go down the drain.

All over the country, adults get fired from their jobs because they just can't get up early enough to show up for work on time.

Some researchers have found evidence that bipolar disorder, otherwise known as manic-depressive illness, is worsened by irregular sleep schedules and is made better by regular sleep schedules.

This section has talked about three long-term goals that may be promoted by regular sleep schedules. Two of them are

A. not getting fired from work, and not flunking out of college,
or
B. greater strength and longer life?

Addictive Drugs

75. What do you guess is the most common cause of mental retardation in the U.S.? (Hint: It does its harm when drunk by pregnant women.) What is involved in about half of all murders? What is a causative factor in close to half of drownings and fatal gun accidents? What also greatly increases the risk of fatal traffic accidents and suicides? What is one of the most preventable causes of liver failure? What drug "hooks" about one in 7 adult males and one in 14 females? The answer to all these questions is alcohol.

According to what you just read, addiction to alcohol causes bad consequences of

A. Mental retardation, violence, accidents, and liver failure?
or
B. brittle hair, a bad smell, and oily skin?

76. But for the last few decades, a substance has caused even more preventable deaths and illnesses than alcohol. This substance is tobacco. It's most widely used in the form of cigarettes. According to some evidence, once someone is hooked on cigarettes, it is as difficult to quit smoking as it is for a narcotics addict to get off heroin.

What you have just read suggests that

A. smoking is not as big a health problem as "harder" drugs,
or
B. smoking causes more deaths and is as hard to quit as "harder" drugs like heroin.

77. There are drugs even more dangerous than alcohol and tobacco. There is some evidence that the drug called "ecstasy" can permanently destroy brain cells and interfere with memory. The most dangerous drug abuse practice of all is sniffing certain types of glue. Such solvents are very damaging to the brain. Permanent brain damage is very likely to occur with glue-sniffing.

Of all the forms of substance abuse mentioned so far, the one the author considers the worst idea is

A. alcohol
or
B. glue-sniffing?

78. So why does anyone choose to use any of these substances? Because in the short run, using them can feel good.

Addictive substances present a clear self-discipline choice point. How much future pain is someone willing to exchange for some present pleasure with these substances?

Unfortunately, for very many people, the answer to the question you just read seems to be

A. very little future pain,
or
B. very much future pain?

Sexual Activity

79. Sexual activity with the right person at the right time can of course have good consequences. One of those good consequences is the continued survival of the human race. Another good consequence is that it helps the relationships between couples. On the other hand, sexual activity with the wrong person at the wrong time can result in bad consequences, for example AIDS and death.

Passing up the temptation of sexual activity that would be fun at the time but a very bad idea is one of the ways in which people use

A. self-discipline,
or
B. work capacity?

Tolerating Low Stimulation Versus Stimulus-Seeking

80. Some people probably inherit a tendency to be "stimulus-seekers." For many stimulus-seekers, even being in danger is often more pleasant than being bored. Having people mad at you

can be more pleasant than not having any emotion stirred up at all. Sometimes stimulus-seekers get the urge to take something that someone else has and run with it, just to make the other person chase. They get the urge to speed in cars or motorcycles, just for the thrill of it. They enjoy mountain climbing, parachute jumping, hang gliding, and the other types of activities that put their lives at stake. They enjoy risking money. They sometimes enjoy trying to trick people, just for the thrill of seeing whether they will be caught or not. People can have the stimulus-seeking trait in various different degrees.

It would not surprise us to learn that people with very high degrees of stimulus-seeking

A. have more deaths from accidents, or
B. find it easier to sit through lectures?

81. If you are a stimulus-seeker, there will be lots of self-discipline challenges that your stimulus-seeking urges will give you. You'll have to think things like, "It would feel really good to drive very fast in this car, but I would risk a very bad long-term outcome (my death, and someone else's)." Or you will think things like, "If I grabbed this person's hat and ran, there might be a fun game of chase at the moment, but I might turn people off to me and lose some friends."

Some stimulus-seekers learn to handle low stimulation by working at it. A good self-discipline activity for a stimulus-seeker is meditation: sitting quietly with the eyes closed, doing any of several mental activities. When you expose yourself to low stimulation, you gradually habituate to it. It does not feel so bad after a while.

When someone habituates to low stimulation,

A. the person puts up with low stimulation so that he can get used to it, or
B. the person gets high stimulation so that he can get his fill of it?

Courage Skills Versus Unrealistic Fear

82. We can divide fears into two classes: realistic fears and unrealistic fears. When we have realistic fears, there is real danger. Our job when there is real danger is to protect ourselves. On the other hand, fear without danger is unrealistic fear. When we have unrealistic fears, our job is to try to reduce the fear.

To be afraid in a situation where we could really get hurt or killed or suffer lots of damage to our reputation is called

A. realistic fear, or
B. unrealistic fear?

83. Here's an example. A teenaged boy gets dared to climb up a telephone pole and crawl upside-down along the wire over to the next pole. Is trying this something we should call brave, or foolhardy? It's a foolhardy act, because it incurs great risk for no benefit.

Anyone who is afraid of doing the stunt you just read about has a(n)

A. realistic fear,
or
B. unrealistic fear?

84. Fear is meant to keep us from taking foolish risks, and realistic fear helps us survive.

      On the other hand, suppose that someone is so afraid of heights that he is really afraid when he's on the fourth floor of a very well built building. He's not really in danger, but he still feels fear.

The fear just mentioned is

A. realistic,
or
B. unrealistic?

85. Someone else is afraid every day that he will throw up at school and be embarrassed. Someone is afraid to raise his hand to answer a question, for fear that he will look silly. Someone is afraid of going to bed at night in the dark. Someone is greatly afraid of riding elevators. Someone is afraid to sleep over at someone else's house. Someone who has prepared very well for a test gets so nervous beforehand that he throws up.

The fears you have just read about are examples of

A. realistic fear,
or
B. unrealistic fear?

86. How do you get over unrealistic fears? Probably most important way is to expose yourself to the scary situation long enough that you can get used to it. You probably remember the word for what happens as you gradually get used to something. It's *habituation*. If someone with a fear of elevators just stands in the elevator long enough, eventually she'll get used to it. If someone who's afraid of answering questions in class raises his hand and answer questions long enough, he'll get used to it.

"To get over an unrealistic fear, face what you're afraid of, long enough to habituate to it." Is that

A. the main point of the section you last read,
or
B. not the main point of the section you last read?

87. Now there's just one catch. Whenever you have an unrealistic fear, it's MUCH more pleasant to stay away from the scary situation than to expose yourself to it. If you're afraid of heights, it's much more pleasant to stay on the ground floor, even though you would like to conquer the fear. If you're afraid of elevators, it's much more pleasant to walk up the stairs than to get on the elevator.

So what do we call the challenge for someone who wants to get over an unrealistic fear? It's a self-discipline challenge, or self-discipline choice point. There's a way of getting over the fear that is unpleasant now, but has a big payoff later. The big payoff is that the fear goes away. The temptation is to run away from the scary situation; the long-term goal is to get over the unrealistic fear.

Why is self-discipline skill so important for anyone with unrealistic fears?

A. Because you have to study and learn so much,
or
B. because you have to put up with the situation until you get used to it?

One Idea, With Many Uses

88. Before you read all this, did it ever occur to you that all these sorts of choice points were so similar to each other? When you were choosing whether to watch TV or do your homework, or to comply with a parent's request the first time versus the fourth time, did you ever think to yourself, this challenge is similar to that of the person who has to choose whether to draw his gun or hold his fire in a moment of anger, or the person who is trying to get off an addictive drug, or the track star deciding whether to work out, or of the weight-controlling person deciding whether to have another serving of food or sip on water instead?

All of the different sorts of situations we have looked at put two things into competition:

A. one person versus another,
or
B. a temptation versus a long-term goal?

89. I have divided self-discipline choice points into three groups, according to whether they are related to productivity and achievement, human relations, or taking care of yourself. Success in these three parts of life is what we cultivate self-discipline for. If you can work well, get along with people, and take care of yourself, you've pretty much got it made! Much of what's left is having a good time doing these things. And one of the ways to do that is by advanced self-discipline!

Other words for the three groups of self-discipline choice points are

A. exploration, relaxation, and insight,
or
B. accomplishments, friendship-building, and self-care?

90. Thinking about these types of choice points is not like memorizing state capitals. This stuff is vital to the quality of life! Look around you at other people. You will see people all around you damaging their lives by bad choices in one or more of these types of self-discipline challenges. If you read the news, you'll read about such sad stories daily. If you walk into nearly any hospital in the world, you'll see people who are there because of serious injury or disease caused directly by bad choices in these areas.

In people's lives, self-discipline-related problems are

A. fairly rare,
or
B. extremely common?

91. What about you? Which is going to be a better summary of your life: "This person aced the self-discipline challenges," or "This person flunked the self-discipline challenges?" To a great extent, you can choose the answer to that question. If you really want to make the best possible decisions in these self-discipline choice points, you can. The remainder of this book will tell you how to develop this crucial skill.

The author thinks that your self-discipline skill is

A. totally beyond your control,
or
B. able to be developed, if you can work on it enough?

Topics for Writing or Discussion

1. This chapter listed 21 different types of self-discipline choice points, 21 "areas" where self-discipline is used. If someone is very self-disciplined in one area, does that give us any guess about how self-disciplined the person is in other areas? Do you think someone can transfer self-discipline skills from one area to the other, if he or she really wants to? Can you think of examples of people who seem self-disciplined across the board? Can you think of examples of people who use lots of self-discipline in one area, but very little in another area? What do you conclude from what you've seen of people so far?

2. Can you think of some important (or unimportant) type of self-discipline choice point that was left out of the list in this chapter?

3. Most of the areas of self-discipline discussed in this chapter, when mishandled, represent tremendous social problems. If you were picked as the representative of your society, and you were given the power magically to wipe out self-discipline

problems in two of the twenty-one areas listed, which two would you pick? Please defend your selection.

4. Why do you think we evolved the capacity for pleasure and pain? Do you think pleasure and pain evolved to motivate us to get what we need and avoid what's bad for us? Why do you think there are so many areas where doing what is pleasurable isn't necessarily what is best? How many of the areas of self-discipline (dealing with abundance of food, resisting the temptation of fast cars, resisting drugs) have been around for very much of human beings' total history? What do you think about the proposition that our brains haven't evolved the instinctive equipment to handle many of these situations, and thus we have to calculate the best solution?

5. Please read newspapers or history books about a person or people who have gotten themselves or others into big trouble. Was there a mistake in one of the 21 areas of self-discipline listed here? Which one or ones?

6. Which of these 21 areas of self-discipline do you think are most crucial in determining quality of life for the people you know?

Chapter 3: Attitudes Toward People With Self-Discipline Problems

92. Self-discipline is a very important skill. It is natural and good to admire the actions of people who use this skill successfully. Admiring these people's actions can help us get the energy to develop our own self-discipline skills.

The point made here is that

A. it's useful to admire self-disciplined actions,
or
B. everyone has to live his or her own life, and what anyone else does is not useful to think about?

93. Sometimes people get very mean and rejecting toward people who have a self-discipline-related problem. For example, someone is an alcoholic, and someone else thinks, "He's nothing but a worthless drunk." Someone is overweight, and someone else thinks, "She obviously has no will power; I don't want her as my friend." Someone has trouble keeping his mind on his work, and someone else thinks, "He's just a lazy goof-off." Someone is addicted to gambling, and someone else thinks, "He's a horrible person for wasting his family's money like that."
But the people who know the most about why people do what they do don't get into calling people bad names and rejecting them because of their problems in self-discipline areas.

This section says that even though admiring self-disciplined actions is a good thing,

A. rejecting people who have self-discipline related problems is what you have to do unless you want to be like them,
or
B. being mean and rejecting to people who have self-discipline related problems is not kind or wise.

94. Let's talk about three reasons why it's not smart or good to be mean or rejecting to people with problems related to self-discipline.
People who are mean or rejecting often assume that it is just as easy for someone else to do something as it is for them to do it. But this is often not the case.
For example, let's think about being an alcoholic. Some people are born with genes that make them feel a little sick whenever they drink alcohol. Other people seem to be born with genes that make drinking alcohol feel really, really good.

Of the two groups just mentioned, which group of people do you think will have more trouble with alcoholism?

A. the people who get a little sick after alcohol,

or
B. the people who feel really good after alcohol?

95. The second group of people didn't ask for the genes that made drinking alcohol feel really good. It is still possible for such people to avoid alcohol. But compared to the first group, it is a lot harder, and it takes a lot more self-discipline. If people in the first group say, "It's easy not to drink alcohol," they mean it's easy for them. They haven't had the benefit of feeling what it's like to have the other person's brain.

The point of this section is that

A. no one with genes for alcoholism can stay away from alcohol,
or
B. people with certain genes need more self-discipline to stay away from alcohol than do people with other genes?

96. In a very similar way, some people seem to get full when they have eaten a certain amount; to eat any more would be very unpleasant. A second group of people can eat huge amounts of food before they ever start feeling full, and the food continues to be just as pleasurable to eat as when they first started. These differences between people, and others that have to do with eating and exercise, also are influenced by what you inherit from your parents.

Which group of people do you think would have more trouble with being overweight?

A. the group that feels full quickly,
or
B. the group that almost never feels full?

97. Is it impossible for a person with a tendency to be fat to lose weight and keep it off? No, it's not impossible, because lots of people have done it. But it probably takes lots more self-discipline than it takes for other people to stay thin.

Felina feels very full fairly soon after she starts eating. She also has inherited a tendency to move around and exercise a lot. She sees Natina, who is overweight. Felina says, "Natina, it's easy not to be fat. All you do is to stop eating when you feel full. That's how I do it, and that's all you have to do too."

What error is Felina making?

A. She's assuming that Natina's body is made just like her own,
or
B. she's assuming that Natina's body may be different from her own?

98. There is even evidence that the type of brain we inherit has to do with behaviors like talking out in class,

interrupting people in conversations, and not finishing schoolwork. For some people, solving these problems takes lots of self-discipline; for other people these problems don't arise.

The point of this is that

A. people can't control their urges to interrupt people,
or
B. some people need a lot more self-discipline to keep from interrupting than others?

99. So far we've been talking about how some people have genes that make it harder for them to make good choices in certain self-discipline areas.

Sometimes people have a hard time for another reason – they have learned things that make it harder for them, or they haven't learned the things that make it easier.

In the family where Drew has grown up, his older brother has hit him, taken his things away, and called him names for years. The only ways that Drew has been able to stop his brother from doing these things were to yell at him and to fight fiercely with him. Drew has also seen everybody in his family yelling and fighting with each other almost every day.

Leonard has grown up in a family where everyone has spoken very politely to each other almost all the time. No one has ever fought physically.

Which person do you think is more likely to have a problem with anger control:

A. Drew,
or
B. Leonard?

100. We can overcome our past learning experiences. But it takes lots of self-discipline. All other things equal, it would probably take Drew much more self-discipline to learn anger control than it would take Leonard. Drew did not ask to be raised in a family where he was almost forced to practice the habit of yelling and fighting hundreds of times. Drew can change this habit, but it requires a very large amount of work.

If we think in this way, we are probably less likely to be mean and rejecting to Drew.

However, our understanding where Drew got his problems with anger control doesn't mean that everyone should sit by and do nothing if Drew hurts other people in moments of anger. Drew should be helped to do the work that he needs to do, to learn to control his temper.

The point of this section is that

A. when people have learned bad habits, they can't do anything to change them,
or

B. people with bad habits should be helped to work to overcome those habits,
or
C. we should be mean and rejecting to people with bad habits?

101. So far we've talked about genes and learning experiences as causes for people's behavior. But often we don't know exactly what causes people's behavior. Even when we don't know why people show low self-discipline, there's a really good reason not to be mean and rejecting to them. That reason is that being mean and rejecting to people usually doesn't help them change for the better. Often it just makes things worse.

A kid is in the habit of interrupting people. Other kids don't like this, and they reject him.

He tries to change. He waits for them to pay attention, but they exclude him. He finds that he can't get their attention unless he is loud and rude. He also finds himself imitating some of the mean things that other kids say to him.

Has rejecting this kid

A. helped him with his problem,
or
B. made his problem worse?

102. A kid is overweight. He finds that people reject him. He loses out on lots of the fun and pleasure that other kids would get from being with friends. He finds that eating is one of the only ways that he can have any fun.

Has rejecting this kid

A. helped him with his problem,
or
B. made his problem worse?

103. What if YOU are the person with a self-discipline problem? If you are, you have lots of company. Most human beings struggle with at least one of the areas of self-discipline listed earlier. And that goes for the author of this book and everyone he knows well!

The things written earlier about attitudes toward others also apply to attitudes toward yourself. Does it help for you to think, "I hate myself for having this problem?" Usually that makes things worse. Does it help for you to think, "There's nothing I can do about this problem, because it's not my fault?" Although this may be better than hating yourself, usually this way of thinking makes you feel helpless about the problem, and it gives you an excuse for not working on it.

How about thinking, "This problem may take lots of work for me to solve. But if I'm willing to work enough, I can make things better. If doing that work makes my life better, it will be worth it." This is the way of thinking that causes success.

Which of the following three statements are most in line with what this book teaches? If you have a problem or a struggle related to self-discipline, you should

A. try to feel very bad about yourself, or
B. if the problem is worth solving, do the work that it takes, or
C. think, "It's not my fault and there's nothing I can do about it"?

104. Why do most people not do the work that it takes? First, doing work takes some self-discipline to begin with. So it takes at least some self-discipline to work on a self-discipline problem.

Usually doing that work is much easier if you have some really nice, supportive person helping you out with it, encouraging you, and celebrating your successes with you. Doing that work is also easier if you get rewarded in some way for each small bit of progress that you make. It's easier if you greatly want the reward. It's easier if you see other people doing the work. One of the major goals of both education and psychotherapy is to rig things up so that ordinary people, without huge amounts of self-discipline, can do productive work. But even in the best of circumstances, goals take work to accomplish.

Work, for most people, is easier to do

A. with models from other people, encouragement from other people, and some sort of reward for doing bits of work, or
B. when you have no contact with anyone else regarding any part of the work?

105. The second reason people don't do the work to increase self-discipline is that they don't know how to. That's the main reason this book was written. The chapters that follow will tell you how to do the work to increase your self-discipline skills.

This book will

A. tell you how to do the work to increase self-discipline, or
B. make it possible to gain self-discipline without even putting out any effort?

Topics for Writing or Discussion

1. Please summarize and contrast the three different attitudes that were written about in this chapter.

2. Suppose someone thinks, "I don't have the self-discipline to work on self-discipline." What sort of circumstances might the person "rig up" to make it easier to do this work?

3. Suppose someone says, "Smokers are inferior people to non-smokers." What

arguments can you think of, to support or argue against this generalization?

4. Suppose someone says, "I think it's useful to think about one act's being better than another. But I don't think it's even useful to think about one person's being better than another person." What do you think?

5. Someone says, "It's all very well and good to think that no one is better than anyone else and that we don't reject anybody. But when you are choosing a spouse, or hiring someone to work for you, or choosing your friends, you're not just choosing actions. You're choosing people, who have certain habits of actions. If you are smart, you select the people with the best habits and reject the ones with the worst habits." What do you think about this idea?

6. Can you think of times when being shamed or ridiculed or harshly criticized had a good effect on you and helped you to improve yourself? Can you think of times when someone's working with you in a kind and encouraging way helped you to improve yourself? Given your own experience, which way do you think works better?

Chapter 4: What's the Point of Self-Discipline? Choosing Goals

106. You can't do self-discipline without goals. Why? Self-discipline equals passing up long-term pleasure, or enduring long-term pain, to accomplish a goal. If there isn't any goal, you can't do this.

What is your highest priority goal? What do you most want to accomplish? Be careful how you answer this question. Bad goals and frivolous goals can sometimes be worse than no goals at all. Bad goals make your work do more harm than good. Frivolous goals waste your time and effort.

What you've just read is that

A. any goal is better than none at all,
or
B. some goals are worse than none at all?

Bad goals

107. A young man sets a goal of proving himself to be the toughest man in town, by getting into lots of fights and beating up as many people as he can. This is what I would call a bad goal: it accomplishes nothing, it uses unnecessary violence, and it causes unnecessary pain and suffering and perhaps death. It is ignorant and immoral.

A young business person sets a goal of persuading as many young people as possible to start smoking the brand of cigarettes his company makes. This is another bad goal: success in it causes unnecessary addiction, suffering, and death.

The bad goals mentioned here are bad mainly because they

A. waste time that could be used for doing people good,
or
B. actually harm people?

Frivolous goals
108. Frivolous activity means wasting time on unimportant things. Suppose someone sets a goal of getting into a book of world records for the longest time of staying up in a tree. While accomplishing this goal doesn't particularly harm anybody, it doesn't help anyone either. It wastes lots of time and effort that the person could have spent on doing kind things for other people or learning things that would prepare him for the future.

Which of the following is the more frivolous goal?

A. Becoming the first person to cross the Atlantic Ocean in a rowboat,
or
B. teaching aggressive people to be nonviolent?

What Are Good Goals?

109. The field of ethics, a branch of philosophy, is devoted to the question, how do you decide what are good goals? One answer that works pretty well is the "greatest good for the greatest number" rule. That is, you set goals that you think will make lots of people lots happier.

The "greatest good for the greatest number" rule implies that

A. it is almost always good to be famous,
or
B. how good you are is in proportion to how much you create lasting happiness?

110. Try to apply the "greatest good for the greatest number" rule to the following question. One person is a professional football player. He gets lots of money and fame. The main result of his work is that lots of people entertain themselves by watching people play football. But if he did not do his work, this result would still take place. The main effect of his choosing to play is that he gets the money and fame rather than someone else.

Another person does research and teaching on how to keep kids from bullying each other. He studies this problem and figures out ways of greatly reducing bullying. He writes about his work, and other people use his writing to reduce bullying. As a result of his work, lots of kids are much happier. If he did not do his work, the work would go undone.

The section you just read suggests that

A. the person who works to end bullying does more good for a greater number,
or
B. the football player does more good for a greater number?

111. An actor stars in movies, and gets lots of money and fame. The movies he acts in are very violent ones.

Another person does research on the causes of violence in society. She gathers lots of information on how often people hit or kick each other. She finds that when people watch a lot of violent movies, over time they tend to hit and kick other people more often. She uses lots of math to try to figure out how much less violence there would be if people didn't use violent entertainment. Many people read what she has written on this subject. A few of them choose not to entertain themselves and their children with violence. Because of this, there are fewer acts of violence in the world. A few lives are saved.

The last section seems to suggest that

A. the researcher does the greater good for a greater number,

or
B. the actor does the greater good for a greater number?

112. The last two sections seem to imply that the world isn't very fair. They remind us that many entertainers such as sports stars and actors and rock stars get lots of fame and money, out of proportion to how much good they really do.

However, the world may not be as unfair as the last section implies. A few athletes and rock stars and actors make big fortunes. But most people who try to make a living in sports, music performance, and acting don't succeed. Most people who dream of getting rich and famous in these ways have to make a living some other way.

Which conclusion follows from the above section?

A. If you want to be a baseball star, devote *all* your effort to it and your dream will come true,
or
B. if you want to be a baseball star, educate yourself for a different profession "just in case."

113. We live in a world where there are love, kindness, wonderful things to find out, amazing discoveries being made, and problems being solved. We also live in a world where violence, poverty, ignorance, unkindness, injustice, destruction of the environment, and disease are widespread. We live with the possibility of widespread destruction from mass warfare. Please, apply your efforts toward making the world a better place and don't waste them on frivolous goals.

The paragraph you just read suggests that

A. the world needs your help in becoming a better place,
or
B. you need to look out for yourself, because no one can change the world?

Where Does Getting an Education Fit In?

114. If you want to succeed at good goals, (or even if you want to succeed at bad goals or frivolous goals), getting the best education you can get is an important means to the end. We are living today in a society where knowledge and intellectual skill, not physical strength, give you power. People who have useful knowledge and skill have a tremendous advantage in getting jobs that put them in a position of doing lots of good. Such knowledge and skill also leads people to be able to earn more money.

A reason for getting a good education, which the last section mentioned, is
A. the fun of campus social life,
or

B. the increased ability to do good for people?

Where Does Anger Control Fit In?

115. If you want to succeed at either work or family relationships, it's very important to be able to keep your temper. The people in our society with the worst anger control problems often end up in prison. People on jobs who scream at or hit their bosses or coworkers are fired quickly. People who threaten or yell at their spouses or children tend to find themselves alone. People who attack other people get attacked back, and often are badly hurt or killed. The skill of keeping cool and carefully deciding what to do when someone does unkind things is crucial for success in this world.

Which is a point made by the previous section?

A. the ability to get angry is part of our genetic makeup, and it's there for a good reason,
or
B. being nonviolent leads to greater success in work and family life?

Some Menus for Goals

116. It is hardly ever a waste of time to think about the question, "What goals are most important to me? What are most worthy of my effort?

Sometimes it's helpful to look at "menus" of goals. For example, the 21 areas of self-discipline listed in the previous chapter are possible goals. Near the end of this book is a copy of the "Psychological Skills Inventory," a list of 62 psychological skills divided into 16 groups. (Self-discipline is an example of a psychological skill!) I often ask people to go through this menu and ask themselves, "How much would I like to get better at each of these?" Getting better at any of these is almost always a worthy goal.

This section implies that

A. your goals should always arise only from within you,
or
B. you can help yourself choose goals by looking at "menus?"

117. Here's another menu for goals.

a. Personal development: Improve in certain psychological skills?
b. Relations with family: Get along better with any family member? Get to know a family member better? Spend more fun times with any family member?
c. Relations with friends: More friends? Become a better friend? Better activities with friends? Better relationship with a friend? Better anger control?

d. Fitness, health, athletics: Sports accomplishments? More exercise? Eating habits? Sleep habits? Other health habits?

e. School achievement: better grades? Specific subjects to get better in? Better organization? Higher fraction homework completion? More work capacity? Better test preparation? Better system for writing? Skills you want to improve? Subjects you are curious to find out more about?

f. School behavior: Make life more pleasant for your teacher? Make life more pleasant for your classmates? Get a better reputation for behaving well?

g. Service to humanity: Make the world a better place in some way? Learn more about how to serve humanity? Join a cause such as nonviolence, reducing poverty, tutoring, improving the environment?

h. Hobbies: Take up a new activity? Improve in an activity you're doing already? Spend less time on a certain hobby? More time?

i. Work: Earn certain amount of money? Learn certain job skills? Get more responsible position? Help people more?

What are some of the goals listed on the menu you just read?

A. Earning money, giving service to humanity, getting along better with people, making better grades,

or
B. Making it into a book of world records for whatever you can?

How Will You Know When The Goal Has Been Reached?

118. If possible, it's good to make your goal statements so specific that it's very clear whether you have reached them or not.

One person sets a goal of "doing better at turning in homework assignments." This person doesn't remember what fraction of the time he's turned in homework so far.

A second person sets a goal of "missing no more than one homework assignment for the rest of the semester."

For which person is the goal stated in such a way that it's easy to tell whether he reached it or not?

A. the first,
or
B. the second?

119. The point we are working on is that making very specific, concrete goal statements allows you to tell whether or not, and when, you have succeeded.

One person sets a goal as follows: "Between now and December 31, I want to hit no one. I want to yell angrily at other people less than 5 times. I want to speak calmly to someone who has spoken angrily to me, at least 5 times." The second person sets the goal as follows: "I want to have better anger control."

For which goal statement will it be easier to see whether the goal was met and to how well it was met?

A. the first,
or
B. the second?

120. The first person sets a goal as follows: "I want to get in better shape." The second person sets a similar goal as, "I want to be able to run a mile and a half in less than 14 minutes by October 23rd."

The second is more specific

A. because it includes a deadline and includes a way of measuring the goal, or
B. because it is written by a more objective person?

121. Specific, concrete goals usually have numbers and dates associated with them.

A first person sets a goal of "losing weight."

A second person sets a goal that "I want to weigh 178 or under by December 31, 2003. I want to weigh 169 or under by March 31, 2004. I want to stay at 169 or under for the year that follows."

Which one has set the goal in such a way that you can tell whether he has met it or not?

A. the first,
or
B. the second?

Writing Your Goals

122. Many people do useful thinking about what their goals are, and then go back to living their lives as before, forgetting about the goals that they have set. One way to avoid this trap is to
1. Write down your most important goals
2. Read your goals list every day.

If you do this, you continually bring your goals to consciousness. You don't let them fall prey to forgetfulness.

The point of writing and displaying a list of your goals is

A. so that others can see it,
or
B. so that you can constantly bring your goals back to your own attention?

123. In this book I will suggest that you write several things to go with each important goal. One will be a list of reasons why you want to meet that goal. Another will be a plan for meeting that goal. Another will be a list of self-discipline choice points you will run

into as you work toward that goal. Another will be a diary of good choices you have made. And still another will be a running record of how much progress you have made toward your goal.

For any given goal, you will be urged to write

A. just the goal,
or
B. several things about the goal?

124. One way to keep track of this is to get a notebook, devoted just to goals. Start a new section for each important goal, and leave lots of room to write about your progress.

Another way to organize your goal-writings is to make a folder on the hard disk of a computer called "goals." Then open one word-processing file for each important goal. I accomplish more when I look at my goals files at the beginning and the end of each day.

The suggestion you are getting is to

A. make a notebook or folder for goals, where you can keep track of them in writing,
or
B. do the things this book suggests in your head only?

Topics for Writing or Discussion

1. Please write your most important goals.

2. If you are a student, please go into detail on what, exactly, your academic goals are. For example: What grade average do you want to get? What fraction of assignments do you want to complete? How well do you want to do on standardized tests? How much progress do you want to make in a certain subject in how much time?

3. Someone sets a primary goal of selecting the other worthiest goals for herself. How would you advise her to do it? How would you advise her to distinguish a more worthy goal from a less worthy goal?

4. Someone says, "I know a good way of telling which goals someone thinks are most important to a certain person. You see how much time the person puts into them. For example, my brother says that his highest goal is to promote world peace, and this is much more important to him than doing well in video games. But he spends about 10 hours a week in video games, and less than 15 minutes a week doing anything about world peace. So no matter what he says, I know that video games are really a more important goal for him." What do you think about this person's

argument? What are its strengths and weaknesses?

5. In this chapter you were advised to make your goal statements very specific, and with numbers that you can measure, so that you can tell whether or not you have reached your goals. What advantages can you think of for this style of goal-setting? Can you think of any disadvantages? Are there some goals that can't be readily measured, such as broadening your philosophy of life? Or would you agree with those who argue that if something can't be measured, it really has no meaning?

6. One person says, "There is no such thing as frivolous goals or bad goals. The goals that one person thinks are frivolous or bad, another person might think are good. It's just a matter of pure opinion, and no one's opinion is any better than anyone else's."

    A second person says, "That's nonsense. Some activities clearly do more good for people than others. It may sometimes be hard to measure how much good they do, but it's possible. The goals that do more good when accomplished are better goals." What do you think?

7. Can you please explain the statement, "Without goals there can

be no self-discipline?" Why would anyone make this claim?

8. Please look around you in the world and see what goals people are pursuing. Which ones do you think they are devoting too much time to? Which ones do you think they are devoting too little time to?

9. Do you think it's better to set very ambitious goals that you may not be able to reach, so as to inspire yourself to strive as hard as you can, or more realistic goals that you can reach, so that you won't be discouraged?

Chapter 5: The Internal Sales Pitch

125. If you are a salesperson, and your job is to convince people to buy something, you get in mind a list of all the reasons why the thing is good. For example: This car gets great gas mileage yet is very safe in crashes. It lasts a very long time. The price can't be beat. This list of convincing reasons to buy something is a "sales pitch."

What about when you are trying to convince yourself to work hard to improve schoolwork, keep your temper, lose weight, get in better shape, or triumph in any other self-discipline goal? You need a sales pitch for yourself.

A sales pitch is a

A. list of reasons why something is a good idea,
or
B. list of ways that something could not work out right?

126. Why is a certain goal worth the effort it will take? If accomplishing the goal means giving up some temporary pleasure, why is it worthwhile to do this? If you don't know the answers to these questions, you are less likely to triumph when you come to self-discipline choice points. But if the answer immediately pops into your head, "It's worthwhile to give up

pleasure now, because this goal will give me X benefits," self-discipline is easier to do.

If you make a list of benefits that come by accomplishing a certain goal, you are making an "internal sales pitch" for that goal. You're making up a set of reasons that sell yourself on doing the work toward the goal.

The point of making up an internal sales pitch is

A. to convince other people that the goal is worthwhile, so they'll help you with it,
or
B. to remind yourself that the goal is worthwhile, so you'll be more motivated to use self-discipline to work at it?

127. Someone sets a goal of getting straight A's in school. Here's the person's internal sales pitch:

Benefits of Getting All A's

1. It's more fun taking the courses if I'm succeeding at them.
2. It's more fun being in school if I get the excitement and suspense of shooting for the top.

3. If I know what's going on thoroughly, I will be able to help other students more.
4. Other students will respect me more if I get top grades.
5. In order to get top grades I'll develop work habits that will help me accomplish other goals throughout my life.
6. I'll get in the habit of being very organized.
7. I'll learn more about some subjects that are interesting or useful.
8. With a better record, I'll have a better chance of getting into a better college.
9. I'll have more of a chance of getting a scholarship, and could save a lot of money.
10. If I educate myself very well I'll be able to get into more fun jobs and more highly paying jobs.
11. With a better education I'll get more pleasure from intellectual discussions with people.
12. I may learn problem-solving techniques that help me to figure out better how to solve real-life problems I get into.

In this book we will use a certain phrase for the list of reasons to work toward a goal, such as the list you just read. This phrase is

A. the "reasons the goal is worthwhile list"
or
B. the "internal sales pitch?"

128. Imagine that another person has a habit of putting off his homework until late in the evening. He sets a goal of doing as much of his homework as possible in the afternoon and early evening. Here's his internal sales pitch for this goal.

Benefits of Getting Homework Done Early

1. I'll enjoy the evening more, knowing that I'm finished.
2. I'll not have to stay up so late to finish, and can sleep more.
3. When there is a lot of work to do, I'll have the evening time to finish up.
4. I will have time to reward myself for doing all my work well by letting myself do something fun afterwards, rather than having to go to bed right after finishing.
5. I'll strengthen my own habit of not putting things off; this habit will help me to accomplish all sorts of other things.
6. If I'm able to have a steady sleep schedule, that will help me feel better in the mornings and all day long.
7. If something comes up in the evening, like a phone call from someone, I'll be able to spend time on it without worrying about my homework.
8. I'll do my work when I'm more fresh and wide awake, and will

probably do a better job for that reason.

9. I will probably get better grades.

The internal sales pitch as it has been written in the examples so far has listed

A. both advantages and disadvantages of achieving the goal,
or
B. just the advantages of achieving the goal?

129. Someone else has a goal of getting to be expert at anger control and keeping cool and calm. Here's the internal sales pitch:
1. I'll be able to keep more friends.
2. I'll not feel so upset so much of the time. Little things won't bother me as much.
3. I'll not get in trouble so much at school.
4. I'll be more prepared to succeed at a job.
5. I'll know I'm doing the right and good thing by being nonviolent and not hostile.
6. I won't provoke people to hit me back or hurt me out of revenge.
7. I won't be as likely to get in trouble with the law.
8. I'll be more likely to be able to have a happy marriage.
9. I'll be able to make more money if I do better at finding and keeping jobs because of better anger control.

10. I'll be able to make better decisions about what to do in situations with other people.

The examples so far illustrate that the internal sales pitch should consist of

A. only the two or three most important reasons for wanting to achieve a goal,
or
B. all the important reasons you can think of for wanting to achieve a goal?

130. It's important to keep reminding yourself of the ideas in your internal sales pitch. I recommend writing down your internal sales pitches for your important goals and reading them every day. I also recommend revising them, particularly adding to them whenever new ideas come along.

So far the main ideas this book has recommended on how to increase self-discipline include

A. realizing that feeling good is not such hot stuff,
or
B. deciding upon, and constantly reminding yourself, what you want to accomplish and why you want to accomplish it?

Topics for Writing and Discussion

1. Please make up a very short story in which someone comes to a self-

discipline choice point, gets the urge to go for the temptation, flashes upon the internal sales pitch, and then chooses to work for the long-term goal.

2. Please write internal sales pitches for your most important goals, the ones you selected after reading the previous chapter.

3. Someone argues, "I think that people should include the disadvantages of a certain goal as well as the advantages in the sales pitches they write. People have too much of a tendency to keep doing things when there's evidence that they should quit and do something else. For example, people keep fighting wars that they never should have started in the first place. If they would constantly remind themselves of the disadvantages of pursuing their goals, they would be able to abandon bad goals sooner." What do you think? Do you think the internal sales pitch should include both pros and cons, or just pros?

4. Someone says, "It's fine to write internal sales pitches. But when the self-discipline choice points come, I don't think about the internal sales pitch for the long-term goal. I just think about the short-term pleasure." Please explain what the person means by this, and tell any suggestions you can think of to help this person with this problem.

5. Can you think of ways of classifying the arguments that you put into internal sales pitches? For example, some of the things you list may be direct payoffs to you. Some may help other people. Some may develop good habits in you that will help you indirectly. Can you think more about the types of advantages of achieving various goals?

Chapter 6: Plans for Goals: Overall Plans and Daily Plans

131. So far you have figured out what you want to do and why you want to do it. The next step is to plan how you want to reach this goal. If you can write down this plan and read and revise it often, you'll be more likely to succeed at your goal.

Suppose there two people, both of whom would like to find a way to cure or prevent a certain type of cancer. One of them does not make a plan. This person just thinks, "Wouldn't it be nice if I discovered something great."

The second one writes this plan: "First, I will finish graduating from college programs that teach about cancer research. While doing this, I will pick which type of cancer I am most likely to succeed with. I will learn everything that is known about curing or preventing this cancer, by reading all the research that people have done. I will keep reading the new research as it comes out. Then I will try to find the person who is doing the best work in this field, and work with that person, so I can learn how to do the work well. I will get into partnerships with the best workers. I will avoid making time commitments in many other areas, so that I can devote almost all my time to this. I will keep good records of how much progress has been made, and I will often ask the question of how faster progress can be made."

Which of the two people do you think is more likely to find a way of preventing or curing a type of cancer?

A. the first,
or
B. the second?

132. Two people want to become better at piano playing. The first one writes this plan:

"I will devote the time between 3 and 4 pm every afternoon to piano practice. I will pick 12 challenging songs, and I will practice them every afternoon until I can play them without missing a note. Then I will tape myself playing them and listen carefully for any problems. I will also get a piano teacher to take a listen to how I do these songs. I will keep going until I can play them in a way that I consider close to perfectly. Then I'll perform them in several places, and try to celebrate that I have accomplished this goal! "

The second person thinks, "It would really be nice to be able to play as well as my friend does."

Which person do you think is more likely to meet the goal?

A. the first,
or
B. the second?

133. Two people set goals of becoming top students.

The first writes the following plan: "I will train myself at note-writing, and write very good notes in every class where it is important to do so. I will study the textbook before the class session, so I'll be able to recognize the ideas covered in class that are not covered in the text. I will make practice test questions from the text and the notes as I go along. I will practice answering the questions I write, and I will keep improving this process until I find myself getting a very good score on test after test. For writing assignments, I will start as far ahead of time as I can, and keep revising until I have a really good piece of writing. I will complete my homework each day, and check it carefully to make sure it's done well. I'll get into a routine of working on schoolwork from 4:00 to 6:00 each afternoon; I'll use as much more time after that as I need."

The second student's plan to become a top student is, "I'm just going to try really hard to get good grades."

Which student do you think is more likely to succeed:

A. the first,
or
B. the second?

134. Two people are unhappy. They both go to a therapist to try to learn to be happier.

The first person plans, "I'll show up for therapy and not drop out. If I need to cancel, I'll call ahead of time."

The second person plans, "I'll be sure to find out from the therapist what sort of work I can do on my own that will help me the most. I will take a notebook to therapy each time and write down what I learn. I will spend at least half an hour a day studying what I've learned, and practicing whatever will help me the most to practice. I will do written exercises. I will ask the therapist what books I should study, and I will study these carefully every day."

One year later, one of the two people says to the therapist, "I've been coming here for a year, and it hasn't helped me." Which person do you think it's more likely to be?

A. the first,
or
B. the second?

135. Sometimes it takes a very long time to find the right plan to achieve a goal. You can often save yourself a lot of time by studying the plans and methods used by people who have already been successful.

The advice just given is

A. don't imitate anyone else,
or
B. use what other people have learned about how to succeed?

136. If you try a certain plan faithfully for a while and it does not work, you can use what you have learned from your experience, to improve your plan. You go back and revise it, or completely redo it.

This paragraph implies that if you could, it would be better to write plans

A. with a word processor,
or
B. with a hammer and chisel, in stone?

137. Rhonda has a goal of losing weight. She plans to use a diet she heard about, in which you eat only grapefruit and cole slaw. After only a couple of days she feels lousy and has a strong craving for almost anything else other than grapefruits and cole slaw. She decides to do more research. She ditches her original plan and makes a plan that includes a more balanced diet.

In this example, Rhonda is

A. improving her plan, which is a good idea,
or
B. failing to follow through on her plan, which is never advisable?

138. You write your *overall* plan for your goal in the file or notebook for that goal. It's also helpful to write down your *daily* plans as well as your overall plans. These can go into a daily to do book or assignment book.

On a Sunday, someone writes a plan about losing weight, as follows. "Each day I will preplan what I will have, and write it down in the morning. I will have no more than what I planned to have."

On the following Tuesday morning this person writes, "Breakfast: bowl of cereal, 1 cup juice. Lunch, 2 cups vegetable soup, 2 cups grapes, 2 cups soy milk. Supper, one veggie burger sandwich, 2 apples, 1 cup juice, 1 bowl peaches."

Which of those plans is an example of a *daily* plan?

A. the first, the one written on Sunday,
or
B. the second, the one written on Tuesday?

139. A person has made an overall plan about making top grades.

She writes to herself, "To do on Wednesday: Biology: Make up practice test questions for the test next Monday, on Chapter 28 and 29. Psychology: Write ideas for the paper that is due next Tuesday."

Are these the sort of things she would write in her

A. overall plan,
or
B. daily plans?

140. It's good to write important resolutions. It's easy to make resolutions in your head, but it's also easy to forget them and change them. If you write your daily plans in a to-do book, you can then check to see how many of your resolutions you kept. You want to shoot for keeping at least 90% of your resolutions. That way you keep up a habit of doing what you've planned to do. If you strengthen this habit, it will help you throughout your life. But this habit has to go hand in hand with the habit of making resolutions that are demanding enough to get the job done, but not so harsh that you rebel against your own resolutions.

The two habits that go hand in hand with each other are

A. making reasonable plans, and carrying out those plans,
or
B. making super-hard resolutions, and making them twice as hard if you don't carry them out?

Self-Starting, Versus Waiting for Others to Nag

141. *Self-starting* means figuring out what is of highest priority to do and getting yourself started doing it, without needing someone else to prompt, command, or remind you to do it. Another word for the self-starting habit is taking *initiative*. Deciding upon your own goals, making your own plans, assigning tasks to yourself, and doing your self-assigned tasks is very hard for many people. Some people never do much self-starting. Some people wait for someone else to remind, command, or nag them before doing important types of activities.

Matilda gets food out of the refrigerator. When her mom or dad asks her to put it back, she does so very cooperatively. But she seldom does it without being asked.

For the task of putting food back in the refrigerator, does Matilda

A. self-start,
or
B. wait for someone to tell her what to do?

142. Two people get hired to work at a store. The first one asks lots of questions of the supervisor. Then she looks all around the store, getting familiar with where things are. Then she finds out all she needs to know about how to use the cash register. As soon as customers come into the store, she asks if she can help them, and she checks them out at the cash register when they buy things.

The second employee stands around talking to another worker. When that worker gets busy, the second person calls a friend on his cell phone to chat. Later the supervisor says, "Why aren't you doing anything?"

The second person replies, "Because you didn't tell me to do anything."

One of the two employees gets fired. Do you think it is

A. the first, who self-started,
or
B. the second, who did not self-start?

143. People who don't learn to self-start eventually get productivity problems. For example, throughout high school, Butch did his homework well enough to get good grades. But he never started his homework before his mom reminded him. When Butch goes to college, his mom is not there to prompt him. He puts off his homework and gets failing grades.

Butch never learned to

A. self-start on homework tasks,
or
B. do homework?

144. Butch illustrates one of the big advantages of self-starting. You don't need someone else to make you productive! This is a very important advantage.

There's another very important advantage. Let's illustrate it with another example.

In the morning, Teresa likes to sleep late. Her mother calls her to get out of bed. She mumbles something,

then rolls over and goes back to sleep. Now Teresa's mother yells at her in an irritated tone of voice. Teresa gets up. Teresa's mom has been reinforced for yelling in an irritated voice.

But as time goes by, Teresa gets used to this irritated tone of voice. It no longer shocks her into getting out of bed. Now Teresa's mom has to keep nagging at her really loudly, in a really angry tone. When Teresa finally gets out of bed, her mom has been reinforced for keeping on nagging very angrily. Without trying to do so, Teresa is actually training her mom to nag her angrily!

Teresa's family gives an example of another big advantage of self-starting. That advantage is

A. that you don't train other people to nag you,
or
B. that you don't have to get up until you feel like it?

145. Why does Teresa not self-start? Partly because her mom is there to prompt, nag, and remind her. Teresa has become dependent on her mom. Why does Teresa's mom nag her so much? Partly because Teresa does not self-start.

Why does Teresa's mom speak in angry tones? Because Teresa doesn't respond to the gentle tones. Why does Teresa not cooperate more with her mom? Because the mom's angry tones make Teresa angry back at her.

When each person's behavior makes the other's behavior worse, the two are part of what's called a *vicious circle*. There are millions of pairs of people who are caught up in these sorts of vicious circles. Some are not very painful, but others are very painful and destructive.

If you can get good enough at self-starting, teach your children and employees good self-starting skills, and choose a self-starting spouse, you may be able to stay out of these very painful vicious cycles.

The author believes that what goes on between people when one keeps nagging another to do something is

A. never a big deal,
or
B. sometimes very destructive, painful, and harmful?

146. There's a third advantage of self-starting. When you get good enough at self-starting, you virtually eliminate boredom from your life.

Two people are waiting for a bus. The bus is late. The first person gets more and more bored. He thinks, "Why do I have to be waiting here? I want to go home and watch TV."

The second person looks at his to do book. He decides that while he is waiting for the bus, he can get some work done. He assigns himself the task of reading an article that he has in his backpack. When he finishes, he thinks, "Hooray, I got that done!" Then he assigns himself the task of starting to write a paper. He thinks of ideas and makes notes until the bus comes. He thinks, "Oh boy, I'm getting some good ideas!"

Which person do you think enjoys the waiting time more?

A. The first, because he doesn't have to work so hard,
or
B. the second, because he's not bored, but enjoying getting his self-assigned tasks accomplished?

147. The "tasks" that people assign to themselves can include what we normally think of as play as well as work.

Two three-year-old children are waiting in a doctor's office. One is bored. One has a great time exploring all the objects in the waiting room, and then making up a little play that she acts out with two of the toy animals there. It's as though the second one had a self-assigned to do list that read,
1. explore objects
2. compose a play.

This story illustrates how the skill of self-starting

A. keeps other people from nagging at you so much,

or
B. does away with boredom?

Topics for Writing and Discussion

1. Please review your own goals. For one (or more) of them, write an overall plan for how the goal can be reached. Use the plans of the first part of this chapter as models.
2. Please write a daily plan, a plan that someone would make for a certain day, on what tasks to do that day to achieve the same goal.
3. Please write a to do list for yourself, for this afternoon, for the next hour, or some other time very soon. As you plan, please notice how difficult it seems to you to carry out the plan. Then please try to carry out those plans. Now as you carry out the plans, please notice again how difficult it is to carry out the plan. Now please write down your observations on the following question: did the plan seem harder to carry out when you were planning it, or when you were doing it?
4. Think of various characters you've run across in books, movies, or television shows. How skilled do you think each of these people is, in the art of assigning themselves tasks and doing the self-assigned tasks? What consequences does this skill have for their lives?
5. Imagine that you were given the gift of lots of time with "nothing to do."

What tasks would you assign to yourself?
6. What ideas do you have about how you might teach your children or employees to self-start?

Chapter 7: Finding the Right Place on the Hierarchy of Difficulty

148. The word *hierarchy* means a bunch of things arranged in order, from least to most. The *hierarchy of difficulty* means a bunch of tasks or challenges, listed in order from least difficult to most difficult.

The word *hierarchy*, as we use it here, means

A. any set of things arranged in order from least to most,

or

B. an organization where some people give orders to other people, and those people give orders to more people?

149. A hierarchy is any set of things arranged in order, and a hierarchy of difficulty is a set of tasks or challenges, arranged in order from easiest to hardest.

　　Someone studies how to teach people to read. The person makes a list of challenges. At the bottom of the list are easy challenges, like listening to some songs about what sounds the letters make. Higher up are challenges such as saying the letter sounds in less than 20 seconds, then in less than 15 seconds. Still higher is sounding out three letter words, then sounding out four letter words. At the top of the list is reading very hard books and correctly answering questions on them.

In this book, the short phrase we use for lists such as this one is

A. the "hierarchy of difficulty,"

or

B. the "list of tasks you have to do to achieve a goal, arranged in order of how hard they are"?

150. A very important idea is that when you work toward goals, you pick tasks or challenges that are not too hard, not too easy, but just right for how skilled you are right now.

　　Suppose that someone is learning to play the piano. Which is smarter: for that person to practice remembering which notes go with which keys, or to practice a very complex song?

　　You can't answer that question until you know how much the person already knows. The first task is lower on the hierarchy of difficulty and the second is higher. Piano students should pick tasks that are just right for their abilities at present.

The main idea is that

A. the harder the task you pick, the better you're likely to do, in the long run,

or

B. you make better progress by picking tasks that are neither too hard nor too easy?

151. What's the main problem with making resolutions that are too hard? Let's answer that question with an example.

Both Jane and Nettie are interested in losing weight. Jane resolves to eat just a little under what would keep her weight the same. She finds that it takes self-discipline to avoid eating more, but she can do it. Nettie resolves to eat far less than that. She resolves to eat an amount that would still nourish her adequately, but which would make her lose weight very fast. By the end of a day, Nettie feels as if she is starving. She thinks to herself, "I think I'll have one last big meal and start this diet tomorrow." So she eats a really big amount that actually makes her put on a little weight that day.

What was a problem with Nettie's very ambitious resolution?

A. It was so hard that she didn't keep it,
or
B. it wouldn't have worked if she had kept it?

152. Sometimes when people make resolutions that are too hard, and break them, they feel guilty. Sometimes they try to take care of their guilt by making even harsher resolutions. Suppose Nettie were to say to herself, "Tomorrow I'll eat even less than I planned to eat today, to make up for all I ate tonight!"

If she did this, she would be making the same mistake she made earlier, which was to

A. make a resolution that isn't challenging enough,
or
B. make a resolution that is too challenging for her present level of skill?

153. Many people are in the habit of constantly making resolutions and then breaking them. This an important habit to stay out of! You want to get strongly into the habit of keeping resolutions. If you break too high a fraction of your own resolutions, you get discouraged with your own ability to do what you plan.

So you start by making easy resolutions to follow. You take into account that you may not have developed the best possible habits yet. You try to arrange success experiences for yourself.

For people who have become very discouraged about keeping those resolutions, the first resolutions should be really easy. A first resolution might be, "I will work on homework for at least 5 minutes before four o'clock comes." Or even, "I will get out of bed at some time tomorrow morning." When you keep your resolution, you celebrate that you are starting to build up the habit of keeping resolutions. Then you gradually move the resolutions up in difficulty. If the resolutions get too hard for you to do them, you can lower the difficulty level.

The suggestion you are getting is to

A. make such hard resolutions that if you ever do one of them, you will have done something great,
or
B. adjust the difficulty of the plans so that you can get into the habit of faithfully performing them?

154. Have you ever noticed that it's sometimes very easy to make resolutions about actions in the future, but hard to do them when the time comes? It's easy to say, "I resolve that tomorrow night I'm going to read a third of the book I have to report on two weeks from now." But when tomorrow night comes around, the task seems much harder. It's easy to say, "I resolve that I'm not going to eat any more junk food for the rest of this day." But two hours later the doughnut on the kitchen counter is irresistible. It's easy to resolve, "Tomorrow morning, I'm going to bounce out of bed the instant the alarm clock goes off!" But when the alarm goes off, the job is much harder.

The hardest part about most self-discipline challenges is

A. making the resolution in the first place,
or

B. carrying out the resolution when the time comes to do it?

155. Here's a tip on getting more harmony between the part of yourself that makes resolutions and the part that carries them out. Use your imagination to bring the two parts of yourself closer together.

Here's an example of what this means. Suppose Nettie starts to resolve, "Tomorrow, I'm going to eat nothing but a bowl of cereal for breakfast and one cup of milk for lunch. And that's it!" The idea of doing this makes her feel good for the moment. But then she vividly imagines what she will feel like at 4 p.m. tomorrow. She pictures herself feeling very hungry. She decides to change her plan. She decides to make her resolution easier, not harder.

She projects herself into the future in her imagination. This helps her to

A. pick a more realistic place on the hierarchy of difficulty,
or
B. expect more of herself?

156. The point we have just made is that when you make plans, it's good to project yourself forward in your imagination, to the time when you will be carrying out those plans. Here's a second point: when you are carrying out those plans, it's good to remember how you felt when you were making them. That way you bring the plan-making

part of the self and the plan-doing part more in touch with each other.

Nettie has made plans for her eating. It is now 4 p.m., and Nettie is tempted to have a huge piece of cake. She thinks back to the time when she was making her resolution. She remembers how determined she felt. She remembers how she felt disappointed over breaking a resolution before, and how she wanted a success experience. When she calls these planning and resolving feelings to mind very thoroughly, this makes it easier for her to pass up the cake.

In the example for the section before last, she imagined doing her resolution at the time she was planning it. In this last section, she

A. recalled the planning at the time of the doing,
or
B. imagined the doing at the time of the planning?

157. So far we've mainly been talking about resolutions that are too hard. But it is also possible to be too easy on yourself with resolutions. Some people fail at their goals because they don't make resolutions. Some students never say to themselves things like, "I'm going to keep revising this paper until I'm sure it deserves an A!" Some smokers never say to themselves, "I really want to quit!" Some out-of-shape people never say, "I want to practice

doing some exercise that makes me breathe fast, every day." It's hard to succeed at a goal if you never make resolutions for yourself.

The point of this is that

A. you should assign to yourself the tasks you need to do to reach your goal, or
B. you should not think about the tasks you need to do to reach your goal, because they will just depress you too much?

Topics for Writing or Discussion

1. Please explain why it is important to pick the right place on the hierarchy of difficulty. Please give some specific examples.

2. Please keep a written record of the resolutions you make for a couple of days. Please also record whether those resolutions were kept or not. As you look over those records, what do you conclude? Are you making too many resolutions, or not enough, or just the right number? Are you making resolutions that are too hard, too easy, or at a just right level of difficulty?

3. Someone says, "One of the biggest problems of education is that the tasks most students are assigned are not at the right level of difficulty. Most of the tasks are either too hard or too easy. This is almost always true when one

teacher is teaching more than two or three students at once, since all will deserve at least slightly different points on the hierarchy of difficulty." What do you think about this idea? Can you cite any observations that support or weaken the case for it?

4. Someone says, "Whenever anyone makes a resolution, there are two things at stake. One is the goal that the resolution works toward. If the resolution is kept, there is progress toward that goal. But the second thing at stake is the person's habit of keeping resolutions. This is usually even more important than whatever goal the resolution is about. If the person gets into a strong habit of keeping his own resolutions, he's more likely to succeed at any goal." Please comment about this. Can you give some specific examples of the point the speaker is trying to make?

Chapter 8: Anticipating and Listing Self-Discipline Choice Points

158. Sometimes you know what the most difficult choice points will be as soon as you write down your goal. At other times, you have to try making daily plans and see which ones are the hardest for you to follow. But it's very useful to answer to the question: "In meeting this goal, what are the situations that will challenge my self-discipline skills the most?" These are called self-discipline choice points.

A person forms the goal of anger control. He wants not to yell at people in anger, and not to hit people.

Which of the following is a self-discipline choice point for this goal?

A. I'm walking down the hall, and a kid purposely bumps into me.
or
B. I'm taking a test, and I know the answers well because I've studied hard?

159. Self-discipline choice points are specific situations where you will have to take action, over and over, to accomplish your goal. Someone has a goal of being a top student. A self-discipline choice point for that person is: "I've planned to review every assignment at 8:30 pm tonight to make sure I've done it well. But when 8:25 comes around, I'm involved in a telephone conversation that I don't want to stop."

Which of the following is the self-discipline choice point?

A. "I want to be a top student,"
or
B. "I've planned to review at 8:30, but at 8:25 I'm in the middle of a fun phone chat?"

160. Someone forms a goal of good anger control. The person writes, "A certain kid at school calls me a wimp. I want to be able to ignore him instead of hitting him and getting in trouble."

The situation being called a wimp is for this person a

A. self-discipline choice point,
or
B. work capacity?

161. Someone wants to have a good diet. The person's overall plan involves eating no more than 250 calories of junk food each day. The overall plan also includes skipping pop at lunch, but having water instead. The person writes, "It's lunch, and I pass by the pop machine. I know I have the money in my pocket so that I could buy the can of pop if I wanted to."

This person has just written a

A. plan,
or

B. a self-discipline choice point?

162. To make things very concrete and specific, anticipate and list the specific self-discipline choice points that could cause you to trip up or to triumph. When you do this, you can then decide what you want to do in these important choice points. You can get clear in your mind the specific, concrete action that will be the better choice.

A later chapter in this book will be about a very important method of increasing any psychological skill, including self-discipline: fantasy rehearsals. To give you a brief preview: in fantasy rehearsals, you imagine yourself using self-discipline in your most important self-discipline choice points. But the first step is deciding what those choice points are.

One of the most important reasons to list self-discipline choice points is so that you can

A. practice in your mind what you want to do in those choice points,
or
B. be sure to realize it and feel guilty when you mess up in those choice points?

163. Here's an example of self-discipline choice points that someone makes when he has the goal of making top grades.

Self-Discipline Choice Points for the Goal of Top Grades

1. I'm in class, and the teacher gives an assignment. I'm tempted to think, "I'll remember it," rather than to write it down.
2. I'm in class, and the teacher is talking for a long time. I'm tempted to let my mind drift away onto a daydream rather than keep listening.
3. I'm at school taking a test, and I finish early. I'm tempted to relax and goof off rather than use every minute checking my work.
4. I'm at home, and I've finished a homework assignment. I'm tempted to go on to the next assignment, rather than checking this one thoroughly to make sure I did it right.
5. I'm at home, and I've finished a homework assignment. I'm tempted to leave it where it is rather than put it in my book bag where I know I won't forget to take it in.
6. I'm studying for a test. I know I will be better prepared if I make up my own practice test and take it, but I'm tempted to skip that.
7. I'm writing a paper. I've finished a draft, and it's pretty good; I'm tempted just to turn it in rather than revise it until it's top quality.
8. There's a classroom discussion. I'm tempted to stay out of it versus make myself raise my hand and get into the action.

9. I'm doing my homework. I'm tempted to ignore my self-talk, rather than to try consciously to reinforce myself.

This set of choice points represents situations where this person

A. wants to use self-discipline,
or
B. wants to do whatever comes naturally?

164. Here's an example of self-discipline choice points that someone constructs for the goal of anger control and keeping his temper.

Some Self-Discipline Choice Points for the Goal of Anger Control

1. I'm telling about something I think, and my brother interrupts me to tell why I'm wrong, before I'm finished explaining.
2. I'm in the middle of a very fast video game that will be over in three minutes, and my mom insists that I come to supper just that instant.
3. I'm at school, and a kid I don't like taunts me, saying, "What's the matter, little poodle dog, aren't you tough enough?"
4. A kid in class keeps taunting me, and when I finally say something to him, very quietly, the teacher punishes me, and the other kid laughs.

The sample lists of self-discipline choice points you see here are

A. only a few of the possible choice points that someone could list for the goal in question,
or
B. all the possible choice points someone could list for these goals?

165. It is never possible to write down every self-discipline choice point that you will encounter on your way to your goal. But if you practice triumphing in every choice point you can think of, you will usually strengthen your self-discipline so much that it will be easier to handle the situations you haven't thought of. And, you can always add more situations to your choice point list.

One of the ideas in this paragraph is that

A. the self-discipline skills you develop with some choice points will help you with other new ones,
or
B. unless you think of every possible choice point and practice it, you're bound to fail?

Topics for Writing or Discussion

1. Please think of a certain goal, and list for it some self-discipline choice points.
2. Please explain what the purpose is of writing a list of self-discipline choice points when you are trying to

achieve a goal. How, exactly, is this supposed to help?

3. Suppose that someone forms a goal, and says, "I have no clue what the self-discipline choice points will be." What ways can you think of, whereby this person could find out what the self-discipline choice points are?

Chapter 9: Fantasy Rehearsal

166. This chapter contains a very important idea, one that can help you improve your performance in almost any area you want to improve in. It has been used by Olympic athletes, professional speakers, musicians, people who want to get along better with other people, and by successful students. The idea is called fantasy rehearsal. The idea is that by practicing things in your imagination, you can get better at them in real life.

Someone doing a fantasy rehearsal practices

A. by moving his body,
or
B. by doing things in imagination?

167. There have been many experiments that have shown that fantasy rehearsal works for learning skills. One of the earliest studies involved ski racers. One group of them practiced in their imagination skiing down the hill as fast as they could. A comparison group did an activity not related to skiing. The group that had used fantasy rehearsal to practice skiing finished the course faster.

Since the time of this early experiment, fantasy rehearsal has been shown to work in letting people handle snakes without fear, letting people be assertive in getting their wants met, and many other skills. It has been reported that most Olympic athletes use fantasy rehearsal in some way or another.

Experiments have shown that

A. fantasy rehearsal can help with athletic skills,
or
B. imagining working out helps you get in shape?

168. Another very interesting experiment used brain imaging. The experimenters asked one group to perform a physical action, and another group to imagine vividly that they were doing that action. The activation of the brain was very similar for both groups. This study suggests that by fantasy rehearsals, you can bring about effects on your brain that are similar to real life rehearsals.

The experiment pointed out that

A. the brain experiences fantasy rehearsal in a way that's similar to real-life rehearsal,
or
B. your brain can't tell whether you're imagining something or doing it in real life?

169. Here is a self-discipline choice point that someone wrote down when thinking about his goal of getting top grades:

"I'm in class, and the teacher gives out an assignment. I'm tempted to think, 'I'll remember it,' rather than writing it down."

How do you make a fantasy rehearsal out of this choice point? Here's an example of what a fantasy rehearsal might sound like.

"I'm in math class. The teacher assigns the next section, and the odd-numbered problems in the problem set. Here is a self-discipline choice point, one that I knew would come up. Right now I'm tempted to try to remember this, so that I don't have to write the assignment down. But I want to build and keep a habit of writing down all assignments. This won't be so hard. This habit will really help me get those good grades I want, for all those reasons I've already thought of. I feel determined. So I get my assignment book, quickly, out of my pocket, and turn to the page for today's to-do list. I write down, 'Math: Study section 10. Do odd-number problems, page 68.' Back in the pocket it goes. Now I feel really good that I wasn't lazy about this. I triumphed in this self-discipline choice point! Hooray!"

What this person said to himself was an example of a

A. fantasy rehearsal,
or

B. a folder on a computer disk?

170. Now let's list the parts of this fantasy rehearsal. We can remember them by STEBC, which sounds sort of like "steps."

S stands for situation. You imagine yourself in the situation, and you describe it, as if it were happening to you right now. You use the present tense, for example "The teacher says this," or the present progressive tense, for example "The teacher is saying this." The more specific you can make the situation, the better. Think of concrete, vivid details.

T stands for thoughts. You say the thoughts, or the self-talk, that you would like to say to yourself in the situation. The person in the example above identified the situation as a self-discipline choice point; this is usually very important to do. Notice that he also thought about his long-term goal of getting top grades. He let his mind flash on how the habit of writing his assignments would help him – in other words, he quickly brought to mind his internal sales pitch.

E stands for emotions. In this fantasy rehearsal he practiced feeling determined to achieve. He did not practice feeling resentful about having to write down the assignments, or feeling too lazy to write them down.

B stands for behaviors. He pictured very specifically the pocket he would reach for to get his assignment notebook, and the page in his assignment book he would turn to, and exactly what he would write. He even imagined returning the notebook to its home.

 C stands for celebration. He took a brief time to pat himself on the back for what he had done, by saying things like, "I triumphed," and "Hooray!"

STEBC stands for

A. Self-discipline over Temptations for Everyone Boosts Courage,
or
B. Situation, Thoughts, Emotions, Behavior, Celebration?

171. It's very important to remember that fantasy rehearsals are what you *want* to do, not what you think you probably would do. You want to practice the best habits you can. You don't want to practice bad habits just because you are already in them. Many people can see the sense in this, but then when they get into a fantasy rehearsal, they say "And then I would probably get really lazy and blow it off," or "and then I would go crazy with impatience," or some other pattern that they don't prefer.

Your job in fantasy rehearsals is

A. coming up with the very best thoughts, emotions, and behaviors for this situation that you possibly can,
or

B. making your response consistent with the "real you"?

172. The more you imagine this "best way" of handling the situation, the more it becomes what you "probably will" do. Some people are tied down by the advice to "be yourself" or "don't be somebody that you're not." Who and what you "are" depends upon your habits, and you can change your habits. If you don't like a habit you have, practice a new habit!

The advice here is that if you don't like a habit you have,

A. accept it, because that's part of who you are, and you should always accept yourself,
or
B. change it, because you can change habits you don't like by practicing?

173. Here's a generic outline for doing fantasy rehearsals of self-discipline. The thoughts listed here are a menu of some types that you might find helpful; you probably won't want to use all of them.

1. Situation:
 Describe the situation. What are the sights, sounds?
2. Thoughts:
 Here's an opportunity; this is a self-discipline choice point.
 What's my highest priority goal right now?

I really want to achieve my long-term goal, for the reasons I listed in my internal sales pitch.

What options are there, and which will work out best?

What I have to endure now is not so bad.

Let me remember a time when I handled a situation like this well. I can do the same thing again.

It will be an accomplishment worth really feeling good about if I can tough this out and handle it well. It will toughen me for the future.

What reward can I give myself, to celebrate finishing this?

If I really play my cards right, maybe I can figure out a way to enjoy this.

I want to reinforce myself for every step along the way.

3. Emotions:

I feel determined.

I imagine myself feeling the way I want to feel: confident, excited, resigned, calculating, proud of the way I'm handling this, or . . .

4. Behavior: I'm doing the option that I chose. I'm doing something that makes sense. I'm working toward my long-term goal.

5. Celebration: Hooray, I did a good job!

When you do a fantasy rehearsal of self-discipline, you should

A. always include everything on this outline,

or

B. use any of the items on this outline that are part of the best response you can come up with?

174. Now let's do another fantasy rehearsal. A self-discipline choice point listed earlier was one in which a student was tempted to drift off in class. He comes up with this fantasy rehearsal, and says it to himself aloud:

Situation: I'm in science class, and the teacher is talking about molecules and how they bind together. I'm tempted to drift off onto thinking about the hiking trip I'm going to take.

Thoughts: This is a self-discipline choice point. I've already decided what's best to do here. I want to pull my mind back onto the science. I need to get my pencil moving across that paper, taking notes or making up questions and answers about what the teacher is saying. If I can do this, really quickly, that will be a big accomplishment. I will deserve to feel good.

Emotions: I'm determined, I'm going to win this one!

Behaviors: I'm tuning back in to what the teacher is saying. I'm writing, very quickly, a question: "What's the difference between ionic bonding and covalent bonding?" and I'm writing the answer. Now I hear something else that could make a good question and answer. I'm writing that too, as quickly as I can.

Celebration: Hooray for me! I did what I wanted to do, and it was even fun. That's advanced self-discipline!

When you do a fantasy rehearsal, it's good to

A. say it aloud,
or
B. never say it aloud?

How Many Rehearsals Are Enough?

175. Suppose someone tries doing fantasy rehearsals five or six times. Suppose he doesn't notice any big change in his self-discipline skills. Suppose his goals don't get achieved with much greater ease. He says to someone, "I tried fantasy rehearsals, but they didn't work." Does this make sense?

 If he had done five *thousand* fantasy rehearsals and had seen no results, perhaps he would have been justified in saying that he had tried it but it didn't work. But doing only a few fantasy rehearsals on one or two or three occasions hardly ever works for anything very important.

The message you are getting is that

A. you have to practice *very* much to gain self-discipline,

or
B. with the secrets in this book, you'll gain self-discipline without effort!

176. Let's compare work on self-discipline through fantasy rehearsals with work on other more familiar goals. Suppose someone wants to learn to play the piano. She spends five minutes studying and practicing a song, on two or three occasions. She notices that she has learned next to nothing. Would she be justified in concluding, "Studying and practicing the piano does not 'work' in getting me better at piano playing?" No. She needs to work at it a lot longer.

The message is that

A. achieving some big goal may take as much work and practice as piano playing does,
or
B. achieving big goals is a snap, now that you have this book?

177. Suppose someone wants to strengthen his chest and arm muscles. He does five push-ups, on two or three occasions. He looks in the mirror and sees absolutely no difference in his muscles. Should he conclude that push-ups, and other such exercises, do not "work" at building muscles? No. He needs to do thousands of repetitions, not just a few.

The main idea is that

A. doing fantasy rehearsals, and exercising, don't really do anything, or
B. if you want to achieve something from fantasy rehearsal or exercising, you have to practice a lot and often?

178. Fortunately, as you get better and better at self-discipline, more and more of your rehearsals can be done in real-life. Choice points come up in real life, you triumph in them, and you get more practice at triumphing in them. For example: someone does enough fantasy rehearsals of anger control that he is able to use good anger control in real life, every day. When he gets to this stage, he can cut down on fantasy rehearsals, because now he is getting lots of good practice in real life. But if he can't rely on himself not to lose his temper in real life, he'd better do fantasy rehearsals in large numbers.

The next chapter is devoted to making the most of your real-life rehearsals of self-discipline.

The main point of this section is that

A. once you get good enough at a skill to do it consistently well in real life, you can cut back on the fantasy rehearsals, or
B. real-life practice can never take the place of fantasy rehearsals?

Topics for Writing or Discussion

1. Please look at a list of self-discipline choice points that you have written, or one of the lists in the chapter on self-discipline choice points. Please write or speak aloud some fantasy rehearsals of good responses to these choice points.
2. Someone says, "If hundreds of fantasy rehearsals are required to achieve a goal, then the technique is useless. No one will be willing to do that much work." Do you agree or disagree, and why or why not?
3. Can video games be viewed as fantasy rehearsals of the behaviors you are practicing in them? Why do you think so or think not?
4. If rehearsing something in your fantasy makes it easier to do that thing in real life, how do you think "shooter" video games should affect the skill of anger control?

Chapter 10: Self-Reinforcement of Steps Toward Goals, or Internal Shaping

The Secret of Self-Talk and Self-Reinforcement

179. Let's imagine two people, each of whom respond successfully to a difficult self-discipline choice point. Both are working on anger control, and both get provoked and taunted by a super-bratty kid. Both manage to stay cool and calm. Both come up with a nonviolent, wise response.

But suppose that the first person says to himself afterwards, "It's too bad I didn't belt that kid. I feel bad about that." The second person says to himself afterwards, "Hooray for me! I did what I wanted to do! I had a success at anger control! I'm getting more and more self-disciplined all the time!"

Which of these two do you think is more likely to come through with good anger control the next time?

A. the first,
or
B. the second?

180. The principle is that if you reward yourself in your own mind for self-discipline triumphs, you'll be more likely to repeat them. Do you agree that the second person is the one more likely to repeat his self-disciplined performance?

Here's an idea that is very important: if you want to make yourself feel good about a certain type of choice, you can cultivate the skill of doing so. You do this largely by choosing what sorts of sentences you say to yourself.

In other words: the way you teach yourself to feel good about the things you want to feel good about is by celebrating through self-talk. You say things to yourself that celebrate your choices. For example: "Hooray for me! I did something tough and strong by turning down that brownie!" or "Yes! I figured out how to do that math problem! Boy, was that cool!" or "Wow, I can't believe I was able to keep cool even with what he said to me! I'm getting more and more in control every day!"

The very important idea of this section is that

A. you can teach yourself to feel good about your own successes, by congratulating yourself with your own self-talk,
or
B. rewards come from outside you, not from what goes on in your own head?

181. Of course, it doesn't necessarily feel good just to form self-congratulating words in your mind. You have to figure out how to let yourself

feel good about these thoughts. You have to do some sort of magic on yourself that lets you enjoy your own compliments.

But if you cultivate the skill of feeling good about your own inner congratulations, your ability to triumph over self-discipline choice points will soar.

The art of feeling good about the compliments you give yourself in your own mind is

A. straightforward and simple, or
B. something you may have to experiment to figure out how to do?

182. Let's imagine three people who are working on writing an article.

The first has very low standards. Her self-talk goes like this: "How quickly can I get this over with? I'll just say this. It may not be the smartest thing, but I don't care. The assignment is stupid anyway.... I'm just glad to be done with this."

The second person has very high standards, and is constantly critical of herself. Her self-talk sounds like this: "Maybe I should say this... no, that sounds stupid. Well, how about this? Oh, I'm not a good writer! Oh, well, I've got to get something down....I started to write it, but I already made an error! My writing is so bad!"

The third person has high standards, but she doesn't feel she has to get to excellence all at once. She reinforces herself for getting started, for making progress. Her self-talk sounds like this: "Hooray, I got started. I'm getting something down. Even if it is only rough notes, I'm making progress! ... Now I have down a draft. It's not bad. With lots of revision, it will be lots better! ... Hey, this is getting better. This was a good choice. Now let's take on this next task. Hey, I improved it again in this way."

What do you think will happen with these three writers? Do you think that the first will turn in something sloppy? Do you think that the second will have a hard time getting anything down, and may not be able to finish the assignment at all? Do you think that the third will probably enjoy herself as she works, and turn in a quality piece of writing?

The third person in this example did something worth imitating. She set high goals, but she complimented herself for every step along the way toward those goals. She had high aspirations, but she used self-reinforcement all along the way.

The other two people did examples of

A. low standards (for one of them) and too much self-punishment (for the other), or
B. self-reinforcement for things that weren't useful (for both of them)?

183. Self-reinforcement means rewarding yourself. If you can learn to reinforce yourself through your self-talk, you will become much more able to accomplish your goals.

You'll notice that the third writer in our example did not wait until the article was totally finished and totally revised, before reinforcing herself. She divided the task up into many, many subtasks, and she managed to feel good about accomplishing each step. The strategy of rewarding each step along the way toward a goal is called *shaping*.

Shaping means

A. getting in shape,
or
B. rewarding yourself for little bits of progress toward a goal?

184. Here's another example of how internal shaping, self-reinforcement, or celebratory self-talk works. Imagine that two people are trying to get physically fit by running. The first one starts out and says to himself, "This feels bad. I hate this. I want this to be over soon. I am obviously not cut out for this. Other people can enjoy this but I can't." It sounds as though this person is not likely to stick with his running program, doesn't it?

The second person starts out running and thinks, "Hooray, I've gotten started! This isn't comfortable, but it's really good for me! I have to

slow down, but I can keep moving! This heavy breathing means that I'm getting more fit! Even though I'm feeling tired, I'm keeping going, and that's good self-discipline! I'll bet within a few days it will be easier, if I keep it up!" It sounds as though this person is much more likely to succeed at his running program, doesn't it?

The main principle of these examples is that

A. if your self-talk makes you feel good after the good things you do, you're more likely to repeat them,
or
B. what you do is important, not what you say to yourself?

185. How much self-reinforcement and how much self-punishment or pessimistic talk has there been in your own self-talk so far? If you're like most people, you probably don't know the answer to this question very accurately. Most people don't pay close attention to their self-talk. Here's another important idea: if you pay attention to your self-talk and monitor how much of it is helpful, you can make it more and more helpful over time.

The idea is that

A. the pattern of your self-talk can't be changed,
or

B. a first step in making your self-talk more helpful is to pay attention to it and find out what it is?

Topics for Writing or Discussion

1. Imagine someone who uses self-reinforcement and internal shaping while doing a homework assignment. Please write or tell the types of things the person might say to himself or herself, while beginning the assignment, while doing each part, and at the finish of it.

2. Imagine a smoker who has recently quit smoking. The person gets urges frequently to smoke, but resists them. Please write or tell what the person's self-talk might sound like if the person uses self-reinforcement for resisting those urges.

3. What do you think creates the "magic" of really feeling good about your own approval? Do you think part of it is really *believing* that the thing you have done is a challenging yet worthy thing to have done? Can you think of other things that might contribute to the ability to feel good about self-reinforcement?

4. What sorts of things do you think people do that makes them *not* feel good about self-reinforcement? For example, what about comparing themselves negatively to other people – as in "It's great that I did this! But – other people my age do it much better than I do." Or what

about letting the accomplishment get lost among all the other things you haven't done – as in "It's great that I did this! But – there's so much I haven't done, it doesn't make any difference." Do you think that sentences starting with a certain word are important in explaining why people's self-reinforcement doesn't feel good sometimes?

5. What sorts of results do you think occur when someone gets into the habit of regularly and severely using self-punishing self-talk? How do you think it would make someone feel to have a steady stream of self-talk saying things like, "You idiot! Can't you do anything right?" and so forth?

6. Please experiment with deliberately trying to congratulate yourself with your self-talk for anything smart or good or self-disciplined that you do for some period of time. Please then write or tell what it was like to do this. Could you remember to do it? Was there a part of you that argued that you didn't deserve the praise? Did you feel good about the praise you gave yourself?

Chapter 11: The Celebrations Exercise

186. The sort of self-reinforcement that we have spoken of so far happens immediately after you have done something smart or good. The celebrations exercise, by contrast, occurs after you have done something smart or good, but not immediately after. To do the celebrations exercise, you remember a smart or good thing you did in the past, and you go over it in your mind again. You congratulate yourself for what you did earlier.

The celebrations exercise is something that you do

A. immediately after doing a smart or good thing,
or
B. a while after doing a smart or good thing?

187. It's also good to try to do the celebrations exercise at a regular time each day. For example, at bedtime, you think back over the things you've done that day. You find in your memory the positive examples that you've done, the things you're glad you've done, and the things that have advanced the cause of your goal. You describe the situation, thoughts, emotions, and behaviors that you did. You write them down, or just remember them, or tell someone else.

You try to feel very good about having done them.

Another characteristic of the celebrations exercise is that

A. you do it at irregular moments during the day, right after you've done a good thing,
or
B. you do it at a regular time each day?

188. Here's an example of how this might look, if someone does it in writing. Let's imagine that the person is working on a goal of high achievement as a student.

10/4: I was at home, working on writing my paper for science class. I had been working for about 20 minutes, and I got the urge to take a break and walk around. But I said to myself, "I'll keep writing until I've done 1000 words, and then I'll take a break and really celebrate my progress." So I checked the word count on the computer and kept going. I got to 1000 words about an hour later, and I really felt proud that I had made so much progress.

This person is celebrating an accomplishment in

A. work capacity,

or
B. kindness?

189. Here's another example of a celebration that someone might write down.
10/5: In history class today I tried a new way of keeping my mind on the subject while the teacher was talking. I wrote down questions about what he said, and wrote the answers to them. I really had to work hard to do so much at once, but it turned out to work well for me. I felt good that I had done this rather than just trying to listen passively during class.

This person is celebrating an accomplishment in

A. good health habits,
or
B. paying attention?

190. Here's another example of something someone might write while doing the celebrations exercise.
10/6: While doing my homework I got a call from Pat Jones, who wanted to get together and ride bikes. I was tempted to get together right at that moment, but instead I figured that I would be at a good stopping point after an hour more of work. So we planned to get together at that time. I got a lot done during the hour, and then had a good time after that. I felt proud that I had saved the reinforcement for after the work was finished.

Going out to ride the bikes right away in this example was a

A. temptation,
or
B. long-term goal?

191. If you want the celebrations exercise to be most helpful to you, there's something very important to do. The three examples we just looked at all did it. The following examples do not do it.
10/4: I kept working instead of stopping, and was very industrious.

10/5: I did a good job of paying attention to what I was supposed to be paying attention to and not getting off on something else.

10/6: I did a good job of resisting a temptation that would have maybe kept me from accomplishing my goal. I felt proud when I did this.

What do these examples fail to do that the first three examples did do?

A. create a specific picture of exactly what happened,
or
B. say anything about feeling good about something?

192. The crucial difference lies in making a concrete, specific picture of exactly what happened. For the first three examples, you can picture what

went on; for the second three examples, you have to make up some definite example if you want to make a vivid picture of it.

Which of the following two examples gives a more concrete, specific, vivid picture?

A. I pushed myself to achieve,
or
B. I went to the Cranberry Community Pool and swam 30 laps in one hour?

193. Why do you want to make your celebrations as specific and definite as you can? Because if you do, you will more nearly relive and reexperience what you did. Each time you bring those very clear details to mind, you are practicing in your mind doing that act and feeling good about it.

The point of this is that the celebrations exercise is not only a type of self-reinforcement, but also a type of

A. fantasy rehearsal,
or
B. temptation?

194. In the celebrations exercise, you are really doing a fantasy rehearsal of something you've already done that is worth doing again. Each time you run a positive pattern through your neurons, you are doing a fantasy rehearsal. If you really feel good about what you've done, then you're reinforcing yourself for the good action that went through your brain circuits.

Many people do all sorts of good things without taking the few seconds required to notice them, remember them, and feel good about them. Taking these few seconds to do these things accomplishes two things. First, it makes you more likely to do the good things again, since you've rehearsed them in fantasy. Second, it makes you a happier person, since you've cultivated the habit of feeling good about the good things you've done.

The two things the celebrations exercise strengthens are

A. good habits and good feelings,
or
B. people and places?

195. Of course, part of the celebrations exercise is knowing what to celebrate and what not to.

Suppose that someone makes the following entry in his celebrations diary.

2/16: Today I put a wad of chewing gum in the chair of that kid Mike Smith who wouldn't give me his cookie at lunch. The gum got all over his pants and all over the chair. It made me really happy to get him back like that, even though I got in lots of trouble for it.

What is the problem with such a celebration?

A. The person is celebrating an unethical act,

or

B. the person is not being definite and specific enough?

196. We have talked about setting up a word-processing file for each important goal. In this file you write the goal, the internal sales pitch for why you should achieve it, the plan for achieving it, the important choice points along the way toward achieving it, and fantasy rehearsals of what you want to do at those choice points. I also recommend that in this file you write celebrations of the choice points you handled well, the ones that advance you toward your goal.

The advice is to

A. write the celebrations down on any old slip of paper,

or

B. write celebrations in the file having to do with the important goal you have chosen?

Topics for Writing or Discussion

1. Please make a celebrations diary. Write celebration-worthy things that you have done in the last couple of days. Include the situation, thought, emotions, behaviors, and celebratory thoughts. Be as concrete, definite, and specific as possible.

2. Please try to do the celebrations exercise, either in writing or in your own mind, at a regular time every day for three or four days. Has doing this for this short time had any effect that you notice? Do you notice that when you do good things, you are starting to say to yourself, "This is a good thing to remember, so I can celebrate it later?"

3. Imagine someone who is very skilled at the celebrations exercise. The person does it as a regular habit, remembers the good acts very clearly, and feels very good upon reliving them. Do you think that this person is more or less likely to get depressed than someone who does not do this? Why or why not?

Chapter 12: External Reinforcement

197. There are several different types of rewards, or reinforcers. When you say to yourself, "Hooray for me! I did a good job!" that is an *internal* reinforcer, or a *self-talk* reinforcer. When something happens outside you that makes you feel good, that's an external reinforcer. There are several sorts of external reinforcers.

The difference between internal and external reinforcement is

A. internal is inside you and external is outside you,
or
B. internal is what happens to you that someone could see, and external is what you think to yourself?

198. Here are some types of external reinforcers. When someone else says to you, "I like that!" that is a *social* reinforcer – some rewarding words or touches from someone else.

Suppose that someone very much wants to go outside and ride a bike, and his parent says to him, "You will get to ride your bike as soon as your room is cleaned up." In that case, riding the bike is an *activity* reinforcer.

Suppose that a child wants a new toy. The parent says, "You can get it as soon as you earn 5000 reading points." The toy is a *tangible* reinforcer, something you can touch and hold.

Suppose that the parent says, "When you earn 300 reading points, you get a piece of peppermint candy." Then the candy is an *edible* reinforcer.

What type of reinforcer is it when someone earns the right to see a certain movie that she wants to see?

A. a tangible reinforcer,
or
B. an activity reinforcer?

199. Jacob is trying to write a book. Just as he is getting ready to write, he gets the urge to get himself some tea and a biscuit. He will enjoy not only the taste of the food, but the activity of preparing it and eating it. But he decides to put off this enjoyment until after his work. In other words, he decides to make the tea and the biscuit reinforcers for writing. He has a program on his computer that measures his keystrokes. He decides that he will give himself the tea and biscuit when he has typed 10,000 keystrokes on his book.

The tea and biscuit are

A. both social and self-talk reinforcers,
or
B. both edible and activity reinforcers?

200. Ralph is trying to get more organized. He really enjoys playing

chess against his computer. He is tempted to spend his time playing chess instead of organizing his room, making his to do list, and checking off the tasks he has done. Ralph sets up a rule for himself that he is allowed to play computer chess on any day when his room is very organized, when he has made a to do list, and when he has done all the essential items on the list. The chance to play chess then becomes a reinforcer for organizing.

In this example, chess is

A. an edible reinforcer,
or
B. an activity reinforcer?

201. Rachel wants to do her homework very thoroughly each day, as well as to prepare for any tests and projects that are coming up. But she finds that she tends to put off her work and surf the Internet instead. Rachel makes a rule for herself that on any day, she will do her academic work first. When all her work has been done really well, she will only then let herself surf the Internet.

Surfing the Internet is an activity reinforcer that comes after, and is meant to reinforce,

A. completing schoolwork,
or
B. finding interesting things on the Internet?

202. In the last three examples, someone did a very interesting maneuver. Jacob faced a choice point between writing and getting something to eat. Ralph faced a choice point between playing chess and organizing his room. Rachel faced a choice point between surfing the Internet and doing schoolwork.

The food, the chess game, and the Internet were, at the moment of these choice points, all

A. long-term goals,
or
B. temptations?

203. The people in the last three examples did not give in to the temptations. But they also did not give up the temptations altogether. They decided to give themselves the rewards, but only after they had done their work toward the long-term goals. Thus the same foods or activities that had been temptations now did some special thing for the work on the long-term goal.

That special thing was

A. to reinforce it,
or
B. to get in the way of it?

204. The maneuver that these three imaginary people did is very useful in cultivating self-discipline. Let's go over it again. First, you have a long-term

goal that you want to work toward. Then you get the urge to give in to a temptation. But instead, you decide to let yourself do the pleasant activity only when you have done enough work on the long-term goal. Now the pleasant activity reinforces the work on the long-term goal instead of interfering with it and competing with it.

The main idea is that

A. the same fun that can tempt you, can reinforce work toward your goals,
or
B. the fun that can tempt you should be given up forever?

205. A woman likes to read adventure novels. But she has a habit of staying up so late reading that she has a bad sleep schedule.

Going to bed and getting up on time is her goal, and reading the adventure novels is the

A. temptation,
or
B. work capacity?

206. The woman considers two options. First she considers just giving up the adventure novels.

The second option is that she makes a rule for herself. When she has gotten herself ready for bed, she will allow herself to read until her planned bedtime. In the morning, if she gets up at her planned awakening time, her reward is that she gets to read for half an hour in the morning.

Which of these two options uses the maneuver that was described in this chapter? That is, which makes the pleasure of reading reinforce the goal of keeping a good sleep schedule rather than interfere with it?

A. the first,
or
B. the second?

207. What is the hardest part of systems such as the ones we have been talking about? It's keeping your own rules. The person who tells himself that he will get the food only after writing a certain number of keystrokes is tempted to go ahead and eat the food before doing the keystrokes. The person who made the rule about the adventure novels is tempted to keep reading even though the appointed bedtime comes. If any of these people break their resolutions, no one will know. All they have to do is to change their minds.

For this reason, following the rules you make for yourself when you set up programs like these is, for most people,

A. hard,
or
B. easy?

208. Following your own rules and waiting until you have earned a reinforcer before giving it to yourself takes lots of self-discipline, particularly if you are setting up a program to follow day after day. For that reason, the plans we have talked about so far in this chapter allow people who already have lots of self-discipline to increase their self-discipline even further.

However, if you start out by fantasy rehearsing a self-directed reward system, you may gradually build up the self-discipline that enables you to follow through with such a program.

The advice you've gotten is that even if you're not ready to do a self-directed reward program yet, you may still benefit from

A. advanced self-discipline,
or
B. fantasy rehearsal of a self-directed reward program.

209. There's another benefit to the sorts of programs where you give yourself a reward only when you have earned it in a useful way. they make life more fun and interesting! It will probably be more fun to work for the right to see a movie than to just see the movie for free. It will probably be more fun to work for a bit of junk food than to just go and get it.

Do you believe that it's more fun to get reinforcement by working for it than just by collecting it for free? If you're not certain, think about these examples.

Suppose you are thinking of buying a video game. Suppose that the reinforcer at the end of the game is to escape from a series of underwater caves and rooms. Suppose you read this advertisement about the game: "To get the triumphant music and screens that show you've won the game, all you have to do is press one button, and it's no secret which one! You can win the game in one second, every time!" Does this sound like a fun game? Most people would get bored with it extremely quickly. It's more fun to have to work harder to win than to be able to win by hardly trying.

In this example, which would people enjoy more?

A. reinforcement you have to work for,
or
B. reinforcement you get for free?

210. Here's another example. Imagine that you are a very good tennis player. You enter a tennis tournament. It turns out that the only other people who have entered the tournament are very young children who can hardly ever even connect with the ball. How long would it take before you feel silly, winning every single point in each game? Wouldn't it be more pleasurable for you to play against other people who are closer to your own level, even though you risk losing? When playing against

the young children, the reinforcer of winning comes virtually for free. When playing against people closer to your own skill level, you have to work for the reinforcement of winning.

In this example, which would people enjoy more?

A. reinforcement you have to work for, or
B. reinforcement you get for free?

211. A mountain climber sets off on an expedition to climb a very challenging peak. The mountain climbing team has spent months planning out how they will be successful on this trip. Just as they begin, a helicopter pilot stops his helicopter near them. The pilot says, "Going to the top of the mountain? I'll be happy to take you there. You'll be up to the top in almost no time." Do you think the climbers would welcome this offer? Or do you think that taking a helicopter to the top of the mountain would defeat the whole purpose of the climb?

Isn't it true that the only thing that makes the reinforcement of arriving at the top of the mountain worthwhile is having to work for it, using skill and determination to get it?

In this example, which would people enjoy more?

A. reinforcement you have to work for, or

B. reinforcement you get for free?

212. Perhaps you can think of other examples, and better examples. The fundamental truth is that having to work for reinforcement makes life more fun.

When you are setting up such a program for yourself, the practical question becomes, how much work earns how much of the reinforcing activity?

Suppose that two people are reinforcing themselves for doing homework by allowing themselves to watch a recorded movie. The first person says, "Getting started is the hardest part. So I'll let myself watch the movie as soon as I do homework for five minutes."

What do you think is the problem with such a program?

A. The reinforcer is so easy to get that you get it before you do enough work, or
B. the reinforcer is so hard to get that you are likely to give up or break the rule?

213. The second person says to herself, "I want to get tough. I'll set high standards. I'll let myself watch the movie only when I've done homework with no mistakes for 30 days in a row."

What do you think is wrong with such a program?

A. The reinforcer is so easy to get that you get it before you do enough work,
or
B. the reinforcer is so hard to get that you are likely to give up or break the rule?

214. Jake decides to do a self-directed reinforcement program. He really likes orange juice. He resolves that he will allow himself one cup of orange juice for each thirty math problems he works in preparation for a test he will be taking. However, when he comes home from school hot and thirsty, he just can't resist the urge to have some nice cold orange juice. At bedtime, he thinks, "I've already broken my rule, so I might as well have some more, even though I didn't do any math problems today."

His plan failed (at least on that day) because of a very common reason: it was that

A. he gave himself the reinforcer without earning it,
or
B. he made the reinforcer too easy to earn?

215. Lucia likes to play with a hand-held video game. She has a goal of becoming a really good piano player. She makes a rule for herself that she will allow herself to use the video game only immediately after she has practiced piano for a solid hour and a half.

She gets the urge to play the video game, but stops herself, remembering her rule. But then she postpones practicing the piano, because she knows that she can't spare as much as an hour and a half. This happens over and over. After a while, she discovers that she is actually practicing the piano less than she was before she made up this program.

What was the problem with her program?

A. She gave herself the reinforcer before she earned it,
or
B. she made the reinforcer too hard to earn?

216. A man is trying to write a book and to lose weight. He loves a certain type of peppermint candy. He resolves that at the end of each day when he has both written 20 thousand keystrokes and has taken in at least 500 fewer calories than he has used up, he will reward himself just before bedtime with one peppermint candy.

He finds that he is able to make this goal about three-quarters of the time. He resists the temptation to eat more than one candy or to eat it without earning it. He finds that the plan is fun, that he gets more writing done, and that he gradually loses weight.

What is the problem with this plan?

A. He made it too easy to earn the reinforcer,

or

B. for him there's no problem with it?

Contracting With Another Person for Reinforcement

217. So far we have talked about external reinforcement that you do all on your own, through deals that you make with yourself. But sometimes it can be a little too easy for people to break the deals they make with themselves. Sometimes they find it easier to make a deal with another person.

Jay and Rita are both interested in losing weight. They make a "weight losing pact" with each other. They decide that they will meet each other every week, and at that time they will both weigh themselves. They will congratulate each other for the weight they have lost. They will tell each other about how they have been successful. If either or both of them haven't been successful, they will make plans for the next time and fantasy rehearse successes.

The type of reinforcement they are using is

A. prizes that you can touch,

or

B. social reinforcement?

218. A woman is trying to quit smoking. She makes a deal with a friend of hers. She give the friend $600 dollars in cash. Every day, she calls her friend and says whether she smoked or not that day. Her friend congratulates her if she has kept from smoking. Every week, they get together. The woman gets back $6 of her money for every day that she has gone without smoking. But for every day that she has smoked, her friend sends off the $6 as a gift to the city, to which the woman already feels she pays too much in taxes. The money that the woman gets back for not smoking, she feels free to use to buy something that she likes, or to buy something her friend likes.

The reinforcers in this deal are

A. the payment of money to the city,

or

B. the congratulations from the friend, getting back the money, and being able to spend the money?

219. A woman has an office in her house that is totally cluttered up with junk. She has a hard time using the self-discipline to organize it.

She is interested in buying a new computer. She makes a deal with her husband, that she will give herself a check mark on a chart at the end of the day when her office is in very good order. He will congratulate her for the days when she accomplishes this. When she accumulates 60 check marks, she will get the new computer.

Between the congratulations and the computer, which reinforcer is tangible (or able to be touched)?

A. the congratulations,
or
B. the computer?

220. Two kids at school want to make better grades. They make a deal in which they will call each other on the phone every night a little before bedtime. They will go over their homework with each other and compare what answers they gave. (Their teacher encourages students to do this, and does not consider it cheating.) They congratulate each other for completing all the work. They also get some pleasure when their answers agree. They also enjoy chatting a little bit with each other too. But they agree that they will not chat if they have not both done all their homework well.

 The reinforcements they give each other are

A. all social,
or
B. all tangible?

221. When you set up reinforcement programs, especially at the beginning it's good to break the job down into small bits. This means that you get a

reinforcer for doing smaller parts of the job rather than waiting until you have finished a very large part before getting the reinforcer.

A man is trying to stop drinking alcohol. He goes to a therapist. He and the therapist decide that instead of talking with the therapist for an hour each week, he will call the therapist and talk for 10 minutes each day. He will report the self-discipline choice points that he came across that day, and together they will celebrate his triumphs. If he ever fails the choice point by drinking, he will do lots of fantasy rehearsals of what he would like to do instead the next time.

When they decided to get in touch every day rather than every week, they decided to break the job of staying away from alcohol into

A. smaller bits,
or
B. bigger bits?

222. A kid has had problems with his behavior at school. On his report card that he gets every three months, there have been bad marks for not finishing work, talking without permission, and some disrespectful talk. The kid really wants to change these things.

The kid enjoys playing a computer game almost every day after school. He and his parents make a deal with the teacher that the teacher will give him a grade each day on his behavior, on a scale from 0 to 10. If he gets 8 or above, he will get to play with the computer game that night; otherwise he won't. Also, his parents and he can celebrate the good days by talking about them joyously.

They are using an activity reinforcer and social reinforcers. They are breaking his job down into smaller bits by getting a report on his behavior

A. every three months,

or

B. every day?

223. A young man goes to college. He has been goofing off and partying too much, and not working enough. His grades are not good. His parents tell him, "If at the end of this coming school year, you have at least a B average, we'll pay for the following school year. Otherwise, you'll be paying for it yourself."

This program seems fair enough. But a problem with it is that the reinforcement that's at stake for the student comes only after a whole year of work. This is a very long-term goal. The reason the student had trouble with productivity in college in the first place was that he was more motivated by short-term goals such as partying and having fun. One of the main purposes of external reinforcement programs is to make the reinforcers come sooner after the behavior they're meant to increase.

This program doesn't do that well enough.

What's the main problem with waiting until the beginning of the next school year for the reward to be given?

A. The young man needs rewards that come sooner after the studying and work that the rewards are meant to encourage,

or

B. the young man may not be grateful to his parents?

224. Suppose that instead the parents say, "We'll get your grades after the first six weeks of school. If after those six weeks, you've gotten a B average or greater, we'll give you the money to pay for your next year, immediately."

The young man works hard for the first six weeks, gets his reward, and then goes back to partying and goofing off for the rest of the year.

What was the problem with this reinforcement program? If the man needs external reinforcement to succeed in the first six weeks, he will also need it to succeed in the rest of the school year. By giving away all the reinforcement at once, the parents left no incentive for the man to work hard during the rest of the school year.

The problem with this program was that

A. There was no external incentive for the man to work hard after the first six weeks of the school year,

or

B. The reinforcement should have come after a whole year of work?

225. After thinking about these things, the parents and the young man work out a different program. They estimate how many tests and papers he will get back during the whole school year. They divide the total amount of "spending money" they're prepared to give him by the total number of graded works he will get. In this way they decide upon a certain amount of money the young man will get for each A or B on any test or paper. As soon as the man gets a test or paper back, he will fax it to his parents. They will send back a check to him at the end of each week, according to the grades he's gotten that week.

In this program they have a better plan for

A. internal reinforcement and the celebrations exercise,

or

B. giving the reinforcement quicker after the behavior, and having the reinforcement apply all the time?

226. This program works well for a few months (partly because the young man is honest enough not to fake tests and papers). Then the young man's great-aunt dies and leaves him $40,000.

Suddenly the small checks that he has gotten from his parents for his grades are not very reinforcing any more, and his grades drop.

This illustrates something important about reinforcement. Things are reinforcing only if you feel at least a little deprived of those things. If you have all you want, for the moment, you probably aren't as motivated to work for that reinforcer. Getting all you want of a reinforcer is called *satiation*. You have to avoid satiation if you're counting on external reinforcement to work.

What's another example of a reward's not working because of satiation?

A. A person training a dog uses bits of food for reward, after the dog hasn't eaten for a day and is very hungry,

or

B. A mom says, "I'll give you a piece of candy when you've finished your math drills," but the child has just gotten back from a party where he has eaten all the candy he can hold?

227. Let's list some of the things you have to do to make external reinforcement work. If the reward is going to motivate you, you have to feel deprived of it and not satiated. This means that there's not an easier way of getting the reward than doing the work. The reward has to come fairly soon after the behavior it's meant to increase. How much you get has to be very

proportional to how much you work. There has to be a good way of measuring productivity. There must not be long times when effort doesn't have a possible payoff. You must not have a way of getting the reinforcer without doing the effort. It's good if you're not be too strongly tempted to lie in order to get the reinforcer, or the program may reinforce lying rather than working. The person giving the reward must be very dependable about coming through when the reward has been earned, and since the rewards have to be paid fairly frequently, this is a big job.

The above paragraph implies that arranging external reinforcement programs that work well is

A. very easy,
or
B. pretty hard to do?

228. It is certainly not impossible to put together external reinforcement programs that work. In most of the workplaces in the world, you will find one. The reinforcer is called "a paycheck" and the behavior in question is called "doing the job." But many people spend lots of time making sure those programs work well. Those people are called "managers."

You can't always count on having a good manager for all your self-discipline challenges, who will rig up an external reinforcement program that is just right for you. For this reason, it's a good idea to strengthen your powers of internal reinforcement and to work toward managing your own external reinforcement programs.

The author feels that

A. external reinforcement is not as moral and good as internal reinforcement,
or
B. there are often practical problems with getting a good external reinforcement program going, so if you're smart you'll try to get good at using internal reinforcement and self-directed external reinforcement?

Topics for Writing or Discussion

1. Please list some self-discipline choice points involved in running a reinforcement program for yourself.
2. Please write or speak aloud some fantasy rehearsals of using self-discipline in some of the choice points that you have made up.
3. Please try to carry out a self-directed reward system. Plan the work toward the goal, and plan what reinforcers you get. See if you can faithfully do the work and give yourself the reinforcers only when you've earned them. In any case, write or tell about what happened. What went on in your mind? What did you do?

4. Please write your thoughts about whether reinforcement you have to work for is more fun to get than reinforcement you get for free. Think about the following examples: someone working at a low wage versus someone receiving welfare; a lion hunting for food in the wild versus a lion being fed regularly in a zoo; someone taking a very easy course at school versus someone taking a more challenging course; being invited into a club that is very selective, versus joining a club that anyone can join.

5. It has been said that earning reinforcement that you value highly, by doing challenges that are for you neither too hard nor too easy, is a very powerful antidote to depression. From what you have seen so far of the world and of people, do you agree with this?

6. If the proposition mentioned in the topic above is correct, it could be that if all people were taught, at an early age, to do self-directed reinforcement programs, there would be a lot less depression in the world. What do you think about this idea?

7. Does making an arrangement with another person for external reinforcement get rid of the problem that you already have to have a certain amount of self-discipline before you can use such a program effectively? If the answer is no, what ways do you have to use self-discipline to be successful in such a program?

Chapter 13: Self-Monitoring

229. Imagine that you are trying to get better at hitting basketball shots. You have a goal and several balls and some practice time. You can do a lot of practice! You even have someone to retrieve balls for you. Unfortunately, however, you are blindfolded and your ears are plugged so that you can neither see nor hear whether your shots went in. You throw the ball a lot.

How effective do you think this practice would be in improving your ability to shoot baskets?

A. very useful,
or
B. not very useful?

230. What is missing in this setup? It's getting feedback on how you're doing. If you aren't able to tell how well each of your tries worked, you don't know how to do it better the next time.

No one would think of practicing basketball this way. However, they try to work towards lots of other goals without keeping track of how they are doing. For example:

Someone wants to save money. When he's been doing this for two months, someone asks him, "How much money do you have now, and how much more is that than you had two months ago?" He replies, "I don't have a clue."

Someone wants to get faster in math. When someone asks, "How fast are you now?" the person replies, "I don't know."

Someone wants to get better grades. Someone asks, "What have been your grades over the last three weeks?" The person replies, "I don't know; we don't get our report cards for a while."

Someone wants better anger control. When someone asks, "How many times have you lost your temper, in a way you didn't like, in the last month?" The person replies, "I have no idea."

The point of these examples is that

A. people should work harder on goals,
or
B. people often try to work on goals without measuring well enough how they are doing?

231. "That which gets measured gets improved." If you really want to get better at something, measure progress accurately and frequently. That way, you will know right away if you are getting off track, and you can correct yourself. You will also get positive feedback if you are on the right track, and you can reinforce yourself for that. Measuring, or monitoring, how you are doing gives you the crucial information you need to decide "Do I keep on doing

102

more of the same?" or "Do I change what I'm doing?"

The reason that monitoring how you are doing is so important is that

A. it lets you decide what to change and what to keep the same about what you are doing,
or
B. it lets you compare yourself to other people and know whether you are better than they are?

232. Through the celebrations exercise, you've learned to monitor your individual self-discipline choice points and to celebrate your triumphs. Self-monitoring is similar, but different. In self-monitoring you are looking at the results that your self-discipline choice point triumphs are producing. You measure the progress that your choices are contributing toward your goal. For example, someone who is trying to lose weight celebrates the choice points of passing up junk food, and self-monitors by writing down her weight every morning.

The loss of weight in this example is

A. the choice point,
or
B. the result that correct choices should be producing?

233. Someone who is trying to get into better shape celebrates the times of working out, and self-monitors by timing himself in a two mile run regularly.

The time in the two mile run is the

A. choice that is made,
or
B. the result of the choices that are made?

234. A person who is trying to be a good student celebrates choosing to study rather than goof off; she self-monitors by keeping track of test grades.

The decisions to study rather than goof off are

A. the choices that are made,
or
B. the result of the choices that are made?

235. Sometimes you can count on other people to measure your performance. If you are a professional basketball player, after every game you can find out what per cent of your shots went in, how many rebounds you made, and many other statistics. But if you are trying to pay attention in class, lose weight, quit smoking, control your temper, or start homework projects early, you will have to do most of the measuring yourself. No one else is interested enough in your goals to do it for you.

The paragraph you have just read has to do with one of the two words in the phrase "self-monitoring." The word is

A. self,
or
B. monitoring?

236. Let's look at some examples of how people do self-monitoring. A person has a goal of losing weight, from 190 pounds to 170 pounds. He weighs himself every morning and writes down his weight on a chart he keeps. He has weekly and monthly goals for the weight he wants to be, and he frequently compares his actual weight to his goal weight.

The self-monitoring occurs

A. when he sets the goal,
or
B. when he weighs himself each morning and writes his weight on a chart?

237. A person has a goal of getting lots of aerobic exercise through walking and running. He gets a pedometer, which he can wear on his belt; the pedometer measures how many steps he takes. He wears it all the time. At the end of each day, he looks at the pedometer and enters on a chart how many steps he took that day. He sets daily, weekly, and monthly goals, and gradually increases them. At present, he aims for an average of 15,000 steps per day.

The self-monitoring occurs

A. when he looks at the pedometer each night and writes the result on a chart,
or
B. when he gradually increases his goals?

238. A person has a goal of writing a book. Every day he gets his computer to count the words in his draft so far, and he enters this number on a chart. He aims for 2000 words added per day. He also has a computer program that counts the number of keystrokes he makes while working on his book. He enters this number in his chart every day also. He aims for an average of 20,000 keystrokes a day.

He uses two ways of measuring his productivity for the day. They are

A. the number of minutes he writes and the number of pages,
or
B. the number of words and the number of keystrokes?

239. A person who has had trouble with alcoholism has a goal of drinking no alcohol at all. He puts a check mark on his calendar for each day that he drinks no alcohol. For any day that he does drink, he plans to write a detailed report of exactly how much he drank of what beverage, what led up to this, what he

was doing at the time, and exactly what effect the alcohol had on him.

He does not particularly enjoy keeping records. In his plan, are the records

A. much easier when he does not drink,
or
B. much easier when he does drink?

240. A student has a goal of making top grades. Every time she gets back some graded work, she writes down the score in a section of her appointment and to do book. She finds out from the teacher how heavily each grade is weighted, so that at any moment, she can compute what her average is.

She is self-monitoring by

A. recording her grades on tests and papers etc.
or
B. recording how many hours she works?

241. A student has a goal of turning in 100% of all homework assignments on time. She writes the assignments in an assignment book. She makes a check mark after each assignment as she finishes it. She makes another line through the check mark when she turns in the assignment. She can flip through her assignment book and measure her success by looking at the marks by the assignments.

Her making these check marks each time she does the behavior that is her goal is called

A. advanced self-discipline,
or
B. self-monitoring?

242. Another student has a goal of getting a high score on a standardized college-admission test. The student buys a couple of books of sample tests. Every day the student takes one thirty-minute section of a sample test, grades that section, and calculates what the grade on the whole test would be if she kept up the same percentage correct. She enters the result in a chart. Some of the tests she has never taken before; some are retakes of tests she has practiced with previously. She keeps one set of records for new tests and another set for retakes. She looks at how the practice test scores increase over time as she uses various study techniques.

One of the main benefits of her self-monitoring is that

A. she can tell which techniques work the best,
or
B. she can study the same test questions that will be on the real test?

243. A person has a goal of making people in his family feel good. He resolves to be joyous and kind with his

family members whenever possible. Every day at the end of the day, he writes down a rating of how good a job he did at these goals, where 0 is a terrible job and 10 is a great job. He looks at his chart each day, and he tries to get the numbers as high as he can. He finds that this helps him in his goal, and his family members seem to be getting happier.

Your joyousness and kindness are harder to measure than things like your weight or your time in the mile run.

Nonetheless, as this section illustrates,

A. you can sometimes measure hard-to-measure things well enough just by giving them a rating,
or
B. unless you can measure something with absolute precision, you should just forget about measuring?

244. Rashad has a goal to keep his work space organized and neat. He thinks that he can get more work done if things are in place. Each night he gives himself a rating, where 10 means that his desk and papers and books are super neat and organized, and 0 means that they are in a total mess. He tries to get the number as high as he can get it.

This is another example of

A. an impossible goal,
or

B. using a rating to measure something that would be hard to measure otherwise?

How Often Should You Monitor Yourself?

245. If a goal is really very important to you, you'll usually do best to monitor your progress very often. I recommend daily monitoring. If you're working on your goal every day, it's nice if you can measure your progress every day.

Some students monitor their success in schoolwork only when report cards come out. Does the paragraph you just read imply that this is usually

A. often enough,
or
B. not often enough?

Sharing Your Self-Monitoring Results With Another Person

246. Accountability usually helps self-discipline. Accountability means that you let someone else know the results of your self-monitoring. Choose someone who will be genuinely delighted if you triumph in your self-discipline choice points, not someone who will be jealous of you. Celebrate your successes with that person. If you have a whole group of people, that is sometimes even better.

What if you would be embarrassed to share the results of your self-monitoring with just any old person? Sometimes people seek out special groups with whom they can share their self-monitoring – groups like Alcoholics Anonymous or Weight Watchers or Recovery Inc.

The idea of this section is that

A. self-monitoring should be kept to yourself,
or
B. sometimes self-monitoring has more powerful effects when you tell the results to other people?

Using Self-Discipline to Develop Self-Discipline

247. Remembering to measure something and writing it in a chart is often very helpful in achieving your goals. But these behaviors are often not the most fun things to do at a certain moment.

Therefore, it takes what skill even to do self-monitoring?

A. self-discipline,
or
B. joyousness?

248. Self-monitoring is meant to help you achieve your goals and use self-discipline. But you have to have a certain amount of self-discipline to use this technique. The more self-discipline

you already have, the more you will be able to increase it by self-monitoring.

I mentioned earlier that it takes self-discipline to use a self-directed reward system. It takes self-discipline to write goals, list choice points, and do fantasy rehearsals. It takes self-discipline to read this book! Almost all the techniques for increasing self-discipline require some self-discipline to begin with.

The point that's being made is that

A. the more self-discipline you have, the more you can use these techniques to develop more self-discipline,
or
B. the less self-discipline you have, the easier it is to improve, because you have more room for improvement?

249. The idea you've just heard doesn't apply just to self-discipline. If you have a lot of money to invest, it's easier for you to make more money. This is the basis for the proverb, "The rich get richer." If you are already well educated, for example by knowing how to read well and understand lots of words, it's easier for you to educate yourself further. If you already have a good reputation, it's easier for you to get good jobs that will make your reputation even better.

The more general idea you've just read is that

A. for lots of desirable things, the more you have, the easier it is to get more,

or

B. for lots of desirable things, the less you have, the easier it is to get more?

250. If you feel that your self-discipline skills are very low right now, you may not be ready to set a goal of daily self-monitoring. You may not be ready to use several of the other techniques, either. But don't let this discourage you. As long as you are having any "success experiences" in any goal-seeking activity, you are probably building greater self-discipline. By success experiences, I mean any examples of trying to do something and succeeding. Focus upon these success experiences, and try to build more of them.

The message of this section is

A. if you can't use self-monitoring and write your goals and do all the other things that are suggested here, just forget developing self-discipline!

or

B. any time you set even a very small goal and through effort succeed at it, you are probably building self-discipline.

Topics for Writing or Discussion

1. Ken has five or six major goals that are very important. But he doesn't have the time and energy to self-monitor every day in all of them. He self-monitors in one of them for a week, then another for another week, and so forth. Do you think this is a good solution to the problem? Can you think of any other solutions?

2. Please try to do daily self-monitoring with one or two goals for at least a few days. How successful were you? What was it like? Was the payoff you got from the self-monitoring worth the effort?

3. Suppose that someone self-monitors, but never takes the time to think about questions like, "Am I getting better or worse? What do I do that makes some days more successful than others? What should I do to make the average for next week better than the average for this week?" Do you think that at least a little time spent pondering these questions is necessary for self-monitoring to be useful?

4. What do you think about this general idea: People who invent ways that people can measure their progress toward goals quickly, easily, and accurately, do a lot of good in helping people.

What do you think about these specific examples? Suppose that there were a computer program that recorded everything you said to family members and gave you an accurate number at the end of the day that measured how kind and cheerful you were. Do you think that this would help people in families get along better?

Suppose that there were another computer program that would analyze a digital photo of your meal, and give you an instant accurate readout of how many calories it contained? Would this help people lose weight?

What measuring inventions can you imagine that would help people the most?

Chapter 14: More on Advanced Self-Discipline

251. Earlier in this book you read about "advanced self-discipline." This can be even more useful to you than "ordinary" self-discipline. Ordinary self-discipline means doing what is best, even though it's less pleasant. Advanced self-discipline means teaching yourself to make the better choice pleasant! With advanced self-discipline, you get not only the long-term payoff, but short-term enjoyment as well, because you have learned to take pleasure in doing what is best to do.

Which of the following two people is using "advanced self-discipline?"

A. One who makes herself do chemistry problems, even though he doesn't enjoy them,
or
B. one who teaches herself to enjoy chemistry problems?

252. In using advanced self-discipline, it helps if you believe two things:
1. It's possible to enjoy doing the better choice, and
2. it's admirable to enjoy doing the better choice.
     What do you think about someone who has trained himself to get much pleasure out of schoolwork? Do you think that this person has accomplished a really desirable feat? Or do you think that the person is a nerd and very uncool?

     Anyone who believes that such a person is very uncool will find advanced self-discipline in schoolwork

A. harder to do,
or
B. easier to do?

253. There are three important reasons why people sometimes decide they *don't* want to learn to enjoy making a more self-disciplined choice: peer pressure, making excuses for their own behavior, and rebellion against an authority.
     Sometimes pressure from other people works against using advanced self-discipline. Suppose that Lenore is with a group of friends. One of them says, "I hate math!" Two others say, "Me too." One says, "What about you, Lenore?" Lenore says, "I love math." All the friends look at her as if she is a freak. "You love math?" says one of the friends, in a shocked and disapproving tone of voice.

What message is Lenore getting from her friends?

A. "You should be like us and hate math,"
or

B. "We admire you for using advanced self-discipline?"

254. Bo trains himself to have a really good time at parties without drinking any alcohol at all. He teaches himself to relax and joke around and enjoy people and not feel self-conscious. He has set a goal of doing this without alcohol because he has learned about all the damage that alcohol can do. His classmate, Lem, thinks that this is the stupidest thing he's ever heard of. He believes that Bo is being a real wimp, and that if he were tough and strong he would prove it by showing how much he could hold his liquor.

Suppose Lem becomes an alcoholic. Do you think that the sort of belief that Lem has will make it

A. harder to break his addiction,
or
B. easier to break his addiction?

255. Sometimes people are in habits of acting in unself-disciplined ways. But they don't want to feel bad about themselves. So they think up some reason to admire people who act in those unself-disciplined ways, and not to admire those who are more self-disciplined. This helps them excuse their own behavior and not feel so bad about it. This helps them excuse their own behavior and not feel so bad about it.
Someone is very overweight. In order to make herself not feel so bad about herself, she thinks, "I can't stand

these people who are always watching what they eat and always exercising. Just because some stupid model looks like she is skin and bones, they think they have to look that way too. They should realize that they have to be themselves."

This way of thinking may indeed make her feel better about herself. But it will probably also make advanced self-discipline in weight control

A. easier for this person,
or
B. harder for this person?

256. Someone is very out of shape. He watches some cross-country runners running. He says, "These people are so stupid to inflict such pain on themselves. They must be hating every minute of what they are doing, but they keep doing it anyway. Where are their brains?"

In the area of exercise and fitness, this person seems to believe that

A. enjoying tough exercise is easy,
or
B. enjoying tough exercise is impossible?

257. It's much easier to use advanced self-discipline if you *want* to enjoy the better choice. Pressure from peers and excusing your own behavior are only two reasons why people sometimes

don't want to enjoy the better choice. Sometimes they don't want to enjoy it because someone is making them do it, and they feel mad about being bossed around. Their attitude seems to be, "I don't have the freedom to keep you from making me do it. But at least I'm free enough to hate every minute of it." This is not a very smart thing to do, especially when they are being made to do something because it is a very good idea. But it's a very human thing to do.

Rena's mom yells at her to clean up her room. Rena yells back at her mom, "Leave me alone!" Rebelling against her mom makes it hard for Rena to think, "I admire people who are able to keep their rooms organized; I want to learn to enjoy doing that myself."

The point of this section is that

A. sometimes people seem to want to hate doing the best thing, because someone is making them do it,
or
B. people always want to learn to enjoy doing what makes things come out best in the long run?

258. Two people have to give a speech, as a requirement for school. The first person thinks to himself, "I wish that no one had made me do this! I'm going to hate this!" He pays lots of attention to how nervous he is. He reminds himself over and over that there's no way he would give this speech if someone weren't making him do it. He does hate giving the speech, but he makes himself do it anyway. He accomplishes his goal.

The second person says to himself, "This isn't the first time I've had to do something I wouldn't have chosen, and it won't be the last time. It will be good for me to learn to enjoy it. How can I think about this in a way that will help me enjoy it?" He concentrates on how useful the information is that he will give to people. He concentrates on how it might help them to hear what he has to say. This makes him feel good. He feels some nervousness, but he considers this unimportant and ignores it. He actually enjoys giving the speech.

Which of these two people has used advanced self-discipline?

A. the first,
or
B. the second?

259. Let's suppose you decide that you really want to be able to enjoy doing the better choice. How do you do advanced self-discipline? You do it by selective attention, habituation, self-reinforcement, and skill-learning. Let's go over each of these one by one.

Selective attention means that you select what you want to pay attention to and what you want to ignore. To do advanced self-discipline, you train yourself to pay attention to the good and fun things about the better choice, and to ignore the parts that aren't fun.

Selective attention means

A. paying attention to how you select things,
or
B. paying attention to certain things and ignoring others?

260. A man trains himself to enjoy working out with weights. He keeps lifting over and over until he feels a burning feeling in his muscle. This is the feeling of his muscle's getting very tired. But he knows that this feeling means that he is stressing the muscle to get stronger and stronger. Knowing this feels good. He also knows that he is teaching himself self-discipline. He thinks that this self-discipline will help him in other ways. This thought feels good. He also notices that the feeling of having tired muscles is pleasant in a way that is the opposite of feeling restless. As time goes by, he learns to pay lots of attention to the thoughts and sensations that feel good, and to ignore the sensations that feel bad. Gradually lifting weights becomes more and more pleasant.

Selective attention in this case refers to the fact that the man

A. selected the parts of the lifting that felt good, and paid attention to them, while ignoring the unpleasant parts,
or

B. got selected by lots of people who paid attention to his big muscles?

261. A girl wants to use advanced self-discipline in practicing piano. As she practices, she imagines herself playing the song really well on a stage. She imagines the audience being really impressed with her work and applauding her. She imagines people telling her afterwards how good her music sounded.

By having this fantasy of a very satisfying success, and paying "selective attention" to it from time to time, she makes her practice time

A. more exciting and pleasant,
or
B. less exciting and pleasant?

262. A boy uses the same technique to learn to enjoy his math homework. While doing his homework he occasionally has a fantasy of being in a math contest. In the fantasy, he is in front of lots of people, and he gets asked a question just like his homework problem. He answers it with ease and grace, and people are very impressed. He feels fairly sure that such a fantasy will never come true in real life, but the image still helps him to enjoy his homework.

Instead of having this fantasy, the boy could have focused his attention on the fun activities he was missing out on while doing his homework. Imagining the contest instead, and paying attention to this fantasy, are the use of

A. selective attention,
or
B. self-criticism?

263. Habituation means that you gradually get used to the parts of the activity that don't feel good. Suppose that a person starts out on a running program, to get physically fit. At first the sensation of running is totally unpleasant. The person does it purely for the long-term benefit.

Is this person so far using

A. ordinary self-discipline,
or
B. advanced self-discipline?

264. Suppose that the same person gradually gets used to the feeling of being short of breath and tired, the more he experiences it. Getting used to something the more you experience it is called habituation.

Gradually the person learns to think, "I'm doing something good for my body." He believes it strongly enough that he feels good as he runs. After a while the sensation of running becomes pleasant for him. He has learned to enjoy, in the present, the activity that produces the long-term gain.

After spending lots of time breathing fast, he got used to the feeling of wanting to breathe fast. Getting used to something is called

A. emotion,
or
B. habituation?

265. As you recall, self-reinforcement means rewarding yourself for your work.

Two people are working at playing the piano. As the first one practices, she says to herself, "That was messed up. Ooh, that didn't sound good. Why doesn't it come quicker to me? I don't like this."

The second one says to herself, "I'm glad I sat down to practice! That took some self-discipline.... OK, that didn't sound bad, let's see if I can make it sound better the next time.... I did! Hooray! ... Oh boy, that was a part that I've had trouble with before, and I did it right this time! It sounded good! ... Wow, now it sounds almost good enough to play for someone to listen to!"

The second person will probably find advanced self-discipline much easier because the person is using more

A. habituation,
or
B. self-reinforcement?

266. Another way to do advanced self-discipline is skill-learning: getting yourself very skilled at the task you are doing. The more you practice, the easier the skill becomes. You don't have to work so hard to do it, and it is more pleasant.

Someone compares what he can gain by watching TV and by reading. He starts a program of watching TV less and reading more. At first it's unpleasant. Reading feels like hard, unpleasant work. But the more the person reads, the more skilled the person becomes at reading, the less it feels like boring work, and the more enjoyable it gets. After some time, the person actually enjoys reading more than watching TV.

We call this "advanced self-discipline" because the person has gradually learned to

A. make himself do what's better even though it's unpleasant,
or
B. enjoy doing what is better for him?

267. Lenore finds math unpleasant. She uses self-discipline to work at math, every day. She practices getting fast at math facts. She practices figuring out how to do harder problems. She keeps going for greater and greater skill. People start referring to her as a math whiz. She wants to enjoy math. Gradually she finds herself enjoying it more and more, the better she gets at it. Finally it becomes her favorite subject.

The technique she used to get more advanced self-discipline was

A. fantasy rehearsal,
or
B. skill-learning?

268. Raymond finds it very unpleasant to do writing assignments. But he is in a program at college where he will have to do a lot of writing.

Raymond takes apart the task of writing into some different skills. He decides to practice each one of them until he is very good at them.

He practices typing until he gets very fast. He gets so skilled at typing that he can type without having to think about the letters; when he thinks a word, his fingers type the right letters.

He works at spelling. He works on being able to spell the most common words in his field without having to stop and look them up or wonder about them.

He studies grammar. He becomes able to find and correct errors very quickly. He becomes able to improve the wording of sample sentences more and more quickly.

He does an exercise where he reads a paragraph in a book and then writes in his own words what he remembers.

He practices putting thoughts into words, each time he has a writing assignment. He practices writing long letters to friends, and making long entries in his own journal.

After several months of doing all these things, he has become much more skilled at writing. Writing has also become much more pleasant for him.

We just described him using what method to develop advanced self-discipline?

A. selective attention,

or

B. skill-learning?

269. Selective attention, habituation, self-reinforcement, and skill-learning are four ways of increasing your enjoyment of a self-disciplined choice. The other techniques we've already talked about also help. It helps to set the goal, use the internal sales pitch, identify the choice points, use the celebrations exercise, do fantasy rehearsals, and so forth.

A good fraction of everything written in this book has to do with learning

A. ordinary self-discipline only,

or

B. advanced self-discipline?

Topics for Writing or Discussion

1. What are three reasons why people sometimes convince themselves that they don't want to use advanced self-discipline in a certain area? In other words, what are three obstacles to advanced self-discipline?

2. If someone does want to use advanced self-discipline, what are four techniques that the person can use?

3. Do you think that someone's skill at advanced self-discipline is very strongly related to how happy the person is? Why or why not?

4. Please make up a story about someone's using advanced self-discipline successfully. Have the main character in the story face some of the three obstacles, overcome them, and use some of the four techniques to learn to enjoy the better choice.

5. What type of self-disciplined choice would you like to learn to enjoy making? Please describe why you would like to learn advanced self-discipline in this area.

6. For the type of better choice you wrote about for question 5, please make up a fantasy rehearsal of enacting that choice, and enjoying doing it.

7. Please think of some type of work that you experience as not very much fun. Try doing this task, using selective attention and self-reinforcement. Were you able to enjoy the task any more than you usually do? Please write about your experience with this.

Chapter 15: More on Work Capacity

270. In this book we have mentioned the idea of *work capacity* several times. Work capacity means how much work you can get done per week, per month, per year. Work capacity is related to how long you can keep going on a certain type of work before you say to yourself, "I've had enough. I need to quit doing this."

One person's work capacity will probably be very different for different types of work. For example, someone may be able to work very long on putting Legos together, but may become restless very quickly when trying to write an article.

Some people, however, seem to have greater work capacity, across the board, for a wide variety of tasks, than other people do. Being able to put in a lot of work helps you to achieve your goals.

A summary of what was just said is that

A. some people can work longer than others, and they're more likely to achieve their goals,
or
B. work capacity depends so much on what sort of work it is, that nobody can be said to have more work capacity than anybody else?

271. Tyra sits down to do homework at 3:30 p.m. At 5:30 she is still going strong, accomplishing a lot, being productive. She has gotten a very large amount done during the last two hours. Her work output on that particular afternoon is at least two hours at high efficiency.

On the other hand, suppose that Zelia starts working at 3:30. After working and accomplishing very little, at 3:45 she stops working and takes a break. She can't get herself to start back. On that afternoon her work output is only 15 minutes at low efficiency.

Who had the higher work capacity, on that afternoon at least?

A. Tyra,
or
B. Zelia?

272. How much work you get done is a combination of two factors. The first is how much time you can spend. The second is how fast you get things done, or your efficiency. If you can keep going for a long time without feeling the need for a break, that helps. If taking short frequent breaks refreshes you and lets you get more done more quickly, that's fine too.

How much work you get done depends on

A. how long you work and how fast you go,

or

B. how much you like the work and who is judging it?

273. If you are sick or very upset, you usually can't get as much work done. Pain and ill health reduce most people's work capacity.

When you have no reason to want to work, you will usually do less. When you want very much to get the work done, you will usually work more. A strong wish to get the work done is called high motivation.

How much work you can do also depends on how skilled you are at the task you are doing. For example, someone who is very strong but not a good writer is able to move for bricks a long time, but wants a break after ten minutes of trying to write a report. For someone else who is a very good writer but not very strong, the pattern is the opposite. The more skilled we are at a task, the longer we can persist at it.

The point of this section is that work capacity depends on

A. your health, your motivation, and your skill,

or

B. your position, your location, and your friends?

274. Some people have a problem with work capacity that is caused by a certain type of bad feeling, a "tired from working" or "bored or restless from working" feeling. This bad feeling rapidly increases as they do almost any kind of work. They have low work capacity. Other people do not get this bad feeling nearly as fast. They can keep working at a wide variety of tasks for a long time at high efficiency. They have a high work capacity.

Your work capacity is greater

A. if you quickly get a bored, tired, or restless feeling from working,

or

B. if it takes a long time for you to get a bored, tired, or restless feeling from working?

275. As you might guess, there is a strong connection between work capacity and success. Benjamin Bloom and colleagues did a study of 120 very talented and successful individuals – neurologists, concert pianists, champion swimmers, and others. These successful people all worked at their particular skill for thousands of hours over many years.

Bloom and the people who worked with him found that

A. when you are talented enough, you don't need to do any work,

or

B. success is usually the result of a lot of work?

276. How satisfied are you with your work capacity? Would you like to be able to get more work done per day, per week, per year? Would you like to accomplish more? Would you like not to get that unpleasant "I need a break" feeling so quickly? Maybe you would like to increase your work capacity.

Having a high or low work capacity isn't just a matter of luck. Although what you inherit makes a difference, you can increase your work capacity by training yourself.

Your work capacity is something that

A. you were born with, and you can't change,
or
B. you can change by training yourself?

277. If you want to increase your work capacity, there is a very important belief or idea that you should cultivate: the *effort-payoff connection.* This is the idea that effort brings payoffs, that work bring rewards, that you can get lots of things you want if you are willing to try hard enough.

The effort-payoff connection is the idea that
A. connections have a payoff that comes without effort,
or
B. effort brings payoffs; work brings rewards?

278. What's the opposite of this idea? Not believing in the effort-payoff connection is sometimes called *helplessness.* Examples of not believing in the effort-payoff connection are the thought that "No matter how hard I work, it won't make any difference." Or "Why try hard? The result will be the same anyway."

Raymond thinks to himself, "It doesn't make any difference if I study math or if I don't. I'm just not smart at math. I can't pass it no matter what."

Would you say that he believes in
A. an effort-payoff connection,
or
B. his own helplessness?

279. Believing in the effort-payoff connection helps you get work done. It also helps you to be happy! Research done by Martin Seligman and colleagues has demonstrated this connection. It makes sense that the idea, "There's nothing I can do about it," is depressing, and the idea, "I can make good things happen by doing the right things," leads to good feelings.

Someone says, "Something very bad happened to me. But I know how to make things better! I believe that my efforts can have a big positive effect!" According to what you just read, would you guess that this person is

A. depressed,
or

B. not depressed?

280. Rachel has always been talented in math. Also, the math classes she has taken in elementary school have been very easy. She has been able to get A's in math even though she has never studied the textbook and even though she has spent lots of time in math class daydreaming. She thinks, "It doesn't matter how much I work – I'll get an A in math anyway." Although most people would not describe her as feeling "helpless," she nonetheless feels that her own work is not what brings success.

Does she believe in the effort-payoff connection for math grades?

A. yes,
or
B. no?

281. When she gets to middle school she takes an honors math course. This course is much more demanding than anything she has seen so far. She finds herself not doing well. She thinks to herself, "I guess I'm not smart in math, after all."

What would be an example of a thought that shows belief in the effort-payoff connection?

A. "The other kids who are doing well are really lucky."
or

B. "If I want to do better, I'll have to work harder."

282. It would be a nicer world, perhaps, if we could get anything we want just by working hard enough at it. But sometimes, in a certain area, there is no effort-payoff connection. Sometimes there really is nothing we can do to achieve a certain goal! Sometimes we have to decide not to waste our efforts working toward one goal, and put our work toward some other goal where we have more of a chance at a payoff.

The idea you just read is that
A. there is always a connection between effort and payoff. If you work hard, you can achieve anything,
or
B. there are some payoffs you can't get, no matter how hard you work. It's good to recognize these for what they are.

283. Rashad is very short, and so are both his parents. He's never been able to run nearly as fast as his friends. He's not very well coordinated. A person who is giving a speech says, "You can do anything you want if you put your mind to it! If you only work hard enough, you can grow up to be better in basketball than Michael Jordan!"

Do you think that Rashad should

A. believe this,
or
B. not believe this?

284. On the other hand, Rashad has been able to do very well in several school courses when he has worked at them. Someone tells him, "Rashad, if you will work hard enough at all your courses, you will be able to go to college, graduate, and learn a profession. If you keep working, you can become a very successful person."

Does the effort-payoff connection here sound

A. more likely to be true,
or
B. less likely to be true?

285. The effort-payoff connection is a confidence that you can get a certain payoff by working for it. How do people build up such confidence? They build it up by successfully getting payoffs by working for them. If you have small successes with small payoffs, that gives you more confidence in the effort-payoff connection for larger goals.

You develop an effort-payoff connection by

A. reading that it exists,
or
B. experiencing, lots of times, that your work gets rewards?

286. Janelle wanted a stuffed animal. Her dad let her earn it by doing chores

and doing drills on schoolwork. Later in her life, she wanted a computer, and she earned the money for it by babysitting. Ruth, on the other hand, had all the stuffed animals she wanted given to her. If she wanted a computer, her parents would buy her one.

Based on these experiences alone, who of these two is learning the effort-payoff connection more?

A. Janelle,
or
B. Ruth?

287. Damon has had trouble learning to read. He has gotten to fourth grade without learning to read well at all. The homework he is assigned is over his head because he cannot read it. He realizes that no matter how hard he tries to listen in class, he can't make good grades.

Can Damon see a reason to believe in an effort-payoff connection for schoolwork?

A. yes,
or
B. no?

288. Then Damon gets a tutor. The tutor does some tests. The tutor says, "Our goal is to learn the sounds of the first five letters, so well that you can tell the answers forty times in a row without missing one. When you can do that,

we'll celebrate." In that very session, Damon works and works and finally gives the right answers forty times in a row. Then the tutor and Damon celebrate by playing a fun game. Damon's efforts have now earned a small payoff.

In his experience with tutoring, is Damon starting to get a reason to believe in the effort-payoff connection?

A. yes,
or
B. no?

289. Getting a tutor was a way for Damon to start learning the effort-payoff connection. Going back to tasks that were not too hard and not too easy was another way. Having someone in your life who approves of your productivity is another way, if you value that person's approval. Sometimes you have to arrange your life experiences so that your brain can learn the effort-payoff connection.

The idea of this section is that you learn the effort-payoff connection

A. simply by someone's telling you about it,
or
B. by having lots of experiences that convince you that effort pays off?

290. Once you believe that work is worthwhile and will bring payoffs to you, there is another way to increase your work capacity. We have used many times in this book the example of getting into physical condition. Suppose that someone is physically out of shape. The person wants to be able to run several miles without stopping, but for now the person gets so out of breath and tired when he runs that he cannot last longer than 20 seconds.

At this point, the person's work capacity for running is

A. low,
or
B. high?

291. How does the person get in shape? He runs every day. He self-monitors how long, how fast, and how far he can run, over time. He tries to increase his running capacity gradually as he trains. He stresses his body enough to stimulate the changes known as getting in shape. He experiences the feeling of being short of breath and tired, but he keeps pushing on, without overdoing it, despite these feelings. He gradually gets used to feeling tired and breathless; he *habituates* to these feelings. Habituation makes the feelings bother him less and less over time. Through daily practice, he develops his work capacity for running.

Getting into good physical shape is really another word for increasing a certain type of

A. work capacity,
or
B. celebrations exercise?

292. You can use the same process to develop your work capacity for reading, writing, math, piano practice, computer programming, or other tasks you do with your mind. You see how long you can go before your score on the "Persistence Power" scale goes way down. You push on a little longer than you did before, despite feeling tired or bored. Thus you give yourself a chance to habituate to the sensation of lots of effort, to get used to it, to let it bother you less and less. In time, it might even begin to feel good to you. You self-monitor and self-reinforce. If you are able to work very efficiently for an hour whereas before you would feel unable to go on after twenty minutes, you celebrate greatly. You realize that you deserve to feel great.

The point made in this section is that

A. increasing work capacity in other areas is very much like getting into good physical shape,
or
B. increasing work capacity in schoolwork is the exact opposite of getting into good physical shape?

293. Here is the "Persistence Power Scale":

Persistence Power Scale

0=I can't stand to keep going on this. I feel that I have no more effort left to put into it.
2= It would be so unpleasant to keep going, and so pleasant to stop, that I feel only a little persistence power for this.
4=I feel some persistence power left to do this, enough to keep going, but it isn't very much.
6=I feel pretty much power to keep persisting, a moderate amount of ability to keep going.
8=I feel a LARGE amount of ability to keep going, a large amount of persistence power.
10=I feel a VERY LARGE amount of persistence power, a very great ability to keep putting out effort on this.

You can use this scale to self-monitor. At the beginning of your training, you might find that you sink low on the scale fairly soon after starting work. If as time goes on you find that you stay high on the scale for longer and longer, you are making progress.

The Persistence Power Scale measures

A. how much effort you think a certain goal is worth,
or
B. how much ability you feel that you have at a certain moment to keep up your effort on a certain task?

294. Here's a shorter version of the Persistence Power scale:

How much persistence power do you feel that you have right now?

0=None
2=Only a little
4=Some but not very much
6=Pretty much, moderate amount
8=Large amount
10=Very large amount

When you use the scale, you can give yourself any number between 0 and 10, including 9, 4.5, or whatever.

You'll notice that this scale asks you about how much you *feel* you can keep persisting. You often don't know how much you *really can* keep going until you do it.

The Persistence Power Scale measures

A. How much longer you can keep going, or
B. the *feeling* of being able to keep going?

295. I made this scale the Persistence Power scale rather than the "bored, tired, and restless" scale for a reason: when you look for something within yourself, you are likely to find it. If you keep asking yourself, "How tired am I? What bad feelings do I have?" you are more likely to notice those bad feelings, because you are focusing on them. On

the other hand, if you keep asking yourself, "What feelings of strength to keep on working do I have?" you are looking for that feeling of strength and you are more likely to find it.

The point of the last section was

A. focus on the feeling of strength inside you rather than on how tired you are,
or
B. pay careful attention to how bored, tired, or restless you are?

296. Sometimes you can have a lot of persistence power despite the fact that you feel very tired, bored, or restless.

Sam is running a marathon. He has run 20 miles. If he were to rate how tired his body feels, it would be at least 9 on a scale of 10. But he has also had that tired feeling for the previous 5 miles. He feels very determined to keep running and do well in the race, and he feels very confident that he can do so.

His rating of his persistence power would be

A. low, because he feels tired,
or
B. high, because he knows he can keep going despite feeling tired?

297. Here's something very important to know when you're training your work capacity. Your brain experiences taking a break after working as a

reward. It feels good to relax after working hard. When you give yourself rewards, you want to reward good habits, such as getting work done, and not bad habits, such as feeling very bored, tired, or restless. So you should plan to take breaks when you've accomplished a certain amount, not when you've gotten so tired that you feel you have to stop.

The advice you are being given now has to do with

A. when to take breaks from work,
or
B. never taking a break from work?

298. If someone says to herself, "I'll take a break after I've written 1000 words," the break will reward getting a lot of work done. That increases her work capacity! If she says to herself, "I'll take a break only when I feel so tired or bored that I can't go on any more," the break will reward her for feeling tired or bored. Breaks of that sort can decrease work capacity! So set goals for reasonable amounts of work to get done, and take breaks when it's time to celebrate achieving those goals.

What's an example of someone's following the advice that you just read?

A. "I'll take a break when my score on the Persistence Power Scale drops to 0,"
or

B. "I'll take a break when I've finished reading this chapter and answering the questions on it."

299. Here's another tip. Doing work with your mind, such as studying or reading or writing, often involves sitting fairly still. The main bad feeling some people get as they work longer and longer is restlessness: the urge to move around. If you're one of these people, try to exercise before working and between work periods. The human body was not meant to sit still all day; it was built to move. If you run, swim, walk, run in place, jump rope, or do sit-ups long enough, you may find that you extend your work capacity on "mind work" just by becoming more able to sit still. I recommend getting up and have a one-minute burst of intense exercise whenever you feel like it.

The advice you just got was that

A. you shouldn't get too tired when you want to work with your mind,
or
B. physical exercise may help you not to be so restless when you work with your mind?

300. Here's another tip about work capacity. Some people are afraid to push themselves to work faster and longer. They think, "If I work too long, I'll make it unpleasant for me. I want to enjoy it. It's better to work a short time

and enjoy it than a long time and not like it."

It is true that you want to give yourself enough time to relax and enjoy life. It's important not to feel that you have to be working all the time. But many people are more afraid of pushing themselves to work hard than they need to be.

When you work hard and long, you habituate to the unpleasant sensations of putting out effort. You get used to those feelings, so that they don't bother you so much. Pushing yourself really hard sometimes makes you enjoy the work a lot more in the future rather than making you hate it.

The advice you just got was to

A. be very careful not to work to the point where the work is unpleasant, or
B. go ahead and push yourself to work hard and long, so that habituation will help effort not to be so unpleasant in the future?

301. In addition to the tips you've gotten so far: just about everything you've read in this book can be applied to the goal of increasing your work capacity. You can set the goal clearly, use the internal sale pitch, list choice points, do fantasy rehearsals, use self-reinforcement, self-monitoring, and the celebrations exercise. You can use selective attention to help you enjoy the work. You can use skill-learning to make the work more pleasant.

The message of this section is that

A. all the techniques of this book can be used to increase your work capacity, or
B. increasing work capacity is a totally different task than the ones this book has to do with?

302. Now let's review some of the ideas of this chapter. Terri is studying for an exam, with a friend. Terri says, "Let's make up a really thorough practice exam, and then take a break. Then we can start back to work, and take our exam."

Terri's friend says, "Let's just keep on working until we can't work any more, and take a break then."

According to the ideas in this chapter, who has the better idea?

A. Terri's friend, because under her plan the break will come when they need it and not when they don't need it, or
B. Terri, because under her plan the break will reinforce reaching a goal rather than getting tired?

303. Jerry is working on writing a long paper for school. He is self-monitoring his work capacity.

Would you urge him to

A. focus his attention on his feeling of power to keep going,
or
B. focus his attention on how much he feels bored, tired, or restless?

304. Sandy is practicing the piano. After 10 minutes, he starts to feel a little tired of practicing.

Would you recommend that he

A. be careful not to practice past the point where he is enjoying the work,
or
B. push himself to practice for longer times, so that he can get used to doing that?

305. Jared tries very hard to increase his work capacity. At the beginning of his training, he finds it very hard to do 100 math facts without taking a break. After training for a few months, he finds that he can do 1000 math facts without stopping, and still feel plenty of energy for more work. He uses the number of math facts that he can do as a measure of work capacity. He measures this number over and over and keeps records of it over time.

 What he is doing is called

A. self-monitoring,
or
B. decreasing work capacity?

306. Rayna studies very carefully and thoroughly for a test. She notices that after all this study, she performs much better than when she has not studied so much. Noticing this gives her a little more belief in the power of studying to help her do well. This helps her to study more for another test.

What Rayna is noticing is called the

A. effort-payoff connection,
or
B. written plans?

Topics for Writing or Discussion

1. What is an area, or a type of task, for which you would like to increase your work capacity? What would be the benefits of increasing your work capacity in this area?

2. Suppose that someone wanted to increase work capacity in a certain area. What tips could you give that person?

3. During most of the centuries of human existence, there were very important experiences that served to teach the effort-payoff connection for most human beings: you go out and forage for food, or else you go hungry. You prepare some way of keeping warm, or else you get very cold or freeze. Do you think that modern life, with all its conveniences, sometimes does a disservice to people by breaking

up the effort-payoff connection? If so, in what ways do you think it does this?

4. There is good evidence that feeling and acting "depressed" is much more common when people have lost the effort-payoff connection. On the other hand, it is much more difficult to feel depressed when someone believes strongly that his or her efforts have a very good chance of making things turn out much better. What do you think about this idea?

5. Please experiment with using the "persistence power" scale. When you start a big task, rate your energy to keep working. As you work, stop every once in a while and write down the time and what your rating is. What happens as you work longer? What are your thoughts about this?

6. Sometimes people work too much in one area of their lives, and neglect other areas. For example, sometimes they work at their jobs too much, and neglect paying attention to their family members. Some people with this sort of problem are called "workaholics."

Someone says, "Workaholics don't need to decrease their work capacity for their jobs. What they need is to *increase* their work capacity for spending quality time with their families."

What are your thoughts about this idea? Do you think that it is too far

fetched to think about someone's "work capacity" for being gleeful and playful?

Chapter 16: Using Stimulus Control

307. Something you see, hear, smell, or feel that prompts you to do something is called a stimulus. What you do when you get that stimulus is called your response.

Suppose someone pokes your back. Startled, you turn around quickly to see what it is.

Which is the stimulus and which is the response?

A. The poke is the response and turning around is the stimulus,
or
B. the poke is the stimulus and turning around is the response?

308. Suppose that someone is at a party. The host puts a tray of brownies out on a table and says, "Have some!" One of the guests, seeing the brownies, picks one up and eats it.

Which is the stimulus and which is the response?

A. The brownies' being put out is the stimulus, and eating one is the response,
or
B. the brownies' being put out is the response, and eating one is the stimulus?

309. Suppose that someone wants to use self-discipline to concentrate fully on his homework.

Which stimulus do you think will most help her to do this?

A. A room with an interesting television show on,
or
B. a quiet room with no distractions?

310. If you purposely arrange the stimuli around you to try to bring out the responses in yourself that you want, you are using *stimulus control*. When you use stimulus control well, you avoid the temptations that would get in the way of your goal. Someone who goes into a quiet room to study instead of trying to study in front of the TV is using stimulus control.

Stimulus control means

A. putting yourself in the sorts of situations that bring out the responses you want,
or
B. learning to make the self-disciplined choice no matter what situation you are in?

311. Suppose that a man is an alcoholic, but he has quit drinking alcohol for a while. He sees a bar where he used to hang out and get drunk often. He thinks to himself, "I'll just go in and say hi to any friends I see there; I won't drink anything."

Would his going into the bar be a wise use of stimulus control?

A. yes,
or
B. no?

312. Since the man has had a habit of getting drunk while in that bar, the place has become a stimulus that is associated with drinking alcohol. If he really does not want to drink, he will be most wise to stay out of it.

Suppose a man has a very bad habit of physically attacking people whom he's mad at. He starts to get into an argument with someone in his family. He knows the argument will not be settled, whether he continues to talk with the person or not.

Which would be a wiser use of stimulus control, if he wants to keep himself from using violence?

A. To excuse himself and go outside for a walk by himself,
or
B. to keep on arguing with the other person?

313. Someone is trying to lose weight. Someone gives her a big basket of cookies and candy.

Which would be a wise use of stimulus control?

A. To get rid of the cookies and candy,
or
B. to keep them at home but try not to eat them?

314. A boy resolves to sit at his desk and do homework every day at a certain time. But he doesn't seem to be able to keep this resolution. His desk is piled with toys and clothes. It's hard to find a place to put these, because the rest of his room is also cluttered up with stuff all over the place.

What's the stimulus that gets in the way of his doing his work?

A. The resolution to work every day,
or
B. the clutter on the desk and in the room?

315. A girl would like to get some exercise today.

In which stimulus situation do you think it will be easier for her to follow this plan?

A. At a movie,
or
B. at a square dance?

316. A college kid is trying to stay out of fights.

In which stimulus situation do you think it will be easier for him to follow this plan?

A. At a bar with a bunch of guys who are drinking alcohol,
or
B. on a hike in the woods with one good friend?

317. A woman has an addiction to gambling. She has lost thousands of dollars by betting on horse races. She is trying to quit gambling. One day she thinks to herself, "Maybe I'll stop by the race track. I won't place a bet; I'll just watch the horses run for the fun of it."

Do you think that this plan is a

A. wise use of stimulus control,
or
B. an unwise use of stimulus control?

318. A boy wastes lots of time playing video games. He wants to accomplish several goals that require his time and effort. He decides that he wants to break his video game habit.

How can he use the principle of stimulus control better?

A. By leaving the video game set up in his room,
or
B. by packing the video game into a box and storing it in his attic?

319. At a certain school, the kids tend to distract each other and fight each other. But when they work one-on-one with an older person, they do not fight with that person, and they don't get as distracted.

Which strategy would make use of stimulus control in a wise way with this bunch of kids?

A. To teach a bunch of high school students to work one-on-one with the younger students,
or
B. to put lots of children in one very large classroom, so that they can learn to get along?

320. A man is trying not to eat so many cookies.

Which plan do you think is most likely to work, according to the principle of stimulus control?

A. To buy lots of cookies, but try to make a box last a long time,
or
B. just not to have them in his house at all?

321. When you are trying to make self-disciplined choices, don't forget about the strategy of stimulus control. People's abilities to resist temptations go up and down. At the moments when your resistance is lowest, you'll still be able to use self-discipline if you don't have handy the materials you need to give into the temptation!

How would you summarize the strategy of using stimulus control?

A. You teach yourself to handle big temptations by exposing yourself to them,
or
B. you avoid exposing yourself to temptation?

Topics for Writing or Discussion

1. Please look at your own goals. For each of your most important goals, please write how you can use stimulus control to help you achieve your goal.
2. As someone grows in self-discipline, do you think it would be a good idea for the person to gradually expose himself more and more to the tempting stimulus, so that he can learn to be around it without giving in to it?
3. Someone says, "Someone's strength of self-discipline varies according to how tired or frustrated the person is. If the temptation is easily available when the person's self-discipline goes down, the person will give in to the temptation." Can you explain this statement? Can you give an example of how someone would use it?

Chapter 17: Momentum Effects: Getting on a Roll

322. Suppose that John Doe is trying to quit smoking. Suppose you want to predict whether or not John Doe smokes on October 15. A good rule is that "What you've done in the recent past predicts what you'll do in the near future."

Which do you guess would help you the most in making a guess about whether he smokes on October 15 or not?

A. whether John Doe said on October 1, "I'm going to quit smoking,"
B. whether John Doe said, "I know how harmful smoking is," or
C. whether John Doe had actually stayed off cigarettes altogether for the whole week before October 15?

323. The person most likely not to smoke on a given day is the person who has not smoked for a good while up until that day. This is the person who has got some "momentum" for the self-disciplined habit.

Who will complete homework, go to bed at a reasonable time, show up at work on time, and triumph in most other self-discipline challenges? The persons who have succeeded in these same challenges for the last few weeks.

After making the self-disciplined choice a bunch of times in a row, you get "on a roll": you build up momentum for making that choice. Conversely, after you make the unself-disciplined choice time after time, you build up momentum for that type of choice.

The main point of this section is that

A. whatever you have been doing, you tend to keep doing,
or
B. the past doesn't predict the future?

324. Part of the way momentum works is simple habit strength. When you repeat an action several times, it starts to become a habit. Life is much easier and happier if you can get into a habit and routine of making certain good choices; you get to save the energy of struggling with them over and over.

According to what you've just read, what is a reason why behavior in the recent past predicts behavior in the near future?

A. The more you do something, the more it becomes a habit,
or
B. people get an image of themselves from what they do, and they act so as to keep that image constant?

325. Another part of the way momentum effects work is that when people have kept their resolution for several times in a row, they don't want to blow the record that they have set. They want to keep making their winning streak longer. They feel that they have more to lose by blowing their winning streak than they would by extending a losing streak a little longer.

Two of the reasons why not smoking for the last 30 days helps people not to smoke on the 31st day are

A. building up a habit, and not wanting to blow their winning streak,
or
B. reinforcement and good models?

326. There's a danger in thinking in terms of keeping up your winning streak. The problem comes when there is one little loss. When people break their resolutions, they often tend to think, "Now I've already blown my winning streak. I don't have anything more to lose. I might as well enjoy myself, and try to start another winning streak tomorrow." And so, rather than drinking just one beer, they have half a case; instead of eating one cookie, they eat the whole box of cookies. Instead of putting off their homework for half an hour, they blow it off for the whole night.

The danger in "winning streak" type of thinking is that

A. you will want to stay on your winning streak and be less likely to break your resolution,
or
B. once you blow your winning streak in a little way, you lose the motivation not to blow it in a big way.

327. But if arrange your thoughts right, you may be able to benefit from momentum effects without letting one small failure push you into total failure. When you have a streak going, you try very strongly to keep it up. You keep yourself aware of the "winning streak" type of thinking, and you realize that you'll be tempted to blow it in a big way. For this reason, you try especially hard to keep up the winning streak.

But you also have a plan in case you mess up. You plan that if you have a little failure of self-discipline, you will tell yourself, "My task is to start back *immediately* on the pattern that will help me reach my goal. A small failure is much smaller than a big failure! The fact that I had a little failure doesn't change the fact that everything counts in either advancing me toward my goal or moving me away from it. Let me review the reasons I want to achieve my goal, and muster my energy toward accomplishing it."

You are being advised to

A. plan to recover as soon as possible if you break your resolution,

or

B. never even think about the possibility of ever breaking your resolution?

328. If you break a resolution in a small way, try not to have all-or-none thinking. With all-or-none thinking, you are either on your diet or off – there is no difference between being off by one teaspoon of sugar and being off by one whole cheesecake. With all-or-none thinking, you are either on your work plan or you are off – there is no difference between being 5 minutes late in starting an assignment and not starting it at all. With all-or-none thinking, you are either off all alcohol or not – there is no difference between taking one taste of wine and drinking the whole bottle. But with respect to achieving goals, there is obviously a big difference. Keep in mind that when you say, "I've broken the rule; it makes no difference now if I break it in a big way," you are saying something false.

All-or-none thinking is what makes people

A. blow a resolution in a big way when they've made a tiny slip,
or
B. recover quickly after a slip and get back working toward the goal?

329. Despite the advice against all-or-none thinking, you probably won't be able to avoid it altogether. For that reason, it's useful to try as hard as

possible to avoid the first slip, such as the first cigarette for an ex-smoker or the first sip of alcohol for the recovering alcoholic. If you tell yourself, "Just one will not make any difference," you are also telling yourself something false, because you run a risk of having your momentum stopped.

The point here is that for certain self-control challenges, especially those like smoking and drinking where you can totally avoid something,

A. you should have a healthy respect for how much damage the first little slip can do,
or
B. you shouldn't worry about little slips, and only focus on the big ones?

Routines

330. If there is something that takes self-discipline for you to do, see if you can do it at the same time each day. To do this is to set up a *routine* for yourself. In this way you take advantage of habit. You set up a habit that will get stronger and stronger the more you follow your routine.

If someone exercises at the same time each morning, that pattern is called a(n)

A. reverse momentum,
or
B. routine?

331. Brenda is trying to write a long thesis for graduate school. She finds it hard to get herself to sit down and write. She decides that she will set aside a time every morning. As soon as she gets up out of bed, she will write for one hour. She is careful not to plan anything that will interfere with that writing time.

It takes lots of self-discipline to get started first thing in the morning for the first three or four mornings. But then she finds it becomes easier and easier. After doing this for a month, she finds that she automatically goes to her desk and starts writing without thinking about it.

This is an example of

A. getting into a routine so as to create momentum,
or
B. breaking a habit by doing something unpleasant each time you do the bad habit?

332. Jared has a problem getting himself out of bed in the morning. He frequently gets into trouble from sleeping too late.

He learns that his brain has a clock-like mechanism that tells him when it's time to sleep and when it's time to be awake. He learns that if he stays up very late and gets up very late, he sets his clock later.

Which do you think would be the best way for him to take advantage of the principle of setting up routines?

A. get a very loud alarm clock,
or
B. go to bed and get up close to the same time every day, at a time early enough so that he doesn't miss things?

333. A man has gotten himself in a lot of trouble by drinking too much alcohol. He has gotten into the habit of stopping at a bar on the way home from work.

He gets out of work at 5:00 p.m. each day. It takes him about half an hour to get home. He has a son who likes to go for walks with him. He decides to make an appointment with his son to go for a walk every afternoon at 5:30. He gradually gets into the habit of this new routine that takes the place of the old one.

This is an example of

A. making a routine for a new activity that will happen at the same time that the bad habit used to take place,
or
B. using an internal sales pitch?

334. Mary is trying to get more exercise.

Which plan do you think is more likely to work?

A. trying to find some time to exercise whenever she can during her busy day, or
B. eating lunch very quickly, then going for a walk every day at lunch time instead of sitting down for lunch?

Topics for Writing or Discussion

1. How would you summarize the advice you are given in this chapter?

2. Imagine that Ken and Bill are both recovering alcoholics. Ken says, "I haven't had a single drink of alcohol in the last five years." Bill says, "I have had only four drinks of alcohol in the last five years, with the last one being six months ago." Who do you think is more likely to keep out of the pattern of getting drunk every day? Why? Can you also argue in the opposite direction?

3. Does the advice you are given seem to contradict itself? For example: if you are a smoker, you should avoid having the first cigarette after you have quit, because that may spoil your momentum. But if you have one cigarette, you should remind yourself that two are worse than one, and try not to let the little slip spoil your momentum. Is it possible to fear the first slip, but also prepare yourself for not letting the first slip spoil all your momentum?

Chapter 18: Organization Skills for Self-Discipline

335. For many people, the biggest barrier to being self-disciplined is that they are too disorganized. They have the self-discipline to rake up all the leaves in the yard – but they can't find the rake. They have the self-discipline to study hard tonight, but they can't find the piece of paper where they wrote down their assignments. They could follow a plan about what to eat today to lose a little weight, if only they could keep track of what that plan was. They could follow a plan of using nicotine gum to help them get off cigarettes, if they could only keep track of what the plan is and where they left the nicotine gum. They make a resolution about anger control that they might be able to follow, if they could only remember what it was.

When the plan or the stuff they need to carry it out is lost, they then do whatever feels best at the moment. In other words, they do the temptation instead of working toward the long-term goal.

In the examples we gave, organization means

A. keeping track of what your plans are and where your things are,
or
B. a group where people work together to accomplish a goal?

336. Staying organized involves two main tasks:

1.Deciding where your things and your pieces of paper belong, and putting them or keeping them there.

2. Writing your plans, including your "to-do" activities and your resolutions, not losing what you've written, and reading those plans often.

These tasks do not do themselves, no matter how much you know about organization. And unfortunately, doing these tasks is often not fun. It's often much more fun to chat with someone or watch TV than it is to put your things where they belong. Thus you need some self-discipline skills to get organized, just as you need some organization skills to get self-disciplined!

The main point of this section is that

A. you need a routine place to keep your written plans,
or
B. it takes self-discipline to keep things and plans in order?

337. Both disorganization and low self-discipline are often seen as signs of attention deficit disorder. I believe that people with attention deficit disorder can improve their lives by consciously trying to spend time putting things in their place and keeping track of their plans and resolutions. In order to be

organized, with or without any kind of diagnosis, you must be willing to spend at least some time, regularly, in organizing.

In this section the author is saying that

A. attention deficit disorder does not exist,
or
B. in order to get more organized, you have to spend time in putting things away and keeping track of plans?

Organizing Objects

If your work area is too cluttered, you might be tempted to run away from it rather than work in it. If you can't find the materials and tools you need to do your work quickly, your work becomes much less pleasant.

The rules for organizing objects are simple:

1. Make a "home" for each object, where that object will go when it's not being used.

2. Choose homes so that things of the same sort are close to each other, and close to the place where they will be used.

3. Get into habits of putting objects back into their homes as soon as you get done using them.

4. Don't get so many things that it becomes too hard to put them away. In other words, de-clutter yourself.

One idea that comes from this section is that when someone gives you something as a present, you have to

A. write the person a thank-you note, or
B. figure out where that thing's home will be?

338. No one has time to waste on looking for objects like keys, wallet, appointment books, pens, glasses, coats, and gloves. You won't waste that time if you put them in their home when they are not being used.

For example: when I'm not using my keys, I carry them in a certain pants pocket; at night they go into a certain box on my desk. My reading glasses, when I don't have them on, are either in a shirt pocket or in the same box. My plans notebook, or to-do book, is returned to either my right hip pocket or the same box when it isn't being used. My warm coat, when not being used at home, is hanging in the front hall closet. My gloves are in the pockets of that coat. If I can resist the temptation to put any of these things down anywhere else, I don't have to look for them.

The author thinks that making fairly rigid rules for yourself about where you allow yourself to put things

A. makes life less fun, because you have to follow those strict rules, or

B. makes life more fun, because you don't get frustrated with losing things as much?

339. Papers are special types of objects. Cardboard file folders, plus a filing cabinet or desk drawer big enough for file folders, are a great way to keep up with papers. A cardboard box of the right size will work if you don't have a filing cabinet or desk drawers.

      The best way to organize files is to make up a title for each file folder, write that title on folder's tab, and put all the folders in alphabetical order. For each of paper that would otherwise clutter up your space, you do something with it, throw it away, or file it.

The best place for papers you aren't using is

A. a flat surface such as a table, or
B. a file folder which is put in its alphabetical place?

The Plans Notebook

340. Part of being organized is to have and use a plans notebook, otherwise known as a planner, or sometimes called a to-do and appointment book. This means that you write down what you have to do rather than trying to remember it all. For the student, this usually takes the form of an assignment book. I use a four-inch by six-inch spiral notebook, one for each month.

When you open the book to any day, the daily appointments are on one page and the daily to do list is on the page facing it. Some people find that electronic versions of such a planner work well for them.

The important point of this section is that
A. your plans notebook must be on paper,
or
B. you should write down what you are supposed to do, rather than trying to remember it all?

341. In the front of the notebook is the "master to-do list." This is where you write down the goals you want to make progress on or complete for the month.

      Whenever something needs to be done or handed in at a certain time, you write it on the appointment page. If you are going to a party, you write on this page the time and place. Each evening you can review what you're scheduled to do the following day. Then, for the time that is not scheduled, you can look at the master to-do list, and also your list of long-range goals, and put on the daily to-do list page the additional things you want to get done. Here's where you can write to yourself what your plans are for making progress on your goals. Here's where you write any resolutions you make for the day. Throughout the day, you then look at these two pages.

The advice is to have

A. an appointment book, a to do list, a resolution diary, and a homework assignment book, all in separate places,
or
B. have all these things in one notebook?

342. After you make a to-do list for the day, it's good to figure out which tasks have highest priority. That is, write 1 by the most important item; write 2 by the next most important, and so forth. You do this because you never know exactly how long things are going to take, or what interruption is going to come up. So you never know whether you're going to get through all the items on your to-do list. But if you get the most important ones done, then at least you're putting your effort into the areas that will pay off the most.

The idea is to

A. do the most important things first,
or
B. save the most important things until later so you'll have more time to think about them?

343. Here's another reason for doing the most important things first. If you get into the habit of working in order of priority, you train yourself not to put off unpleasant or difficult activities. When a task's number comes up, you do it, like it or not.

The idea here is that by doing things in order of how important they are, you can train yourself to

A. avoid putting unpleasant tasks off,
or
B. get more work done per minute?

344. Here's a game useful to play with yourself every now and then. For one of the items on your to do list, before doing it, write a guess as to how much time it will take. Then time yourself and see how long it actually takes. It you do this enough, you will get better and better at estimating how long things really take. The ability to estimate work times helps you know how to take on not too much, not too little, but just the right amount of work to commit yourself to.

This section suggests keeping track of how long certain tasks take, so that you can

A. get rewarded according to how long you work,
or
B. get a better sense of how long things take to do?

345. When you finish an item on the to-do list, check it off, and congratulate yourself for finishing it, and try to feel good about what you have done! If you can train yourself to feel good when you

finish an item, you will get much more done.

In other words, you do the things that were talked about in the earlier chapters on

A. self-reinforcement and the celebrations exercise,
or
B. goal-setting and stimulus control?

346. When you're making a to-do list, it's better to break down large tasks into small parts, so that you'll be able to check off an accomplishment and feel good about it more often. For example, rather than having just one item for "Do Science Experiment," you write subtasks under this task, such as
1. Search for articles on the subject
2. Read articles
3. Learn how to use the equipment
4. Write blank data forms
5. Write out the procedure
6. Do the measurements with the subjects
7. Punch the numbers into the computer
8. Analyze the data
9. Print out graphs
10. Write the article

Breaking a job down into small parts is often a very important step in overcoming resistance to getting it done.

Following the advice of this section results in writing

A. more things on the to do list,
or
B. fewer things on the to do list?

347. What if, as the day goes on, you decide that some task not on your to-do list is what's most worth doing? Of course, you can change your to do list any time you want. Some people write tasks on their to-do list and check them off, sometimes even after they've done them, just to have the satisfaction of looking at the accomplished task.

What reason is just mentioned why people would ever write down tasks and check them off after they had already done them?

A. to be able to look at the checked-off task and feel good,
or
B. to be able to have a permanent record of what was done?

348. When you do a task so automatically and routinely that you don't need even to think about whether and when to do it, your reward is not having to write it down. For example, most people never write, "Brush my teeth" on their to-do lists, because it is an automatic ritual.

Which of the following would someone be more likely to write on a to do list?

A. wait for the school bus,
or
B. start reading about the science project?

349. I think it's a good idea to write resolutions on the same planning-book page as to-dos. Resolutions are like to-dos, in that they are things you want to do. But they are different in one way: you want to get as close as you can to keeping 100% of resolutions. With to-do tasks, you want to do as many as you can, starting with the most important, but not worry if you can't get every one done today.

If someone writes, "No alcohol today," that's a resolution. Or if someone writes, "Be hungry when I go to bed," that's a resolution. Or "I must finish writing the research proposal by tonight." Or, "Finish the first 5 items on my to-do list" can be a resolution.

The difference between a to do task and a resolution is that you aim for

A. 100% following of resolutions,
or
B. 100% of all to do tasks finished each day?

350. Many people get into habits of making lots of resolutions, which they then break. For example, the person trying to lose weight resolves, "I'll skip supper." But he gets tempted and eats something good. "This is the last one," he resolves. But it tastes so good that he changes the resolution: "Only two more." But after those two there's a similar change in the resolution. Some people can repeat this process over and over, day after day. It leads to a feeling of failure and a feeling that you can't trust yourself.

Life becomes much happier when there is a habit of keeping resolutions. It helps if you write down the resolutions on the to-do page and celebrate greatly when the resolutions are kept.

The advice here is to

A. think twice before making a resolution, but try to keep all resolutions,
or
B. make lots of resolutions without intending to keep many of them?

Getting Into Routines

351. Which of the following sounds more pleasant for you?

To do laundry when you notice that no clean clothes are left, or to schedule laundry at certain regular times each week?

To pay bills when you wake up in the middle of the night wondering if the phone will be cut off, or to have a certain scheduled time once a week for bills and paperwork?

To write your daily to do list whenever you can remember it, or to have a certain routine time in the daily schedule for writing it?

To change the oil in your car when you start hearing strange noises or seeing warning lights come on, or to do it when the time comes up on your appointment book?

Having regular routines rather than reacting to the negative consequences of letting tasks go usually seems to be a more pleasant way to live.

What's another example of following the advice in this section?

A. taking back library books when you get an overdue notice in the mail,
or
B. having a regular time to back up computer files, before the hard disk crashes?

Task Analysis and Fantasy Rehearsal to Get Into Routines

352. How long does it take you to get organized into a new routine? For example, if you're a student, how long does it take you to get into a routine that will let you get the right books and papers where they should be at the right times? If you're a worker, how long does it take you to get into habits of going to the right place with the right stuff in hand or in briefcase?

If the answer is "too long," or "forever," task analysis combined with fantasy rehearsal might help.

We are getting ready to talk about

A. a way of making decisions more carefully,
or
B. a way of getting into routine habits quicker?

353. Task analysis means writing down the steps in carrying out a procedure, such as completing a day of school, performing a surgical operation, or cleaning a house. You take a procedure or complicated process, and break it down into its individual parts.

Let's do an imaginary task analysis for someone in high school who has a locker in the hall, switches classes every period, and finds it convenient to stop by the locker before each class. This student likes to carry a book bag to all classes.

Let's start the task analysis as the school day begins.

1. Pick up book bag I left on my desk last night and check one more time to make sure all my books and papers and my assignment book are in it. Take it with me to school.
2. Before the first class, stop by my locker. Check what books, pencils, pens or papers I need for the first class, and put them into the book bag.
3. At the first class, turn in my homework paper when asked to do so. When I get a homework assignment, take my assignment book out of the book bag, open the assignment book to

that day's date, write the name of the subject, and write the assignment carefully. (If there is no homework, write "none.") Check to make sure I wrote the assignment correctly. Return assignment book to the book bag.

4. Do steps 2 and 3 before all the other classes.

5. Before going home, stop at my locker and open my assignment book. Look at each assignment and make sure the books or papers I need to do each assignment are in my book bag. Take the book bag home.

6. At homework time, look at the assignments. Get out of the book bag what I need. Do the first assignment. Check it off in the assignment book. Then put the completed paper back in my book bag, in the file folder for that subject.

7. Do the same thing with the other assignments until all are finished.

8. Return the book bag to the top of my desk.

A task analysis is

A. figuring out why a task should be done,

or

B. breaking some task down into its little steps?

354. If there's a procedure you do repeatedly and you keep forgetting steps, it's a good idea to write a task analysis. The next job is to go over the task analysis repeatedly and memorize it. Next, you very vividly imagine yourself carrying out the procedure or do fantasy rehearsals of it.

Here's how a fantasy rehearsal might start for the task as analyzed above.

"It's morning, and I'm about to leave for school. I'm seeing my book bag on my desk, and I'm checking to make sure all my books and homework papers are in it. I'm picking it up and taking it with me. Now I'm at school, and it's before my first class. I'm stopping at my locker. I'm pulling my assignment book out of my locker and looking at it. I see what I need for my first class, and I'm making sure I've got that book in my book bag. I'm glad I checked carefully. Now I'm at my first class, and the assignment is written on the board. I pull my assignment book out of my book bag, and I write the name of the subject and copy the assignment. I'm checking it very carefully; yes, I've got it right, good for me . . ."

As you do a fantasy rehearsal, remember to congratulate yourself for carrying out the steps well.

The purpose of doing these fantasy rehearsals is to

A. get into the habit of remembering to do certain things at a certain time,

or

B. change how you feel about what you are doing?

355. Sometimes a task analysis takes the form of a checklist. Before a pilot takes off in a plane, she refers to a list of things to check that could possibly cause trouble during the flight. This is really a task analysis. Sometimes it's helpful to check it off at some time during the day. You don't break the job down into every little muscle movement. You ask yourself, "What could I possibly forget to do?" You include each of those items on the checklist.

For example, a student makes the following error-reduction checklist for finishing homework:
1. Did I write down all the assignments?
2. Did I do each assignment and check it off my list?
3. Did I put each completed assignment back in my book bag?
4. Did I put my books back in the book bag?
Did I put the book bag in its home?

The idea of such a checklist is to include

A. every part of the job that you could forget,
or
B. every single motion that you have to make in doing the job?

356. If the steps of your task analysis don't work well in real life, then revise them to improve the plan. Then you fantasy rehearse the new plan.

When you no longer have any trouble remembering what to do and when, your reward is that you can throw out your task analysis.

The idea of fantasy rehearsals of the steps of task analyses is to

A. do it forever,
or
B. do it until you get into routines that you don't have to think about?

357. The following checklist summarizes the points we've covered about organization skills.

Organization Skills Checklist

Are you willing to put time into putting things and papers in their homes, writing to yourself about goals and tasks and plans, and keeping up with what you've written?

Do you get and keep no more objects and papers than you really need?

Do you have a "home" for each object, especially the important ones?

Do you have enough file space and file folders to keep organized files of all papers you want to keep?

Do you have a plans notebook (paper or electronic) that is almost always near you?

Does the appointment notebook have in it adequate space to write daily appointments and daily to-dos and to see both of them without having to turn pages?

Do you keep a master to-do list?

Do you make a to-do list each day?

Do you put numbers by your to-do tasks, to order their priorities?

Do you check each task off the list as you do it?

Do you remember to feel good when you check a task off the to-do list?

Do you use your appointment book to remind yourself to do things before some bad consequence prompts you to do them?

In adjusting to complicated routines, do you write out a task analysis and do fantasy rehearsals?

Before taking on a new commitment, do you carefully consider whether you will have the time and energy to do it well, and say no to it if the resources aren't there?

The purpose of all these things is to be able to

A. make plans to achieve goals, and follow those plans,

or

B. impress people that your life is orderly and neat?

Topics for Writing or Discussion

1. Has disorganization caused any problems for you? If you can think of a time when being disorganized caused a problem, please tell about that time.
2. Why do you think it is an advantage to be able to make plans and keep them rather than doing everything on the spur of the moment?
3. Which of the techniques of this chapter do you want to use at this point in your life? Why do you choose those?
4. Please write some to do tasks for at least one day, put them in order of priority, check them off as you do them, and celebrate in your mind each time you finish one. What was this like? How is it different when you have a to do list from when you don't?
5. Please write some fantasy rehearsals of making good choices regarding organization skills.
6. Please write some celebrations of good choices you've made in real life regarding organization skills.

Chapter 19: Self-Talk and the Twelve Types of Thoughts

358. We've already talked about how what you say to yourself makes a big difference. Let's think again about the example where two people are writing an article. One is saying things to himself like "What I just wrote is no good," and "Why did that person make me do this stupid assignment?" A second person is saying things to himself like, "Let's see, what could I say here: this or this, I think I like this better. Hey, I'm making some progress!"

In this example, the first person is making himself feel bad by the things he is saying to himself. If he does this every time he writes, he consistently punishes himself for writing. Writing will probably be very painful for him. On the other hand, the second person is making himself feel good by using self-reinforcement. If he consistently does this, he will probably enjoy writing.

The main point of this section is that

A. writing is hard work, and can take lots of self-discipline,
or
B. what you say to yourself can make a job like writing either more pleasant or more unpleasant?

359. Here's a very important idea. You are probably already familiar with it from previous chapters. But it's worth repeating.

You can choose the types of things you say to yourself. You can make this choice according to what *results* you want to achieve. If you're in the habit of getting down on yourself too much and not celebrating your own choices enough, you can change that habit. You can arrange your self-talk in such a way that you are most likely to accomplish your goals. Choosing useful self-talk is often very important in determining whether you succeed or fail at your goals.

The very important idea is that

A. self-talk is very important, and you can choose your self-talk according to what's most useful,
or
B. self-talk is something that we can't change, because it comes too quickly?

360. Here's the important idea for this chapter. We can choose more easily the type of self-talk we want to do, if we have words for the important types of self-talk. Having words for things makes it easier for us to think about those things, to recognize them, to consciously do them.

This important idea is that

A. words can't express many of our types of thoughts,
or

B. it's helpful to have words that label types of self-talk?

361. Let's divide things that people say to themselves into twelve types of thoughts. Let's go through them one by one. The twelve types of thoughts apply no matter what situation you're in. We'll stick to the article-writing situation as we give examples.

1. If someone were to think, "It's terrible that I have to write this dumb article, I can't stand it!" that would be called *awfulizing*.
2. If he thinks, "What I just wrote sounds really stupid," he's *getting down on himself*.
3. If he thinks, "Why did that no-good person have to assign this to me," he's *blaming someone else*.
4. If he thinks, "This isn't such a big deal to have to write this. I can take it," he's *not awfulizing*.
5. "What I just wrote is not great, but I don't want to punish myself for that," is *not getting down on himself*.
6. "I don't like this assignment, but I don't want to spend my energy blaming the teacher who gave me the assignment," is *not blaming someone else*.
7. "My goal at this moment is just to get down as many ideas as I can; later I'll go back and revise them," is an example of *goal-setting*.
8. "Let's see, I could talk about this next, or I could talk about this other thing. I think the first would be

better," is an example of *listing options and choosing*.
9. "I wish I had started this article longer before the deadline; for next time, I'll remember to start earlier," is an example of *learning from the experience*.
10. "I'm glad that I happened to find these articles – they'll really be helpful in writing my article," is *celebrating luck*.
11. "I'm glad I got the teacher gave me this challenging assignment; it will stretch my abilities and help me improve," is *celebrating someone else's choice*.
12. "Hooray! I'm making progress! I'm really glad that I've gotten myself working!" is *celebrating your own choice*.

These twelve types of thoughts are

A. ways of talking to yourself in any situation that you find yourself in,
or
B. ways of talking to yourself only when you write articles?

362. Now let's talk about the effects of these different types of thoughts.

Awfulizing, getting down on yourself, and blaming someone else all tend to make you feel some unpleasant emotions: for example scared, ashamed, or angry.

Not awfulizing, not getting down on yourself, and not blaming someone else all tend to make you feel less bad. For example, thinking "It's not such a big deal," helps you not to feel so bad about whatever it is.

Goal-setting, listing options and choosing, and learning from the experience all help you figure out what's the best thing to do or remind yourself what's the best thing to do, and why. (Goal-setting can include reviewing the internal sales pitch.)

Celebrating your own choice helps you feel good about it when you do something good; it helps you feel good about the things you can control. Celebrating luck and celebrating someone else's choice help you feel good about the things other people or luck control.

The main point of all this is:

A. you can choose the thoughts that will produce the result you want,
or
B. there's no connection between what you think and how you feel or act?

363. So what does all this have to do with self-discipline? When you want to use self-discipline, you want to use thoughts that choose your goals and your plans very carefully, that make you feel good about progress toward your goal, and that make you not feel too bad about what you have to put up with to reach your goal.

Suppose that someone wants to use self-discipline to exercise a lot and get in really good shape. Suppose the person thinks, "This feeling of being out of breath and tired is not such a bad feeling. I can get used to it." What type of thought is this an example of?

A. blaming someone else,
or
B. not awfulizing?

364. The thoughts that we choose to say to ourselves have a big influence on how easily we achieve our goals.

Is the person's "not awfulizing" about the feeling of being out of breath and tired likely to be helpful in achieving his goal?

A. yes,
or
B. no?

365. Suppose the person runs a little farther today than he has run before.

He thinks to himself, "Yes! I set a new record! That's really great!" What type of thought is this?

A. listing options and choosing,
or
B. celebrating his own choice?

366. Celebrating your own choice usually makes you feel good.

Do you think that this type of self-talk will be helpful for achieving his goal?

A. yes,

or

B. no?

367. Suppose that someone has a big problem with alcohol. She has many times drunk a lot of alcohol without being able to stop. She has used very bad judgment as a result. She is trying to stay away from alcohol altogether.

She goes to a party, thinking that no alcohol will be served there. But people are offering wine and beer and other alcoholic drinks.

Suppose that you could choose her self-talk in order to help her. One of your choices is "awfulizing," like this: "It's a bummer that all these people can drink and I can't. It isn't fair!" Another choice is goal-setting, like this: "I remind myself that staying off alcohol is my number one goal, more important than fitting in at this party, more important than even staying at this party."

Which of the above two sentences of self-talk, which do you think will be most helpful to her?

A. awfulizing,

or

B. goal-setting?

368. Someone is working on anger control. The person finds that while his car was parked in a parking lot, someone else dented it. But the person left a note on the windshield with a name and phone number and a promise to pay for the repair.

Suppose you could choose this person's self-talk for him as he prepares to talk to the other person on the phone. One of your choices is celebrating someone else's choice: "I'm really glad he was honest enough to leave the note." The other choice is blaming someone else: "How could that idiot not watch where he was going and hit a parked car?"

It should be pretty clear which of these would make the person less angry. Which is it?

A. celebrating someone else's choice

or

B. blaming someone else?

369. Someone is trying to follow a plan about losing weight. The person sees some food that she has planned not to eat. Suppose you could choose her self-talk. One possibility is getting down on herself, like this: "I'm just going to fail at weight loss, I'm a hopeless case. So it really doesn't make any difference whether I have this food or not." Another option is celebrating her own choice, like this: "I'm really glad I became aware that I'm in a self-discipline challenge situation! That's a very important step toward triumphing in this challenge!"

Which of these two types of self-talk do you think will help her to use self-discipline more effectively?

A. getting down on herself,
or
B. celebrating her own choice?

370. Someone is trying to lose weight. But as she monitors her weight over time, it is not going down, and even is slowly creeping up again. Which of these two types of self-talk do you think will be more useful to her? The first is blaming someone else: "If my family members wouldn't buy all this junk food and leave it lying around, I wouldn't be tempted to eat it. They are doing this to me, those bad people!" The second is listing options and choosing: "How can I be less tempted by the junk food that is left lying around in my house? One option is that I can have a special place where I keep my own food, and start a custom of only eating the food that's kept there. Another option is that when I see their food left out, I will put it away. Another option is asking them to put it away to help me out. I think I'll start by trying the first and third option."

Which do you think is more useful to her:
A. blaming someone else,
or
B. listing options and choosing?

371. Someone has resolved to get out of bed in the morning at a certain time to get some work done. But when that time comes, he is tempted to go back to sleep. Suppose you could choose his self-talk for him. One option is goal-setting, like this: "I really wanted to get an early start on my work. It will make me feel good all day long to do it. And if I get up at a reasonable time this morning, that will help me set my rhythm so that I can get up early the next mornings more easily!" Another of the options is awfulizing, like this: "I'm so sleepy! What a wrenching feeling it would be to get out of this nice warm bed. I can't take it!"

Which type of thought will be more helpful to him in using self discipline?

A. goal-setting,
or
B. awfulizing?

372. Suppose that the person who wants to stay away from alcohol takes one sip of a drink. One option for self-talk is not awfulizing: "This isn't such a big deal. One sip never hurt anybody." Another option is awfulizing and getting down on himself followed by goal-setting, as follows: "I just blew my record. That was stupid. My goal right now is not to drink another drop, so that I can cut my losses to a minimum."

Which do you think will be more helpful for his use of self-discipline:

A. not awfulizing,

or

B. awfulizing, getting down on himself, and goal-setting?

373. We talked earlier about how it's useful to refresh yourself and "recharge your batteries."

    A person is taking a break from work. He goes outside for a walk. Which self-talk would you choose for him? Your first option is celebrating luck: "Wow, what a nice day it is. It's wonderful that I get to take a walk in this park! It feels good to be alive!" Your second option is a type of goal-setting: "I've got to do so much work today. I need to finish at least five more today. I really need to get this done."

If the priority at this moment is relaxing and refreshing himself and recharging his batteries, which self-talk would you choose?

A. celebrating luck,

or

B. goal-setting?

374. Suppose that someone is trying to make top grades in school. Most of the time when he sits down to study, his older brother comes and tempts him with some way to play and goof off. Gradually he figures out something: his older brother doesn't want him to succeed in school work, because the older brother himself didn't succeed.

His older brother is purposely trying to distract him from his work.

    Suppose that you could choose the younger brother's self-talk. Which of the following two possibilities do you think would be more helpful in meeting his goal? The first is blaming someone else, awfulizing, and goal-setting: "That brother of mine is trying to make me fail like he did! He is being very selfish. What a bad thing, that my own brother is really trying to harm me! Now I have another reason to want to succeed: I want to show myself that he can't do this to me!" The second is not awfulizing: "It's not such a big deal if I don't do well at school. It's not the end of the world."

Which do you think is most helpful:

A. blaming someone else, awfulizing, and goal-setting,

or

B. not awfulizing?

375. Sometimes bad feelings can be very useful. Sometimes it's useful to feel guilty or disappointed or angry. In the example we just gave, perhaps the younger brother could use his anger at his older brother to help him succeed and use self-discipline. It's a good thing that we can feel painful feelings. Painful feelings can alert us to problems that need to be solved, and they can help motivate us to solve them. For this reason, awfulizing, getting down on

yourself, and blaming someone else are sometimes useful things to do.

However, two bits of advice about these types of thoughts are helpful. First, try not to overdo them. You want to feel just enough bad feeling to motivate you in a good direction. Very large amounts of bad feeling can get in the way of goals. The second piece of advice is not just to keep on thinking the thoughts that make you feel bad: go from these types of thoughts to goal-setting. When there is something bad about the world, yourself, or someone else, figure out what you want to do about it. If you can change it, set that goal. If you are sure you can't change it, and you want to put up with it, set that goal. As soon as you make any progress toward your goal, you can celebrate and feel good.

The idea of this section is that

A. you want to avoid bad feelings, so don't ever awfulize, get down on yourself, or blame others;
or
B. bad feelings can be useful, if you keep them from being too huge and if you harness them to working toward a good goal.

376. Think about the central idea of this chapter.

What's the main idea of this chapter about how to choose the thoughts you want to include the most in your self-talk?

A. Choose the thoughts that help you meet your goals,
or
B. choose your thoughts so that you feel a little bit good about progress to meet your goals and you feel extremely bad about every little failure to make progress toward your goals?

Topics for Writing and Discussion

1. Please take any situation, any choice point. Describe the situation, and then make up 12 examples of how someone could think in that situation. Make up an example of each of the twelve types of thoughts that were defined in this chapter. This is called the "twelve thought exercise." If you do it a number of times, it helps you to be flexible and choose your thoughts rather than to be stuck with only one thought pattern.

2. Please summarize the general strategy of choosing thoughts so as to increase your self-discipline. Do you want to avoid all bad feelings? Do you want to feel huge bad feelings? What do you want to feel a little bad about? What do you want to feel very good about? What do you want to figure out and decide?

3. For some time, try to be aware of the types of thoughts that go on in your own mind. Of the twelve types

that are defined in this chapter, which do you think are the top three or four for you? In other words, which three or four types of thoughts do you use most frequently? Are these the ones you find most useful? If not, which ones would you like to use more often?

4. The strategy this chapter talks about is consciously choosing your own self-talk. Why might this be a hard thing to do? What are the obstacles to using this strategy? Can you think of ways to overcome these obstacles?

Chapter 20: Modeling

377. How do people learn to do what they do? A large fraction of what we learn is from *modeling* and by *imitation learning*. People see people doing something, and they tend to do the same thing.

Two researchers named Meltzoff and Moore studied newborn babies. They made faces at them, and took videotapes of the faces that the babies made. The researchers found that the babies imitated the facial expressions they made.

The researchers concluded that people are born with a tendency to imitate what they see other people doing.

The main point of this section is that

A. people tend to do more often what gets them a reward,
or
B. people tend to do more often what they see others do?

378. One of the ways of measuring self-discipline has been to give people a choice between a small reward now and a greater reward later on. To pass up the small reward now and wait for the larger reward takes some self-discipline.

Two researchers, Albert Bandura and Walter Mischel, did an experiment. They showed children someone else who was making this choice. The children tended to imitate the person they saw. Children who saw someone choose the greater reward later on were influenced to use self-discipline in that way. Children who saw someone choose to get the smaller reward right away were influenced to make the same sort of choice. This influence took place even when children heard about the choice and did not see it in real life.

What is the point of this section?

A. that modeling can influence whether you use self-discipline or not,
or
B. that modeling has a lot to do with skills such as singing or figure skating?

379. Some models of behavior come from people we deal with in real life. We get real-life models of behavior from our friends, our family members, and from the other people we come into contact with.

If modeling is a very important method of influence, then it's a good idea to pick carefully which friends we hang out with. Like it or not, we tend to imitate our friends, just as they imitate us.

The main idea of this section is that

A. since we tend to imitate friends, it's good to pick them carefully;
or

B. since we tend to imitate TV shows, it's good to pick them carefully.

380. So far we have spoken about real-life models, such as family or friends. But models that come from books, movies, television shows, and video games are also important. A great deal of research shows that we store in our minds images of behavior that we see or read about; when we choose our real-life behavior, the images we have in our memory are available to pick from. If we read about or see certain models over and over, we increase their influence.

The main idea of this section is that

A. models from books, movies, video games, and TV shows influence us,
or
B. what goes on in fantasy entertainment does not affect our behavior at all?

381. How can you take the most advantage of the power of modeling? By collecting written or recorded examples of the type of self-disciplined behavior you want to do more often, and purposely exposing yourself to those models over and over.

  You will notice that throughout this book there are lots of models of self-disciplined actions. The last few chapters of this book contain many examples of how people might work toward various self-discipline goals. I hope that you can use the models contained in this book to help yourself.

What is the main advice of this section?

A. look for models in movies and videotapes, not in books,
or
B. expose yourself often to whatever are the best models of self-discipline you can find?

382. Suppose you start looking at what's on TV and movies and videogames and thinking, "Is this a model that I want to imitate?" You will probably find that there are lots of models that you don't want to imitate. Don't kid yourself into thinking that bad models have no influence on you. Every time you turn on a television, you are receiving someone's efforts, not just to entertain you, but also to *influence* you. Advertisers put billions of dollars into the mass media, not for charitable goals, but to try to influence you to buy their products. And they would not spend this money if the influence didn't work.

The purpose of television is

A. purely to entertain you and make you feel good,
or
B. partly to influence you to spend your money in ways that benefit the advertisers?

383. The messages that say, "Buy our product," are very clear and obvious. But in most advertising and most entertainment, there are more subtle messages about what is good, what is fun, what is cool, what people should do.

Here are some words from an advertisement for a video game.

"Armed with chairs, pool cues and tables, you'll smash your way through over 50 rooms, crushing Skeletons, kicking Ninja Imps, bashing Vampire Chickens and hordes of other dirty fightin' ghoulies. All the while, trying to avoid being bitten, burnt, and even mummified. So take a deep breath and get over your fears, you've got a house to wreck."

Think about each of the following messages, and think whether the ad seems to send you this message.
1. Our video game is cool.
2. Doing the things you'll do in this game is brave.
3. Physical fighting is cool.
4. Smashing things is fun.
5. In conflicts, careful, patient thought is cool.

Does the ad send
A. all these messages,
or
B. all these messages except the last?

384. Here are some words from another video game ad. "Slaughter mercilessly....Hurl enemies into objects, impale them on sharp objects, or throw

them off ledges.... Feed your dark hunger by sucking the blood and devouring the souls of enemies to survive."

Think about the following messages, and decide which of these the ad sends.
1. Violence is very enjoyable.
2. All good people should feel sorry for others who are hurt or killed.
3. Ending violence should be the highest priority for the human race.
4. When you have enemies, you should try to solve the conflict peacefully.
5. You should use violence only as a last resort, and even then you should not take pleasure from it.

Does the ad send

A. just the first message,
or
B. just the last message?

385. How would you like to live in a world where everyone thought that hurting other people was very enjoyable? What would it be like? I think that you would live in constant fear. Every person you encountered would be dangerous. A species of people who felt this way would probably become extinct very soon. They would kill each other off quickly. The idea that making other people feel good is pleasant and making people feel bad is unpleasant is one of the main ideas permitting human society to exist. But if you want to strengthen this idea

in yourself, the videogames advertised as above won't help.

The author feels that the messages given by the videogames and their advertisements are

A. not very important one way or another,
or
B. very bad, in a very important way?

386.   Here are some words from a recorded song by Eminem.
"But if I had a million dollars
I'd buy a ... brewery, and turn the planet into alcoholics...
If I had a million bucks
It wouldn't be enough, because I'd still be out
Robbing armored trucks."

Two things the imaginary character in this song seems to enjoy thinking about doing are

A. getting people addicted to alcohol and committing robbery,
or
B. helping people break addictions and learning to earn money successfully?

387. Many people say, "But video games and songs are about imaginary things. They just have to do with your fantasy; they don't have anything to do with real life."
     The reply is that many, many scientific studies have been carried out about the effects of entertainment violence. Most of these have involved television. The results are clear that watching lots of violence tends to make people more violent in real life. Not everyone who watches violence becomes violent in real life. But a higher fraction of those who watch lots of violence become violent in real life than of those who don't watch much violence. The scientific studies of TV violence have just been one more piece of evidence that modeling and fantasy rehearsal influences what people do.

Which of these statements does the scientific evidence support?

A. If you want to succeed at anger control, don't entertain yourself with fantasy violence,
or
B. if you want to succeed at anger control, entertainment violence doesn't have anything to do with that goal?

388. Of course there are lots of images of helping and kindness and self-discipline that are available through the electronic media. Here are some lines from a song entitled "Lean On Me" by Bill Withers.
"If you have a load that you can't bear, that you can't carry,
I'm right up the road, I'll share your load, if you just call me.
Lean on me when you're not strong,
I'll be your friend. I'll help you carry on.

For it won't be long till I'm gonna need somebody to lean on."

The message that this song seems to give is that

A. working together and helping each other are a good way to do things, or
B. no one can trust anyone else?

389. Do you want to swallow whatever messages the electronic media send your way? Or do you want to want to think about your goals, and pick and choose what sorts of images from the electronic media will most help you to reach those goals? One purpose of this chapter is to suggest that you pick your entertainment carefully. Think about what your entertainment is causing you to store in memory and rehearse in fantasy. Think about whether those memories and rehearsals help you make self-disciplined choices for the sake of productivity, kindness, and self-care.

The message is that

A. whatever entertainment is most fun, do it, or
B. pick your entertainment so that the fantasy rehearsals help you reach worthy goals?

Topics for Writing or Discussion

1. Please audiotape or videotape a portion of a television show. Then please copy into writing a little of what was said. Or copy down some song lyrics, or some dialogue from a movie. Or copy what an advertisement tells you.

Then please analyze what sorts of messages are being given about the topics of this book, i.e. self-discipline in the service of productivity, kindness, and self-care.

It's probably beneficial to do this assignment lots of times.

Is it easier to find positive messages, or negative ones?

2. Someone says, "Violent entertainment such as gory video games couldn't be *that* harmful. *Everyone* does it these days." What do you think about the strength of this argument? Are you convinced by it? Why or why not?

3. Mohandas Gandhi was one of the "nonviolence heroes" of all time. He was leader of India's successful nonviolent struggle for independence during the 20th century. His methods were a model for Martin Luther King's methods used during the American civil rights struggle. In the passage below, from his autobiography, Gandhi is writing about incidents that happened when he was about 12 years old.

"Somehow my eyes fell on a book purchased by my father. It was ... a play about Shravana's devotion to his parents. I read it with intense interest. There came to our place about the same time itinerant showmen. One of the pictures I was shown was of Shravana carrying, by means of slings fitted for his shoulders, his blind parents on a pilgrimage. The book and the picture left an indelible impression on my mind. 'Here is an example for you to copy,' I said to myself...

There was a similar incident connected with another play.... This play-*Harishchandra*-captured my heart. I could never be tired of seeing it. But how often should I be permitted to go? It haunted me and I must have acted *Harishchandra* to myself times without number. 'Why should not all be truthful like Harishchandra?' was the question I asked myself day and night. To follow truth and to go through all the ordeals Harishchandra went through was the one ideal it inspired in me. I literally believed in the story of Harishchandra. The thought of it all often made me weep. My common sense tells me today that Harishchandra could not have been a historical character. Still both Harishchandra and Shravana are living realities for me, and I am sure I should be moved as before if I were to read those plays again today."

Please comment on what Gandhi wrote. What do you think it has to do with what was said in this chapter?

5. Someone starts a project to collect and store lots of positive models of self-discipline, productivity, kindness, and self-care, so that people can hear songs, see movies, read stories, and get just about any type of entertainment that they want in a way that encourages worthy goals. What do you think about such a project?

Chapter 21: Reading the Instructions

390. How many people in the world have a self-discipline problem? Nearly all of them! How many of those people have ever read a book, or even an article, about how to solve that problem? Almost none of them!

What fraction of the people with violent tempers have ever read anything about anger control? What fraction of people with procrastination problems ever read a book about how to stop procrastinating? What fraction of people with alcohol problems frequently read about how to stay off alcohol? What fraction of children with problems with attention and impulsiveness read books about how to pay attention and think before acting? What fraction of children who make bad grades in school ever read anything about how to make better grades? The fraction is very small.

The instructions are out there in the libraries and the book stores (as well as in the book you're reading now). They are readily available, and they are cheap. But it takes self-discipline to read them.

The main point of this section is that

A. reading takes self-discipline, because many authors write on boring topics,
or
B. people should take advantage more often of what has been written about how to live their lives better?

391. There are at least two purposes in reading about psychological skills. The first is to teach yourself things you didn't know before. Scientists are constantly accumulating new information on how to increase your psychological skills. You can learn these new things. Most people are very much aware of this purpose.

The second purpose is to remind yourself of things you already know. In other words, you bring back to your awareness the important ideas that you might not otherwise think about. You motivate yourself by bringing important ideas and images to the forefront of your mind. This is a reason to read often, not just to read once and be done.

The author's attitude is that

A. once you read something, you've got it in your memory, and reading it again is a waste of time,
or
B. by reading and re-reading ideas about self-discipline, you remind yourself of what you already know and make yourself able to use it.

392. Tammy has a goal of becoming a very successful student. She reads a book entitled *How to Get Straight A's*. She thinks that the book has lots of really good ideas in it. After she's read it once, she starts a custom: every day,

she picks it up again and flips through the pages until she finds one idea that she wants to remind herself of. She thinks about that idea and how she can use it for her goal. This takes her less than two minutes each day. But it revs up her thinking about how she can be successful.

When she reads a little in the book each day, she is using the book to

A. find out things she never knew,
or
B. remind herself of things she's already learned?

393. Ralph was dependent on alcohol, and is now trying to stay off alcohol. He reads a book called *What Science Tells Us About Alcohol and How to Stay Off It*. He finds that the book has many useful ideas and facts. As part of his program for staying sober, he reads a little of the book every day, as soon as he wakes up in the morning.

By doing the reading at the same time each day, he is making use of the principle of

A. self-reinforcement,
or
B. using routines to create momentum?

394. Here are some of the messages that you get by reading instructions on psychological skills:

It's not impossible; you can reach this goal if you try hard and long enough in the right way.

Your choices are important. Some ways of working toward a goal work much better than others.

Other people have used these methods and have succeeded, and you can too.

It is exciting and interesting to work on this goal.

If you succeed, you will have done something very much worthy of feeling good about.

All these messages tend to have the effect of helping you

A. put out effort,
or
B. relax and not think about the goal?

Topics for Writing and Discussion

1. If you are going to spend a lot of time studying a book on how to live well, you want to pick a book that gives good advice. Can you think of, or find, examples of books that have given bad advice? What ideas do you have on telling which books are trustworthy and which are not?

2. Some people find it pleasant and interesting to read about how to achieve their important goals, and others don't. Can you think of any reasons why some people would find this more pleasant than others?

3. Suppose that someone wants to follow the advice of this chapter, but doesn't know how to read. How easy or hard do you think it would it be for the person to do the same thing using audio or video recordings?

4. Have you ever read a nonfiction book more than once? Have you ever read a book lots of times, to remind yourself of the things in it rather than to learn them for the first time? If so, please tell about this experience. If not, please tell what you imagine it would be like.

Chapter 22: Time on Task

395. This chapter tells about a fact that should not be surprising to anyone. Yet most of us at least sometimes wish that it were not true, or act as if it were not true. If we get used to this fact, and learn to live with it, and accept it, we are more likely to be successful.

Here is the fact: the more *time* you spend *working* on a goal, the more likely you are to *achieve* that goal well.

Another way of saying the main point of this chapter is that

A. the more you work, the more you accomplish,
or
B. the faster you work, the less time it takes?

396. The phrase, "time on task" means not just spending time, but spending time paying attention to, and doing, what you want to accomplish. If you have an imaginary (or real) stop watch that times how long you have worked on something, you click it off when your mind and effort get off that task. You click it back on when you start working on the task again.

Erica's goal is to clean up and organize her room. While she is picking things up, deciding where they should go, and putting them away, she is "on task." She picks up a magazine off the floor and happens to notice that an article in it looks interesting, so she starts reading it.

If the task is cleaning up the room, then while she is reading the article, she is

A. on task,
or
B. off task?

397. The room gets cleaned only during the on task time, and not during the off task time. This is not surprising. But people sometimes forget this fact. Suppose that after being "on task" for two minutes and "off task" for 28 minutes, Erica were to say to herself: "I've been doing this for half an hour, and I've gotten nowhere on it. There's just too much work to do; I'll never get it done!" She would be acting as if the main point of this chapter were not true.

What would she say to herself if she were to realize that this main point is true?

A. "The job is not possible,"
or
B. "If I want to get it done, I need to put the time in on the task."

398. Someone starts seeing a therapist for some problems. The person misses the appointments with the therapist most of the time. The therapist assigns the person work to do in between the

visits, but the person never does this homework. After six months, the person has talked to the therapist four times and has done zero work outside the sessions. The person says to the therapist, "I think that your therapy is no good. I've been seeing you for six months, and my problems are still as bad as they've ever been!"

The person is acting as if there is an imaginary stopwatch that starts ticking at the first visit with the therapist and doesn't stop. The longer that time goes on, the better the person should be.

What the person doesn't seem to realize is that

A. the stopwatch runs 24 hours a day,
or
B. only the time that is actually spent working on the problems helps solve them?

399. A high school forms a chess team. They get together a bunch of very smart kids who like to play chess every once in a while. The kids go to play against another team. They lose every single game. They think to themselves, "Those kids on that other team are geniuses!" Then they find out that the other high school has championship chess teams year after year. They think, "What is it about that high school? What's their secret? I guess lots of really smart people go there."

It turns out that championship chess team does have a "secret." They get together to study chess and practice chess for two or three hours a day, all year round. They accumulate hundreds of hours more in training than the other teams do.

The secret of their success is

A. brain power,
or
B. time on task?

400. People have done studies of how children do on tests of math and science and reading, in different countries. In some countries, the children always do better than in other countries. Why do they do better? The principle of this chapter holds.

In the countries where the kids do better, guess what has happened? The number of hours they have spent working on those subjects is

A. greater,
or
B. the same?

401. The children who do better on their achievement tests have spent more time on task, as you might expect.

The same finding holds for children in the same country. Those who go to schools where they spend more time working on math tend to do better in math. Within any given school, the students who spend more time working tend to do better.

The same is true for sports teams and for athletes. How many Olympic athletes have just dabbled around in their sport, found that they have enormous talent, gone to the Olympics, and won a gold medal? Approximately none. They have usually devoted hours every day to training, over several years.

Of course, how they train is important. They use the best training techniques. They and their coaches try very hard to get the most out of every training hour. They are careful not to injure themselves. They train smart as well as long. But the smartest training doesn't work if it's only for a short time.

The point of this section is that

A. high achievers are unusually lucky, or
B. high achievers put in lots of time on task?

402. Some young children are called autistic. They are born with a problem in how their brains work. They have very big problems in learning to speak and in learning to relate to people. Many children with this problem have never been able to go to a regular school, have friends, and get jobs. Many of them have been very handicapped all their lives.

A man named Ivar Lovaas started a way of helping these children. The children who went through Lovaas's program did very much better than those who did not. They could speak and relate to people much better. Many of them could go to regular schools and succeed. The effects of the program on these children were almost miraculous.

What was it that worked so well? In this program, people were assigned to work individually with each child. These people worked day after day to teach the child to talk and to get along with people, bit by bit. They would work at this for 30 or 40 hours a week, for at least a couple of years. This comes out to three or four thousand hours of work.

Of course, what the workers did during those hours was very important. They figured out things that the child could be successful at. They figured out ways of rewarding the child for successes. They had a very systematic plan and they stuck to it. They were very patient.

Nonetheless, the best plan in the world would not have worked if they had only had ten or twenty or fifty hours in which to do it. It took thousands of hours.

The point of this section is that the very dramatic positive results came about through

A. a brilliant plan only,

or
B. the combination of a good plan and many hours of putting it into effect?

403. When we use the idea of time on task, we can think of two meanings of "wanting" something.

Meaning #1: How much you feel it would be nice to have it.

Meaning #2: How much time you are willing to spend working for it.

A man tells a counselor, "I want to have a happier marriage. I want it more than anything else in the world." The counselor assigns him a book to read on how to have a happy marriage. He says, "I just couldn't find the time to read it." The counselor assigns to him and his wife certain exercises to do together. He says, "I just couldn't get around to doing them." The counselor suggests that the two of them just spend some time together trying to have some fun. He says, "There were too many other things to do."

If we define "wanting" by how much time you are willing to spend on something, how much does the man want a happier marriage?

A. more than anything else in the world, or
B. not very much?

404. Two people both say they want to be wealthy. They both say they want it 10 on a scale of 10. The first one of them spends several hours each week studying how to earn money, working for money, preparing for better ways of making money, and studying how to invest money better once it's been earned. The second one spends some time each week fantasizing about how nice it would be to win the lottery.

According to our second definition of "wanting," which person wants more to be wealthy?

A. both of them, since they both said they want it 10 on a scale of 10, or
B. the first one, since the first was willing to spend much more time working at it?

405. There are lots of reasons why people are not willing to work toward goals. Sometimes their past experience leads them not to believe that through effort they can achieve goals – they don't believe in the effort-payoff connection. Sometimes they don't know what sort of work to do. Sometimes the sort of work that they start doing is so unpleasant that they can't keep it up, and they don't realize that there are ways to make the work more pleasant. Sometimes they start with something too hard for them rather than starting with something easy enough and working their way up. Sometimes they have already promised their time in other ways, that they don't feel they can get out of. Sometimes they just have too little work capacity. Frequently, they

have just never fully realized and thought through how many hours of effort and what sort of effort it will take to get what they want. Sometimes they can't set aside the time because nobody knows how many hours it will take.

The main point of what you just read is that

A. there can be several different reasons why people are not willing or able to put in enough time toward their goals, or
B. we needn't bother listing the different reasons why people don't work enough on their goals?

406. People sometimes fail to think about where their time is going. Here's a useful exercise for you. List your three most important goals. Take your best guess about how much time each week you spend on each of those goals. Then list the three activities you spend the most time in. Estimate how much time each of these activities gets. Then you can answer this question: do I spend my time on what's important, or what's unimportant to me? You may decide to shift some of your time away from unimportant goals and toward your more important goals.

This exercise asks you to

A. estimate how much time you spend on your important goals, compared with how much you spend on unimportant goals, or
B. estimate how long it will take you to achieve your important goals?

407. Here's an example. Jay lists as one of his most important goals writing a book for children on how to control their tempers. When he thinks back carefully, he estimates that he works on this book an average of one hour a week. On the other hand, he finds that he is spending about twelve hours a week on the Internet. Many of those hours are spent looking on the auction sites for good deals on laptop computers. Since he already has enough computing power, he rates the goal of getting another laptop computer as about 1 on a scale of 0 to 10 importance. He rates the goal of writing his book at 9 on a scale of 10 importance. He has been working on the unimportant goal about 12 times as much per week as he has been working on the important goal!

Jay decides to shift his time use to match how important his goals are. Unlike some people who have no choice but to spend time on things unimportant to them, he is free to shift his time use. He decides to work on his book ten hours a week, and reward himself for his productivity with a couple of hours on the Internet.

The point of this section is that if possible, you should

A. avoid surfing the Internet too much, or
B. devote enough time to your important goals?

408. Here's another example. Alex lists his three top goals as 1) succeeding in school, 2) building good relationships with friends, and 3) making the world better somehow. He finds that his three most time-consuming activities are 1) watching television, 2) playing videogames by himself, and 3) skateboarding by himself. He is spending lots more time on these activities than on anything to do with his three biggest goals.

As a result of his analysis, Alex should decide that

A. He should leave they way he spends time just the way it is, or
B. he should take some of the time he spends on activities he thinks are unimportant, and spend it on goals more important to him?

Topics for Writing and Discussion

1. Please list some of your most important goals. How much time do you estimate that you spend working toward each of them each week? Now please write about some of the least important things that you spend your time on. How much time do you spend on these?

What conclusions do you come to, from thinking about this?

2. Suppose that someone has as a very important goal, getting better at the skill of self-discipline. The person asks, "There's not really any way I can spend time working on this skill, is there? I just have to try to do better at it in my daily life, and that's about all I can do, right?" How would you reply to this person? Are there specific ways that the person could devote time to this goal?

3. Can you think of an example of a time when you considered a goal to be important to you, yet you didn't spend enough time working on that goal to accomplish it? Can you recall the reasons why you did not spend more time working on the goal?

4. How much total time do you think it takes to do certain things? Please make up some tasks or goals, and take a guess at how long it would take to complete them. The more specific the task is, the clearer the answer will be. Get someone else to take a guess, and see how much you agree.

5. Think of questions like the following: How long do you think it takes to learn to play the piano? How long do you think it takes to become a good writer? How long does it take to learn to have good anger control? Can you think of reasons why it is very hard or

impossible to answer these questions as
they are stated?

Chapter 23: Ways to Restore Your Persistence Power

409. Self-discipline and persistence power are in many ways like a muscle. You can develop persistence power by exercising it. You can also get it tired.

Suppose that Mr. Johnson takes very difficult examinations all morning. He uses persistence power to keep his mind on the tests. Then all afternoon, he spends time with an important business client who is very irritating. Still, Mr. Johnson persists in trying to be very nice to him. As he drives home from this, there is a big traffic jam. Mr. Johnson keeps on persisting, to keep himself concentrating in the traffic.

Mr. Johnson has also been trying to lose weight. But when he gets home, he eats a whole carton of ice cream.

At the moment he gets home, Mr. Johnson probably feels as if his persistence power

A. has been used up,
or
B. is greater than ever before?

410. Mr. Johnson probably felt as if his persistence power had been lost or used up.

Have you ever felt this way? Probably most people have. When one situation after another forces you to do something unpleasant, sometimes you feel you have run out of the strength to resist when you get the chance to do something pleasant, even if it isn't good for you.

People who are trying not to drink alcohol probably are more likely to start drinking again when

A. they feel their persistence power is used up,
or
B. they feel their persistence power is filled to the brim?

411. When you feel that your persistence power has been used up, how do you get it back? What sorts of activities "recharge the batteries?"

This is a question that hasn't been studied much. A lot of useful research is left to be done on this question. But I can tell you what my guesses are.

The question, "How do you restore your persistence power" is one that science

A. has fully answered,
or
B. has not fully answered?

412. Here are my first few guesses for ways to restore persistence power.

1. Sleep, rest, relaxation, or meditation
2. Exercise
3. Socializing, being with someone
4. Time alone

5. High stimulation, excitement
6. Low stimulation

What do you notice about this list? It has things on it that are just the opposite of each other, doesn't it? But this is because at different times, you need different ways to restore your persistence power, depending on what you did to use it up!

The author is suggesting that

A. different things work to restore persistence power at different times,
or
B. one thing will always work to restore persistence power?

413. Suppose that you have been using your persistence power to sit still all morning and work on writing an article. You might find your persistence power restored best by taking a nice run, walk, or swim.

Suppose that you have been helping to put out a forest fire. You have been using your persistence power to keep working hard even though you are physically exhausted. You might find your persistence power restored best by taking a nap.

The experience that helps you restore your persistence power in these two examples is probably

A. the same as the experience that used up your persistence power,
or
B. the opposite of what used up your persistence power?

414. Marva works in the customer service department of a store. All day long she has listened to people complain, and has used her persistence power to be nice to them even though they are angry and irritating.

Seth is a college student. All day long he has used his persistence power to keep writing a paper for a course, despite feeling lonely.

Which of the two do you think would be more likely to get the "batteries recharged" by spending some time in a quiet room, away from people?

A. Marva (the customer service person),
or
B. Seth (the college student)?

415. Jake is an emergency room doctor. He has had a very hectic morning. He has run from one patient to another, trying to keep everything straight in his mind, trying to juggle several tasks. He has had to make very important decisions constantly. Life-or-death situations have happened frequently.

June has just got off a very long plane flight. She has had to keep sitting in the same place for a very long time.

Think only about the idea that you often restore your persistence power by doing the opposite of what used it up. Which of the two people do you think would best "recharge the batteries" by doing a very highly stimulating, such as playing some rock music in front of an audience?

A. Jake (the ER doctor)
or
B. June (the traveler off the long plane flight)?

416. How do you know whether you need rest or exercise, time with people or time alone, or low or high stimulation? You have to cultivate the skill of noticing how you feel. It's always easier to notice feelings if you have words for them. Let's think about how "feeling words" go with the things we've talked about.

The word for needing physical rest is easy: *tired*. What's the word for needing physical exercise? These don't come so easily to mind. *Restless*, *edgy*, or *antsy*, perhaps.

The word for needing to be with people is *lonely*. What's the opposite of lonely, the word for needing some time alone? I'm not sure that there is a good one. A phrase, such as feeling *the need for time alone* may be the best we can do.

The word for needing more stimulation and excitement is *bored*. What's the word for needing less stimulation, needing to get away from high-stakes decisions, needing to shut off the flow of sights and sounds coming at you? Again, our language

probably doesn't have a way to put this well into one word. Overstimulated, harried, or frazzled come fairly close. Maybe best is to use the phrase "need for less stimulation."

The author can't think of perfect ways to put into one word

A. needing time alone, and needing less stimulation,
or
B. needing to be with people, and needing some stimulation or excitement?

417. I believe that there's a reason that the words for the need for exercise, the need for time alone, and the need for less stimulation are harder to come up with. I believe that people are less "in touch" with these feelings, less accustomed to thinking about them. And I think that this is because in the days when our language was being formed, these feelings weren't as common.

The author feels that people are more "in touch" with their feelings of

A. tiredness, loneliness, and boredom,
or
B. need for exercise, need for time alone, and need for less stimulation?

418. Think about exercise. A hundred years ago, most people used walking for transportation much more than they do

now. Even school children who had to sit in class usually got to school by walking. Most people did physical work for most of their days. Feeling tired was much more common than feeling antsy from having to sit still too long.

It's only in the twentieth century and after that people have had to sit for so long while machines move them or do their work for them.

The author is making the point that
A. the feeling of "need for exercise" is one that the human race hasn't needed to practice recognizing as often, until the twentieth and twenty-first century, or
B. We will all be healthier if we get more exercise?

419. Let's summarize what this chapter has told you so far. Suppose you feel that your persistence power is running out, and you need to restore it. Try to figure out whether you feel tired (needing rest), bored (needing stimulation), lonely (needing company), or needing exercise, needing aloneness, or needing less stimulation. These feelings may be important clues about what will restore your persistence power.

The author is suggesting that when you need to restore your persistence power,

A. you should always rest, be alone, and have low stimulation, or

B. you should try to be aware of several important feelings, which will give you clues about how to restore persistence power?

420. Here's a caution that is also mentioned in another chapter. If you feel bored, tired, restless, or otherwise in need of a break from working, please try to time your break so that it occurs after you have done a certain amount of work rather than after you have reached a certain amount of bad feeling. This is because breaks from work reinforce whatever comes before them. If you take a break after finishing something, you reinforce finishing. If you take a break after getting tired, bored, or restless, you reinforce developing those feelings.

So try to time your breaks so that they will reinforce your effort rather than your fatigue.

The advice you have just heard is to think things like,

A. "When I have finished the thirty math problems, I'll take a break." or
B. "When I feel restless 10 on a scale of 10, I'll take a break."

421. Here's another strategy for getting back your persistence power. It's letting your mind drift and do "whatever it wants" rather than directing it toward a goal. Using self-discipline and persistence power is by definition

working toward a goal. Sometimes a good way of restoring persistence power is letting your mind do whatever comes naturally, without trying to make it do anything in particular.

The idea you've just read is that

A. when you've been working toward a goal, a good way of resting may be ceasing to try to do anything,
or
B. you should never stop trying to do worthwhile things?

422. One way of *meditating* is letting the mind drift without trying to direct it. You define whatever your mind does as a success at this form of meditating.

You might try the following way of meditating sometime. (It's very different from some other ways of meditating.) Sit down and close your eyes. Just be aware of what thoughts, images, feelings, and memories come to mind. Just observe them without trying to change them. Do this for anywhere from a minute to twenty minutes, whatever seems most comfortable to you.

The way of meditating you've just read about consists of

A. focusing your attention on a certain thing, such as your breathing,
or
B. letting your attention go wherever it will, and just observing what happens?

423. Doing this type of meditation while sitting down with your eyes closed is particularly good if you need rest and low stimulation. What if you need exercise and higher stimulation? Then you might try letting your mind drift to whatever it wants, not sitting with eyes closed, but while walking around with eyes open! For example, someone goes for a walk and observes whatever is happening around him, as well as what's going on in his own mind.

Letting your mind drift with no particular goal in mind is something that

A. you must do sitting in a comfortable chair with eyes closed,
or
B. you can do while taking a walk, or even riding a bike?

424. Now let's talk about another very important way of restoring self-discipline, persistence power, and work capacity. It's getting success experiences. It's trying to rig things up that the work you do gets reinforced (or rewarded) rather than punished.

Suppose that Todd is learning reading. He is sounding out a list of words. But the words are too hard for him. Over and over he tries to sound out the words, and each time he gets corrected. With each one of them, Todd gets the message, "No, you didn't do that right." He's not having any success experiences; he gets no experiences of doing just what he tried to do. Even though his tutor tries to correct him in a nice way, Todd starts feeling more and more discouraged. His persistence power drops quickly.

In this example the persistence power dropped quickly because

A. Todd needed exercise,
or
B. Todd was not getting enough success experiences?

425. Now suppose that Todd's tutor realizes what is going on. She says, "Todd, I think we need to work some more on some easier lists. We can work our way back up to this harder list." So they do that. Now Todd is successful in sounding out the words. Nearly every time he tries to sound out the word, he hears from his tutor, "Great! You got it!" He gradually works his way back up toward the harder list, getting almost all the words right.

Todd is now having
A. frequent success experiences,
or
B. not very frequent success experiences?

426. Todd finds that working at the correct level of difficulty and having successes actually *increases* his persistence power. The work he is doing, rather than tiring him out, makes him more confident, less discouraged, and more able to use self-discipline!

This example illustrates that

A. work always uses up your persistence power,
or
B. work, when it results in success experiences, can actually increase your reserves of persistence power!

427. Todd's experience illustrates a very important strategy called "down the hierarchy and back up again." The "hierarchy" we are talking about is the hierarchy of difficulty. This is the list of tasks to accomplish a goal, ordered from easiest to hardest.

Mary is getting some tutoring in math. She tries some problems, but she is totally frustrated by them. She can't figure out any of them.

Her tutor says, "Let's go down the hierarchy a little bit. Try this problem." The tutor makes up a problem that is part of what makes up the harder problems, only much easier. Mary does problems like this for a while. Then the tutor makes up other easy problems that give practice on things Mary needs to know for the harder problems. After doing problems like these for a while, and gradually working up the hierarchy, Mary is ready to try the first set of problems again. This time, she does them successfully!

The strategy that Mary's tutor used was to

A. go down the hierarchy and work the way back up again,
or
B. keep trying the same task until you finally succeed at it?

428. Sam has gotten a failing grade at writing. He has become very discouraged about writing, and his persistence power in it is very low. He gets a tutor to help him with writing over the summer.

The tutor watches him try to write. The tutor says, "Let's go down the hierarchies and work our way back up, in several ways." They practice some very easy typing exercises, and gradually work the way up, so that Sam learns how to type more skillfully. The same typing exercises drill Sam in how to spell, starting with the most common words in the language and going to the harder ones. As another part of each lesson, the tutor types for Sam while Sam dictates, and Sam practices putting ideas into words this way. Sam gradually puts more and more complex ideas into words.

So far there have been several different hierarchies which they have gone down and are working their way back up. How many are there?

A. Three: typing, spelling, and putting thoughts into words while someone else writes them,
or
B. Two: grammar and handwriting?

429. Sam's tutor also gives Sam exercises in restating out loud paragraphs that he has just read, to give Sam more practice in putting ideas into words. They start with easy paragraphs and work their way up to harder ones. The tutor asks Sam to study grammar and practice correcting grammar errors, starting with easy rules and progressing up to harder ones. Then they start writing papers together; at first the tutor does most of it, and gradually Sam takes over more and more of the work. On each of the six different hierarchies that they used, the tutor tries to keep Sam at the level that is not too hard, not too easy, but just right.

As a result of all this, Sam's ability to write well grows greatly. So does his persistence power for writing.

The point the author is trying to make with this example is that

A. if you do lots of work on writing skills, it pays off,
or
B. if you go down the hierarchies for a complicated task and work back up, you can have the success experiences you need to get back lost persistence power?

430. Sally is a beginning piano student.

She plays some songs that she has learned, in front of a group of friends. They really like her music. They clap for her. They say things like, "I really like that!" They run and get other people to listen. Sally plays several songs. With each song, she feels even more enthusiastic about playing more and more.

The work that Sally is doing on piano songs is

A. decreasing her persistence power, because she is having failure experiences,
or
B. increasing her persistence power, because she is having success experiences?

431. Sally has a substitute piano teacher who expects way too much of her, for how much she has learned so far. Sally goes to the teacher and plays the same songs she played before her friends. The teacher criticizes every song, telling Sally all about everything she is doing wrong, and how to improve. Every time Sally plays, she hears about the things she did badly. She feels as if she is failing on every song. She very quickly starts feeling, "I want to quit."

The work that Sally did this time
A. decreased her persistence power, because it resulted in failure experiences,
or

B. increased her persistence power, because it resulted in success experiences?

432. Years later, Sally is an expert pianist. But she wants to get even better. She knows she can play well. But she wants to find out the things that would make her really sound great.

Sally goes to a person who judges piano contests. Sally's goal is not to impress this person. Her goal is to get as many tips as possible on how to improve.

Sally plays a song. The judge tells Sally all the things she did wrong, and how she can improve. Sally thinks, "Great! I got some good tips! These will help me improve!"

Sally plays more songs, and her experience is very similar.

This time she is getting constant criticism, but she doesn't feel discouraged. She thinks, "I am succeeding at getting the information I wanted! This will help me to be a better player!" She finds that her persistence power stays very high.

Sally's persistence power stayed high because
A. she was failing to impress the teacher that her playing was perfect,
or
B. she was succeeding at getting the information she was trying to get?

433. The last example illustrates something very important. What are

"success experiences" and "failure experiences?" It depends on what goals you have. If your goal, your definition of success, is "doing it perfectly this time," you will not succeed very often. If you define success as "doing something that helps me improve," you will succeed much more often.

Which of these two thoughts is more likely to make someone feel a success experience?

A. I should have done it perfectly,
or
B. hooray, I learned something that will help me do better next time!

434. Another way of arranging for success experiences is to look, very systematically, for the type of job or activity you will be most successful at. This means finding a job or activity that's a good match with your own talents.

    Mike is a salesperson. He is very shy. All his life, he has hated to talk with people he doesn't know well. He avoids calling on people to try to sell things, doesn't sell much, and feels himself to be a massive failure.

    Mike talks with a counselor about his work problems. They consider going down the hierarchy and working up, learning how not to be shy with strangers.

    But the counselor finds out that Mike only got the sales job because no one was hiring computer programmers

at the time. Mike is good at computer programming, and enjoys this job. Mike decides to look harder for a job in this area. When he finds one, he starts getting success experiences. He finds that his persistence power increases in all other areas of his life.

Mike used a strategy to get more success experiences. It was to

A. go down the hierarchy and back up again,
or
B. find a job that matched his talents?

435. Let's review what this chapter has said about getting back your persistence power when it has gone down.

    You can try to figure out whether you need rest and relaxation, exercise, time with people, time alone, high stimulation, or low stimulation. You can then try to get the type of experience that refreshes you. You might also consider the activity of letting your mind drift wherever it will, and just observing its activity, rather than trying to focus your mind on achieving a goal. You can do this sitting down or walking around.

    You can try to get more success experiences. One way to do this is to go down the hierarchy to easier tasks and work your way up. Another way is to redefine in your mind what success is – for example success is learning and improvement rather than perfect performance. And another way is to find a job that taps into your natural talents.

This chapter has focused on ways of

A. getting more organized,
or
B. getting your self-discipline levels higher when they sink low for a while?

Topics for Writing or Discussion

1. Please notice the ups and downs of your own persistence power over a day or more. When you feel that your persistence power is low, try some strategy to restore it. Tell or write about how well that strategy worked.

2. Is there some goal that you are working toward every day, or almost every day? For example, are you working on keeping up with schoolwork, watching your diet, getting enough exercise, or keeping your temper? Try an experiment. On some days, try using as many of the suggestions from this chapter as you can, to keep your persistence power and self-discipline high. On other days, do whatever you would normally do. On which days do you accomplish your goal best?

3. Someone tries to let his mind drift, without trying to do anything. But then he notices that he naturally starts to try to figure out problems or to try to imagine what will happen if something else happens. He says, "When I try not to try anything, I fail!"
Someone else advises him, "Here's what it means to let your mind drift. You define anything your mind does as a success, and nothing that your mind does as a failure!"
Do you think this advice should take care of the problem of "trying not to try anything, and failing?"

4. Can you think up, or make up, words for the feelings of "needing to be alone" or "needing lower stimulation" or "needing exercise" that you think would be better than the language used in this chapter?

5. Please watch for an opportunity to use the strategy of going down the hierarchy and back up again. If you can use this strategy, please tell about what your experience with it was.

6. Although it's good to have lots of success experiences, it's also good to have some experience with failure, so that you learn how to handle it. It's good not to let the fear of failure keep you from sometimes trying difficult things.
Think about times in your life that you have succeeded and that you have failed. What did these experiences do for you? Have you been able to learn from or otherwise benefit from failure experiences?

Chapter 24: Other Ingredients for Success

436. What is self-discipline for? It's for achieving worthy goals. Let's think some about the big picture of achieving worthy goals. Let's think some about what you need to do, in addition to using self-discipline.

1. You have to set a goal in the first place.
2. The goal has to be one that is "worthy" of your effort – this means something that makes you and/or others happier.
3. You have to avoid setting too many other goals that would compete for your time and energy.
4. You have to have accurate information on how to reach the goal.
5. At choice points, you have to list enough options.
6. You have to predict the consequences of those options.
7. You have to reason well in making your choice.
8. You need to have gotten the skills (other than self-discipline skills) to carry out the option that you choose. Finally,
9. You need to use self-discipline to enact your choice, and keep working at it long enough.

These are all useful abilities that are part of the process of

A. increasing self-discipline,
or
B. achieving worthy goals?

437. Let's think about some examples of these, by looking at reasons people fail.

A boy goes to school. He never thinks about what he wants to accomplish. He works when he feels like it, but much of the time he does not feel like it. He ends up with rather bad grades.

Why does he not achieve the goal of becoming a top student?

A. Because he didn't have accurate information on how to achieve that goal,
or
B. because he never set that goal in the first place?

438. Another student is very interested in getting top grades. But she is also interested in being a top athlete, socializing very much with her friends, playing in a band, taking art classes, taking singing lessons, and working to make money to make car payments. She does lots of work, but she just doesn't have time to do the studying to make top grades.

Why did she not meet her goal of becoming an excellent student?

A. She had too many competing goals,
or
B. she did not have good work capacity?

439. A girl was interested in being very healthy. She grew up in a time when people believed that lots of sunshine and a dark tan were very good for your health. So she went out in the sun a lot for many years. When she grew up, researchers learned that sunshine was actually bad for your skin. The woman stopped exposing herself to the sun, but it was too late; she got skin cancer.

Why did she not succeed at her goal of being very healthy?

A. She did not list enough options,
or
B. she did not have correct information about how to achieve this goal?

440. A man has a goal of keeping himself safe. While he is driving, his brakes fail. He tries to steer to safety, but runs off the road and hits a tree, hurting himself. Later someone says, "Why didn't you use the emergency brake?" He says, "Oops, I never thought of that."

Why did he not achieve his goal of keeping himself safe?

A. He did not list enough options,
or
B. he never set the goal?

441. A kid wants to be safe. But one day this kid, who has never skateboarded before, sees a skateboard on a sidewalk. Without a moment's thought, he gets on it without a helmet and tries it out. He falls and hurts his head.

Do you think he had a failure at his goal of safety because

A. he had too many other competing goals,
or
B. he failed to predict the possible consequence of his action?

442. A leader of a country gets elected during the time his country is at war. He has a goal of promoting peace. He has accurate information that continuing to fight the war will waste lots of lives and will accomplish very little. He thinks of the option of simply pulling out of the war and stopping fighting. He predicts that this will save lots of lives and lots of money. But then he thinks, "I can't do that. That will mean that the people who have already died in the war will have died for nothing." So he keeps his country in the war for a lot longer, and a lot more people die for nothing.

He makes what is called the "sunk costs" error. He fails to realize that his choice only affects the future, and nothing he can do will change what happened in the past.

He had a failure in his goal of promoting peace because

A. he made a reasoning error, called the "sunk costs" error,
or
B. he did not list enough options?

443. A person reads a newspaper article that advocates a harmful and wrong course of action. The person has a goal of helping his community make good decisions. The person lists options and predicts consequences and decides that the best thing to do would be to write a very eloquent letter to the editor of the newspaper, making a very persuasive case for the other point of view. However, the person unfortunately is not a good writer. Even though he works hard on his letter, he can't write it well, and the newspaper rejects it.

Why did he fail to achieve his goal?

A. Because he lacked important skills other than self-discipline,
or
B. because he lacked self-discipline?

444. A man sets a goal of going over a big waterfall and living to tell about it. He studies very carefully where he should go, and where he can land safely. He trains hard for the swimming he will have to do to get into the right place. He uses self-discipline to make himself go through with his plan despite the fear he feels. He goes over the waterfall and lives, even though he breaks a couple of bones and requires a rescue from the local police.

There is something lacking that keeps this from being called a great achievement. What do you think it is?

A. The man set too many other goals,
or
B. the man didn't set a "worthy" goal – his goal didn't accomplish anything for anybody.

Topics for Writing or Discussion

1. Please make up some more examples such as the ones given in this chapter. Have the main character fail to accomplish a worthy achievement because of one of the nine ingredients was missing. Ask your reader to identify which ingredient was missing.

2. Please identify an achievement that you think really was very worthwhile. Please see if you can explain how each of the nine ingredients was present.

3. Do you think that these nine ingredients for successful achievements are worth memorizing? If so, can you make up a mnemonic that will help people remember them? For example, you might summarize each by one word, write the first letters of those

words, and remember those letters by a
word or a sentence.

Chapter 25: Preparing for a Test

445. This chapter will give lots of examples of the self-discipline techniques that were explained in the chapters that went before. In this chapter we will imagine someone using these techniques to do better on tests. A boy has been bored with school. As he thumbs through a book at the library, he sees the words, "How not to be bored at school." After looking it over, he decides that he will study this book carefully, because it has a lot to do with what makes him happy or unhappy every day.

We can call what he did

A. using stimulus control,
or
B. reading instructions?

446. The book says the following:
"Lots of students think that school is very boring. But some do things inside their heads that make school exciting. They manage to get the same sort of pleasure from school that other people get from sports contests or other games. They try very hard to do well on tests and writing assignments. When they get a good grade back, they feel as if they've won a game. When they get a lower grade back, they feel determined to raise it the next time. They let the tests and papers and grades be for them what keeping score is for an athlete. They let striving for high grades be a fun game."

The book is saying that working to get good grades can be made fun.

Having fun in working for good grades would be called using

A. self-monitoring,
or
B. advanced self-discipline?

447. The book continues, like this:
"How do you make school fun rather than boring? It has to do with what types of thoughts you choose to say to yourself.

"Imagine that two people are playing chess. Imagine that the first one is thinking, 'What good is all this mental effort going to do me in life? When is this going to be over so that I can do something else? What is the point of it all? This is stupid that I have to work on this.'

"The second person is thinking, 'Let's see, what is the best move I can make right now? This would be a good one.... Hey, here's one that's even better! Let's see if making it has the effect I thought it would. Yes, it did! I won a piece! Hooray!'

"The first person is thinking in a way that we can call 'awfulizing.' The second is 'listing options and choosing,' and then 'celebrating her own choice.' The thoughts that you choose to think have a lot to do with whether you enjoy any game."

The technique the book is talking about now is

A. the internal sales pitch,
or
B. choosing consciously among twelve types of thoughts?

448. The book continues:

"Of course, the chess player who is setting goals, monitoring whether she is on target for those goals, and celebrating greatly every step of progress toward those goals is the one who is having more fun. If you do the same thing with the 'game' of getting good grades, you will enjoy your schoolwork much more too!

"But much more than board games and sports, the game of getting good grades is one that encourages you to learn skills that will be extremely useful for your life. Learning to read, speak, and write well will enrich your life very much."

The boy who is reading this book thinks about the goal of doing well at school. He decides, after much thought, that doing well on the tests he takes is one of the most important goals that he can choose.

This is an example of

A. exposure and habituation to increase work capacity,

or
B. careful goal selection?

449. The boy goes to the self-discipline folder on his computer, and opens a file called "tests." He writes the following in this file:
Reasons for Learning to Ace Tests
1. It's fun to ace tests, just as it's fun to win games.
2. Working hard for something and getting it will make school less boring to me.
3. Good test scores will help me get into a good college.
4. Good test scores will help me get scholarship money to college.
5. Being successful in school will help me get a better job and earn more money.
6. More success in learning will help me know how to do more good for people.
7. Learning lots of interesting things will help me to enjoy reading and learning throughout my life and to be a happier person.

The list that the person is making is called

A. the internal sales pitch,
or
B. the list of choice points?

450. The boy reads more books about how to do well on tests. Later, he writes in his "tests" file the following.

Plan for Acing Tests

I want to start preparing early. I want to find out as far ahead of time as possible when the next test will be. Especially I want to plan for the next "big" test, the one that counts a lot toward my final grade. I want to get myself ready for that test as far ahead of time as possible, and then stay ready by reviewing.

"When I anticipate the next test far ahead of time, I will have time to find out what the test will be like. Often, teachers will be willing to tell me lots about what types of questions will be asked. Will the questions be multiple choice, fill-in-the-blank, essays, or problems to solve? Is the teacher going after memory of little details, or understanding of big ideas? Sometimes I can look at tests that were given in previous years. Sometimes teachers will give study guides that ask the same sorts of questions that are on the tests. Sometimes I can find out from students who have taken the course before what sorts of questions are on the test. If the teacher gives little quizzes, that gives another type of clue about what will be on the big tests."

The boy is working on

A. writing an overall plan for accomplishing his goal,
or
B. choosing consciously among the twelve thoughts?

451. He continues to write his plan, as follows:

"I don't want just to read the book and look over the notes and show up for the test. My plan is also to practice, often, answering test questions that like the ones on the real test. I want to keep practicing until I can answer questions very accurately and fast enough that I'm sure I can ace the test. If there isn't a copy of the test that is like the one I'll take, then I will make up my own test. This will help me learn the material well, also."

The principle that he is referring to in this part of the plan is called

A. rehearsal, which is practicing the skills he needs,
or
B. stimulus control, which is avoiding tempting situations?

452. He writes in the same file,

"Here are some situations where what I do is important.

1. I'm in class, and I have the chance to ask the teacher about what will be on the test, or just let it go.

2. I'm at home studying. I have the choice between just relaxing and reading my textbook or notes, or writing questions while I read.

3. I've made a lot of sample test questions; do I actually practice answering them?

4. Do I measure and record how accurately and how fast I perform on practice tests?

5. Do I keep practicing until my practice test scores are super good?

6. I've gotten the real test back. Do I compare it to the practice test, and learn from all my mistakes, and celebrate all my successes?"

What he is doing now is called

A. listing choice points,

or

B. the celebrations exercise?

453. He continues to write, as follows:

"In class, I want to use any chance I get to find out what the teacher looks at when making up the test questions. I want to ask whether it's the class notes, the textbook, both, or something else. My teachers are usually willing to answer the question of what the test will cover, if I ask it.

"As I study the textbook, I want not to just sit back and read; I'll write questions as I go. After I read my math book and do problems, I want to make up more of my own problems that are like them. As I study my class notes, I will write questions as I go. Making up test questions will focus my mind upon what I am studying. To make up questions, I will have to process the information very actively. I will be more likely to remember it."

What he is doing now is called

A. deciding what he wants to do in the choice points,

or

B. frequently reading instructions?

454. He continues to write:

"With each batch of test questions that I make up, I want to answer those questions soon after making them up. That way I will not forget much between test-making and test-taking. If I'm short on time, I can answer them in my mind; if I really want to practice thoroughly, I will answer them on paper, as if I were taking the test. I want to review the questions often enough that I don't have time to forget."

He is

A. deciding clearly what he wants to do in choice points,

or

B. collecting positive models?

455. For another choice point, he decides to imagine himself doing what he has decided to do. He says to himself,

"I've finish answering my test questions. But I'm reminding myself that I'm still not finished! There are several answers that I'm not absolutely sure I got right. So I'm going back to my text and the notes to check out the original material. I'm comparing my answer to the explanation in the text.

I'm finding some answers I didn't get just right, and I'm going back and revising them. I'm thinking, 'This took self-discipline to keep going until I was really finished! Hooray for me!'"

This is an example of

A. an internal sales pitch,
or
B. a fantasy rehearsal?

456. He reads some more in a book. The book says,

"As the days go by, you make a test and practice it for more and more lessons. But unless you review, you may be forgetting the past lessons as fast as you learn the new ones! If you wait until the night before the test to review all the previous lessons, you probably will have forgotten much of what you learned in the lessons that took place a few weeks ago. So you keep reviewing the past lessons as you do the new ones. And how do you review? You skim the book or notes that you got the questions from, and then you practice answering the questions again. You read the book or the notes again, if necessary, to make sure you got the answers right."

His reading this book is an example of

A. advanced self-discipline,
or
B. reading instructions?

457. The book continues:

"One important secret is to get familiar with your own 'forgetting curve.' Your 'forgetting curve' is a graph that shows what fraction of a certain lesson you remember as the days go by after it, without review. Suppose that someone remembers 90% the first day, 50% the second day, and 0% the third day. The information doesn't stick in the student's mind very readily without review. On the other hand, suppose that someone remembers 90% after one week, 80% after six months, and 80% after a year. Then this information sticks tightly in this student's mind without review."

The book is making the point that

A. there is one rate of forgetting for all people and all sorts of subjects,
or
B. there are very different rates of forgetting for different people and different subjects?

458. The book continues:

"Here's an important point about getting to know your own forgetting curve. It is much quicker and easier to get 100% of the information back in your mind when you're starting at 90% than when you're starting at 30% or 0%. So if you forget a certain type of information quickly, you will want to review it very soon after learning it. If your mind hangs on to this type of information really well, you can afford to let more time go by before reviewing.

"The more you review some information and bring it back to mind, the more it tends to go into 'long-term memory' where it will stick and not be forgotten nearly as fast."

One point the book makes is that you should review more often if you tend to

A. forget the information more quickly, or
B. forget the information more slowly?

459. The boy studies a chapter in science. It takes him an hour to get to understand and recall the information perfectly. But the next day, he checks to see how much he remembers. He guesses that he has forgotten about one tenth of what he's learned. But he now spends 10 minutes reviewing, and he gets himself back up to the level that he was the previous day.

Three days later, he reviews again; he thinks he remembers about 90% of what he learned. But in 10 more minutes of review, he is back up to 100%. In three more weeks (the night before the test) he is down to 90% again, but 10 more minutes gets him back up to 100%.

He's taken 1 hour for the original learning, and a total of 30 minutes reviewing. He's done the same thing for all 5 chapters that the test will cover. That means that the night before

the test, he only has to study for 50 minutes.

The strategy that he is using is to

A. review when he has forgotten all about the subject, or
B. review when he still remembers almost all about the subject?

460. The boy remembers what usually happened when he didn't review at all until the night before the test. He figures that his memory of the first 4 science chapters would have gone down to about 5%. He now would have to start all over again, relearning all the material he forgot. He would have to spend close to an hour on each chapter that he forgot. Plus, since would be trying to cram it all into his memory in one evening, he would not be able to hold it all. After a certain amount of time, he would feel that when one fact gets crammed into memory, another fact gets crowded out!

The moral is that it's a good idea to

A. review often, for short periods of time, before you have forgotten very much of the material, or
B. review infrequently for very long periods of time?

461. The boy figures that this idea has been so helpful to him that he wants to practice it a lot in the future. So he practices it in his imagination. Here is what he says to himself:

"I've just finished my homework assignment in history. I'm feeling glad that I'm done. But now I'm at a self-discipline choice point. If I don't review for just a few minutes what I learned last night and a few days ago, I'll forget it. It won't kill me to do a little more work. I can handle it. I feel determined to do really well on the next big test, for all the reasons that I've listed, including it will be fun. OK, now I'm skimming over the chapters in the textbook for the past lessons, and I'm looking at the questions I made up, practicing answering them in my mind. Here's one I'm not sure of – let me look it up in the book. OK, that comes back to mind now.... Now I've finished, and that wasn't so bad. I feel really good that I had the self-discipline to review!"

What he has just done is called

A. self-monitoring,
or
B. a fantasy rehearsal?

462. Here's another big idea that the boy learns from reading about human memory. As you take your practice tests, go first for accuracy, but after that, keep practicing until you can answer the questions *fast*. You keep answering the same questions until you can do them without hesitating at all. When you have learned to do them really fast, your brain has really mastered them, in a way that is different from when you have to sit and ponder each question.

When you get fast, you will be able to have more time during the actual test to check your answers and make sure you didn't make any careless errors.

The idea of this is to

A. try to answer the practice test questions accurately,
or
B. keep practicing the same questions until you can answer them fast and accurately?

463. Here's another big idea. Often a certain skill is made up from a combination of simpler skills. Sometimes, if you are having a hard time getting fast and accurate at some skill, it is best to practice the simpler skills that are part of it.

The boy is studying algebra. He is learning to "factor quadratic expressions." He is having a hard time with this. He figures out that when he does this advanced skill, he uses a lot of adding, subtracting, multiplying, and dividing. And he figures out that his being really slow at these basic math facts is what mainly holds him back in the algebra skill he's trying to learn.

The boy times himself each day at 100 facts each for addition, subtraction, multiplication, and division. He starts out at about 12 to 15 facts per minute. He writes this number on a chart. Each day, he writes his best time for the day on the chart. He gradually gets faster and faster. Over a few weeks, he gradually gets to over 80 facts per minute! He finds that this helps him a lot with his algebra.

When he kept a chart every day where he wrote down best time for each set of facts, this was an example of

A. reading instructions,
or
B. self-monitoring?

464. The boy decides that there are other skills, in addition to the basic math facts, that are very important to be able to do quickly, because they are the building blocks of so many other skills. Spelling the most common words, typing, handwriting, and using rules of grammar and punctuation are examples of skills that he resolves to learn to do very fast. He figures that when he can do these fast, he can do them automatically or by "second nature," so that he won't have to think much about them. That means he'll have more brain resources to use in thinking about how to solve the math problem or how to say what he's writing about.

His resolving to get faster on these basic skills is an example of

A. advanced self-discipline,
or
B. goal-setting?

465. The boy trains himself to do drills for much longer than most other people are willing to do them. There are times when he has worked on them for a long time, when he feels the need to restore his persistence power. He has been doing the drills while sitting still, alone, and focusing his attention intensely. He restores his persistence power by taking a walk, chatting with his brother, and letting his mind drift.

This section describes the strategy of

A. daily self-monitoring, as an aid to keeping his motivation strong,
or
B. restoring persistence power by doing something different from the activity that used it up?

466. The boy has at some times had "test anxiety." This means that he has gotten so nervous that his fear has made him do worse on tests.

He remembers what he has said to himself while taking tests. He remembers that he has said things like, "What if I fail? That will be terrible!" and "I can't get it, I'm not smart enough!" He decides that he would like to do much less of this awfulizing and getting down on himself, and would like to do more goal-setting and listing options and celebrating his own choice. He decides he would like to say things like, "I want to give this next problem my best shot, and concentrate. Let's see, I could use this strategy, or this other one; which one would be better? ... Good, the strategy I chose is working, hooray!" He also decides that he would like to talk to himself in a calm, reassuring tone of voice.

The technique he is using here is

A. consciously choosing among the twelve types of thoughts,
or
B. self-monitoring?

467. After he gets clearly in mind the ways in which he wants to talk to himself when he is taking a test, he does lots of practicing in his imagination. For example, one day he speaks to himself like this:

"I'm ready to take my math test. I'm waiting for the teacher to give out the test booklet. I'm remembering the time I really concentrated well on the test last week; all I have to do is to do the same sort of thing with my brain. I'm remembering how I thought fast and accurately when I did my practice tests. Now I get my test. I feel my heart pounding, but that's OK, I can concentrate anyway. Here's the first question. I know the strategy.... Yes, I think I got it right! I'll go back and

check it when I'm done. Concentrate on the next one! Write out the steps ... Hey, I'm doing just fine! ... Here's one I'm not sure how to do. This isn't the end of the world. Let me think of a few options... Still no progress on this, OK, I'll come back to it when I've reached the end. Concentrate on the next one. Great! I got it!"

The boy is using the technique of

A. the internal sales pitch,
or
B. fantasy rehearsal?

468. The boy gets to the end of the test. He has an urge to turn his paper in and be done with the test. But this was one of the choice points that he listed and did fantasy rehearsals with. He now does just what he fantasy rehearsed: he goes back and works on any questions that he isn't sure of, and checks as many questions as he can. He uses every second until the test ends. He finds several questions that he would have gotten wrong.

This section reveals that he got a better grade partly because he used the techniques of

A. listing choice points and fantasy rehearsal,
or
B. self-monitoring and external reinforcement?

469. After the test, he comes to another choice point. He has the urge just to forget about the test. But instead, while the test questions are fresh in his mind, he looks at his practice test. He thinks, "There were questions like this on the real test! Hooray, my practice test was done well! Let's see, I remember a type of question that was on the real test, that I didn't have here. Let me write it down, so I can make up questions of that type for the next test or for the final exam."

Comparing his practice test to the real test is not as much fun as relaxing. But it helps him more to reach his goal. Because of this, the situation is an example of

A. an external reinforcement,
or
B. a self-discipline choice point?

470. When the students get their graded tests back, some of them put them away without looking at them. But the boy has tried to train himself to enjoy feeling very curious about what he got right and wrong. He looks over the graded test very carefully, and figures out exactly what he did wrong on all the problems he missed. He celebrates that he has found the exact source of the error, so he will be less likely to make the errors again. He looks at the hard problems that he got right, and he celebrates. Over time, he comes to enjoy this process more and more, so

that he can hardly imagine not analyzing his graded test.

The fact that he has cultivated the ability to enjoy this makes what he did an example not just of self-discipline, but also of

A. the internal sales pitch,
or
B. advanced self-discipline?

471. So far we've kept in mind the sorts of tests your teacher makes up. But the ideas also apply to standardized tests, the type made up by testing companies. The most famous is the SAT. Here's a word to the wise about standardized tests. For just about every standardized test, from elementary school through graduate school, there are "test prep" books that give either actual test questions that have been used in the past, or test questions that closely match the sorts you'll find on the tests. If you really want to do well on standardized tests, get these books and practice. Any questions that you can't answer, figure out how to answer. Can you make up similar questions? Can you answer the questions in the time that the test allots, with some time left over to check?

The author feels that

A. you should stick to your textbooks,
or

B. you should find test prep books and use them thoroughly?

472. If you use the method that this chapter has just described, I feel very confident that you'll ace lots of tests. But there are lots of self-discipline choice points involved. For example:

1. I just finished my science homework for tomorrow. In ten more minutes, I could review the chapter I studied a few days ago. My memory of that chapter that has probably gone down from 100% to 90%. Do I try to bring it back to 100%, or call it quits?
2. I'm reading my history chapter. I have the urge to just lie back and read, and let my mind drift off sometimes. Do I do that, or do I sit at the keyboard and make up questions while I read?
3. I feel fairly confident that I know most of the material. Do I bother to take my practice test, or do I just go into the test and hope for the best?
4. I have just taken my practice test. I think I did fairly well. Do I relax and do something else, or do I check my answers?
5. It's the day of the test, and I've just answered the last question. Do I sit back and relax, or do I keep revved up and check until the last moment?
6. I've finished a test. Do I just put it out of my mind, or do I recall the types of questions on it, and compare them to those on my practice tests?
7. I've gotten back a test where I missed only a couple of questions. Do I celebrate how well I did? Do I also analyze what went wrong with the questions I missed? Or do I just go on to the next thing?
8. I've done my regular schoolwork. I had resolved also to spend some time practicing for the standardized test coming up. Do I practice, or do I call it quits?

The point of this section is that

A. the method described in this chapter is so quick and easy, you can't possibly fail,
or
B. the method described here takes lots of self-discipline?

473. How can you practice making a self-disciplined choice in each of those choice points, at this very minute? You can do fantasy rehearsals.

If you're a student, you will also have plenty of chances to practice in real life! The more your practices are of good study habits, the more you'll strengthen the habits that will help you later.

You may find that you are able to do well enough on tests without going through the steps that were listed here. If so, keep in mind that some day you are likely to run into a subject that is hard enough for you that you will benefit from the steps listed here.

The author's attitude is that

A. if you don't use this method, it's almost impossible to do well,
or
B. people sometimes do well in some courses without using this method, but they should still consider the method for the future?

Topics for Writing or Discussion

1. Please summarize, by making a list, the advice you were given in this chapter.
2. Please explain the reason for reviewing often.
3. To what extent have you been able to enjoy the "game" of doing well on schoolwork? Would you like to enjoy it more?
4. Some people say that the best way to learn something is to teach it. Do you think that teachers often learn from making up the tests they give their students? Why or why not?
5. One person argues that it's best not to enjoy learning things that aren't helpful in real life, for example in a job. That person argues that being bored with useless information keeps you from wasting your time on it. Another person argues that it's better to be able to enjoy learning than to hate it, even when the information will not be useful to you. As long as you have to go to school, this person argues, you might as well learn to enjoy it. What are your thoughts about this? Can you think of ideas to add?
6. Suppose that tests are easy enough for some people that they don't need to do any of the things mentioned in this chapter. The idea of working so hard to prepare for a test seems crazy to them. They don't study for tests at all. Can you think of ways in which the habits they are developing may not serve them well later on?

Chapter 26: Doing Written Assignments

474. What do you do when you have an article, a story, or some answers to essay questions to write? Some students simply start writing the first thing that comes to mind, reach the end of what they wanted to say, and call it quits. Others start to write, but then they start criticizing their own word choice and the organization of what they are saying, and their spelling and punctuation. They feel so bad about what they are starting to write that their productivity grinds to a halt.

Between these two options the more painful would be

A. the first,
or
B. the second?

475. In the process that I recommend, you work hard to make your writing good. But you don't try to do everything at once. You divide the job up into stages. I remember these four stages by the letters GIOW.

G stands for generating ideas. In this stage you try to get down onto paper or onto your word processing file anything you might want to say. You don't worry about the grammar or word choice or anything else. Sometimes generating ideas can come from your own head. Sometimes it comes from reading works that other people have written. When in doubt about whether the idea is worth including, write it down quickly.

In the generating stage, you want to "turn off your internal critic." You want to silence the part of yourself who would criticize your sentence structure or your punctuation. You want to reinforce yourself for everything you write down. You even want to have fun.

The point of turning off your internal critic is that

A. sentence structure and punctuation aren't important anyhow,
or
B. you want to devote your whole mind to thinking up things that are worth saying?

476. The next stage is I for inclusion: you now go through and decide which, of all the ideas you generated, you want to include. The ideas that you don't want to include, you either delete or move into a separate file.

O stands for ordering. Of all the things you want to say, in what order do you want to say them? You think about outline structure, and ways of organizing your ideas. You figure out which sequence of saying things makes things clearest to the reader. In this stage you use a lot of cutting and pasting, moving ideas around till they are in the right places. You make headings and stick the ideas under them.

Sometimes your decisions about inclusion can only come when you've thought about ordering. Sometimes people go back and forth between ordering and inclusion, for good reasons.

The idea you've just heard is that

A. you must stay rigidly in the GIOW order, never going back to a previous step once you've gone on to the next one,
or
B. you stay flexible, using the steps as guidelines to help you not do everything at once.

477. W stands for wording. Here you figure out and write the particular words that best express your ideas. You make your sentences as clear and vivid as you can. At the end of this stage, you pay attention to capitalization, punctuation, grammar, and spelling. Often it's good to go through what you've written once for each of these, so that you can concentrate on each one at a time.

By separating the big writing task into several little tasks, you allow your brain to give its full attention to each part, without being distracted by the other parts. The result is a better piece of writing.

The important principle of this advice on writing is

A. break down a complicated task into several simpler tasks,
or
B. allow the brain to experience things holistically?

478. Once you're done with GIOW, if it's permissible and not cheating, try to give your composition to someone else to read. Get that person's feedback and suggestions. Sit down and revise your composition again, taking into account your reader's reactions.

If it's not legal to get feedback from someone else, read your own composition and give yourself feedback one more time, as if you were reviewing someone else's writing. Then revise as if you had received the feedback from someone else.

The next desirable step after GIOW is

A. concentrating on the wording,
or
B. getting feedback from a reader?

479. In the beginning stages, you turned off your internal critic so that it would be easy to get your ideas down. As the stages progress, you gradually turn your internal critic back on. By the final time you are reading your composition, the internal critic is looking for every possible error, so that you can correct it.

As you gradually get your article or story completed, the internal critic is to get

A. more active,
or
B. less active?

480. The plan is that you get something down in a hurry, and then you keep improving on it. By now you know that self-reinforcement is very important: every time you improve your composition, try to remember to say to yourself, "Hooray! I made it better than it was!" And at the end, if you like what you have written, you say "Great job! I wrote something that I really like! It was work, and I did it!" Part of your job as a writer is to reinforce yourself enough that you will look forward to your next writing stint rather than dread it.

Even as your internal critic is getting more active, you try to

A. feel bad about your imperfections in what you have written,
or
B. feel good about the improvements you are making in what you have written?

481. When you get back your composition from your teacher, graded, make sure to analyze how you did. If your teacher gives any criticisms, take these into account the next time you write.

The type of thought that you are being advised to do after you get a graded composition back is probably best called

A. learning from the experience
or
B. blaming someone else?

482. I have one more suggestion that will make writing more pleasant for you. Practice handwriting, typing, spelling, grammar, and punctuation, until you can do these tasks very quickly and automatically. The more these become second nature, the more you can use your brain to think about ideas. It can be very pleasant simply to think and watch your thoughts appear in print. This is the way it feels when you have practiced the mechanical tasks of writing until they have become automatic.

The advice of this section is to

A. make the mechanics of writing automatic, so you can concentrate on ideas,
or
B. concentrate fully on the mechanics of writing each time you write?

483. If you ace your written assignments as well as your tests, your success as a student is assured. But there are lots of self-discipline choice points involved in what I've suggested here. For example:

1. I'm writing, and I'm tempted to try to do everything at once so that I'll get it out of the way quicker, rather than divide the task up into stages. Which do I do?
2. I'm slow at handwriting and typing, and I resolve to get on a schedule of practice to get myself faster. The appointed time comes. Do I do this practice?
3. I am generating a nice bunch of ideas. Do I remember to reinforce myself for them, even though they are not in final form yet?
4. I've finished generating ideas. I'm tempted just to turn in what I've written so far. Do I keep working and go through the stages of improving my composition?
5. I've finished with GIOW (generating, inclusion, ordering, and wording) decisions. It's legal to ask someone else for feedback. Do I do so, or do I just call it quits?
6. Someone else gives a lot of criticisms of my composition. Am I grateful for them, and do I use them to improve the writing, or do I get mad at the person for not saying my writing is perfect?
7. I get back a graded paper with lots of criticisms by my teacher. Do I get mad and think how little the teacher knows, or do I use the information I've gotten to do better next time?
8. As I do each stage, do I try to take joy in the process?

Given what you've read in previous chapters, what might be an activity that will help you triumph in these self-discipline choice points?

A. internal criticism,

or

B. fantasy rehearsals?

Topics for Writing or Discussion

1. Please summarize the advice on how to write that was given in this chapter.

2. Someone says, "Learning to write in an organized way is learning to think in an organized way. We use words to think with, just as we use them to write with. Anyone who wants to learn to think better should learn to write better." What do you think about this idea?

3. Someone says, "Breaking complicated tasks down into simpler tasks and keeping track of them using writing is a way of doing smarter things without having to get an improved brain to do it. You don't have to have a brain that can hold everything in memory all at once. By letting your brain do one thing at a time, you can do things you never could have done if you tried to hold it all in memory at once." What do you think about this idea?

4. Someone makes a plan to increase her ability to do the mechanical parts of writing automatically. She first

practices copying writing from a book, to exercise her handwriting and typing skills and to get an "eye" for correct writing. Then she practices writing from recorded dictation someone has prepared, so that she can practice spelling and capitalization and punctuation as well. Then she practices using a grammar book, correcting sentences with errors in them. What do you think of her plan? How would you advise her to change it, if at all?

Chapter 27: Improving Concentration

484. This chapter will give examples of someone's working toward the goal of improving concentration. It will ask you to identify concepts and techniques you have learned earlier in this book. Someone notices that she gets off task a lot while she is doing homework. It takes her a very long time to do work that should be finished much sooner. She sets a goal: "I want to learn to concentrate better." Later she writes more about this goal. She writes, "I want to be able to finish my homework in an average of two hours instead of four hours. I want to be able to keep my mind on what I'm doing at least 90% of the time while I'm working rather than about 40% the way it is now."

When she wrote more about the goal, what did she do?

A. She imagined concretely and specifically what it would be like to accomplish the goal,
or
B. she used external reinforcement for a self-discipline triumph?

485. She writes more in her file about her concentration goal. She writes, "Every day when I do my homework, I will stop every 10 minutes and rate what percent of the time I had my mind on task. When I concentrated really well, I will try to remember what I did and keep doing that more."

What she is writing is part of a

A. use of stimulus control,
or
B. a plan for how she will achieve her goal?

486. She decides that her work area where she does her homework has too many distractions. She removes all games from the area. She clears off all things from her desk that she would be tempted to pick up and read. She puts away her radio and CD player. She tries to have nothing in the area other than what she is working on.

She is using

A. the twelve-thought exercise,
or
B. stimulus control?

487. While riding on the bus, she imagines that she is doing her homework. She imagines herself getting off task, becoming aware of this right away, getting back on task, and congratulating herself for her fast recovery of attention.

She is using

A. stimulus control
or
B. fantasy rehearsal?

488. While doing her work, she gets the urge to call up a friend and chat on the phone. She says to herself, "I know! I'll use that as a reward. When I finish this assignment, I'll call my friend then."

She is planning to use

A. external reinforcement for a self-discipline triumph,
or
B. careful goal selection?

489. She writes the following in the word processing file that she keeps concerning this goal. "Here are some advantages of getting better at concentration. 1. I'll finish my work sooner and have more time to play. 2. I'll do better on tests, and I'll make better grades. 3. I can enjoy reading books more. 4. I'll accomplish more in my life. 5. I won't be so frustrated by not finishing things."

What she has written is called the

A. list of self-discipline choice points,
or
B. internal sales pitch?

490. One afternoon she is working on her homework, and she sets a timer to go off after fifteen minutes. When it goes off, she thinks, "Wow, during those fifteen minutes I kept on task constantly! I was working solidly for the whole time! Hooray for me!" She

feels very good about this accomplishment.

She is using

A. careful selection of her goal,
or
B. self-reinforcement?

491. She keeps track, every day, of how long it takes her to finish her homework. She notices that the time gradually decreases as she becomes more efficient.

This is an example of

A. the internal sales pitch,
or
B. self-monitoring?

492. She tries to get into a habit of working on homework at the same time and place every day. She knows that if she can get a steady habit going, she will make things easier for herself.

This is an example of

A. using routines to keep up momentum,
or
B. doing the celebrations exercise?

493. One afternoon she finds herself worrying about a bad problem in her family. She finds herself thinking, "You're not doing well. You should be concentrating. You're goofing off." But

then she thinks to herself, "Getting down on myself isn't helping anything. Let me list options and choose, instead. One option is that I could stop working right now and think what to do about this problem. Another option is that I could plan to think about it as soon as I finish this assignment. I think I'll try the second one. And if I don't concentrate as well as I usually do, there's a reason, and I'll try not to get down on myself."

What she did was an example of

A. choosing consciously among twelve types of thoughts,
or
B. writing the most important self-discipline choice points?

494. She finds that when she has planned a time to think about the family problem, she can concentrate better on her work. Later she concentrates on the family problem. She comes up with some good ideas about how to help her family.

Later, she writes in the file that she keeps on this goal. She writes the date, and jots down a how she was successful at concentrating on one thing at a time. She writes that she feels good about the strategy she used.

Her writing is an example of

A. exposure and habituation,
or
B. the celebrations exercise?

495. She often reads whatever she can find about the topic of concentration. She finds some writings about something called "precision teaching." The idea that she gets from this is that you can increase concentration by measuring over and over your speed at doing certain tasks, and trying to get faster and faster. For example, in order to solve a bunch of math problems, touch type, or read and answer questions very fast, you have to concentrate well.

In this example she is

A. frequently reading instructions,
or
B. using advanced self-discipline?

496. For each of her subjects in school, she figures out a set of tasks that she wants to learn to do very fast. In math, she picks a set of important problems. In English, she picks a set of sentences with mistakes; her task is to find and correct the mistakes. In science, she makes a list of questions over what she has been reading, and the task is to answer them out loud. In music, her task is to name notes on the musical staff. In typing, her task is to type a certain couple of paragraphs with speed and accuracy. In spelling, the task is for her to spell each of a list of words out loud after someone says the word to her. In handwriting, the task is to copy a

certain paragraph with very clear and legible writing.

Then for each of these tasks, she makes a chart. She writes down on the chart how long it takes her to do the task.

Then she practices timing herself over and over. She goes for greater and greater speed. She greatly celebrates when she sets a new speed record. She keeps going until she can do all the tasks very fast. Her speed and automaticity help her with her schoolwork. She also finds that she can concentrate better.

Measuring her speed on tasks and keeping charts and records of how fast she goes is called

A. advanced self-discipline,
or
B. self-monitoring?

497. She is so excited about this method that she tells a few of her friends. They are excited, too. But they never get around to doing the timing and practice, because when their regular homework is over they don't want to put in any more time on schoolwork.

The girl succeeded in improving concentration, but her friends did not.

This is because she was willing to put in more

A. time on task,
or

B. self-reinforcement?

Chapter 28: Thinking Before Acting

498. A person finds that he does things that he later thinks are stupid, because he does not think before acting. He gets urges to do things, and does those things immediately. He doesn't think first of other possible options that might work better, or the possible consequences of what he does. He works to overcome this problem.

He makes a list of the types of situations he later regrets. Here are some of the situations:
1. I see someone do something I think is not smart, and I have the urge to say something critical or make fun of the person.
2. Someone dares me to do something, and I have the urge to prove that I can do it right away.
3. Someone is doing something illegal like using drugs, and the person asks me to help out in some way, like hiding something. I have the urge to go along with them.
4. There is a group of people having a party, and I have the urge to show off and draw lots of attention to myself by doing something loud and silly.

What the person is doing is called

A. listing choice points,
or
B. using stimulus control?

499. He writes in a file that he keeps for this goal: "Here's why I want to do more thinking before acting. 1. I'll have a better reputation; people won't think I'm such a loose cannon. 2. By stopping myself from doing something unsafe, I may save my life. 3. I will get into lots less trouble. 4. I will not turn people off so often by what I say. 5. I'll feel better about myself, because I'll feel more in control of my life."

This is an example of

A. stimulus control,
or
B. the internal sales pitch?

500. He decides that each day, he will write down how many times he did something impulsively that he later regretted. He also will write down how many times he caught himself before doing something impulsive and reconsidered what to do. He'll try to decrease the impulsive acts and increase the reconsidered options.

He is figuring out a way of

A. using exposure and habituation,
or
B. self-monitoring?

501. He takes the choice points he has written and practices in his mind listing options for what he could do. He also takes a bunch of those options and practices listing their advantages and

disadvantages. He does this for a large number of imaginary situations. As he does this over time, he gradually strengthens the habit of thinking about what to do before doing it.

He is using

A. an internal sales pitch,
or
B. fantasy rehearsal?

502. He often goes to the library and searches for what has been written on the subject of thinking before acting. He finds a book called *The Options and Consequences Book*. He skims it to see what it has to say about the subject of thinking before acting.

He is giving an example of

A. frequently reading instructions,
or
B. describing specifically what achieving the goal would be like?

503. He finds that *The Options and Consequences Book* has a long list of situations for people to practice with.

He decides that the book will be very helpful for him because it will greatly expand his

A. external reinforcement,
or
B. list of choice points?

504. He takes the imaginary situations listed in the book and practices listing options and predicting consequences and listing advantages and disadvantages.

His doing this is an example of

A. fantasy rehearsal,
or
B. stimulus control?

505. For each situation in the book, he gives himself one minute to list options or consequences. He sees how many of the ideas listed in the book he can come up with in one minute. He makes a chart, and sees if he can come up with more and more of them over time.

This is an example of

A. self-monitoring,
or
B. the internal sales pitch?

506. He works on this sort of exercise almost every day for ten or fifteen minutes.

His logging in this time, day after day, is an example of being willing to put in

A. time on task,
or
B. avoiding negative models?

507. Sometimes in real life he catches himself before he acts on an urge. He

reconsiders. Sometimes he figures out a better way of handling the situation. Sometimes he decides to go ahead and do what he had the urge to do. But in either case, he tries to say to himself, "Hooray for me! I thought before I acted!"

He is using

A. self-reinforcement for bits of progress,
or
B. organization techniques?

508. One day he sees a bike that isn't locked up. He doesn't know whose it is. He gets the urge to hop on it and ride it around some. Then he thinks to himself, "Wait, do some listing options and choosing."

He thinks to himself, "It would feel good to do a little bike riding. But if the owner of the bike saw me riding without permission, that person might be very mad. The person might think I am trying to steal the bike. They might call the police or try to knock me off the bike. What other options are there? I could look for the owner, and ask if I could take a little ride. Or I could go by my own apartment and get my own bike and take a ride on it. Or, I could go ahead to the library, and do the work there that I was starting out to do, and maybe take a ride on my own bike after I'm done. I think I'll do the last one."

He is

A. consciously choosing to do one of the twelve types of thoughts (listing options and choosing)
or
B. using routines to keep up momentum?

509. Immediately after he makes this choice, he says to himself, "I got the urge to do something really stupid, but I thought before I acted! Hooray for me!"

This is an example of

A. self-reinforcement,
or
B. daily plans?

510. That night, he makes a brief entry in a little diary: "Had an urge to ride someone else's bike without permission, but I predicted consequences, listed options, and made a good choice! Eventually rode my own bike some."

This is an example of

A. the celebrations exercise,
or
B. careful goal selection?

511. One winter's day the boy is in the park. A man and his kids come to do some sledding. The man makes sure all the kids have helmets on. They all check very carefully to see if there is anything dangerous along the slope.

There is a tree that isn't really very close to where they are planning to go, but the man takes some bales of hay that are in the park and makes sure they are in front of the tree just in case a kid should ride the sled toward the tree. Then after all this careful checking and planning, they start sledding and they have a great time. They do lots of laughing and playing and making noise and having fun.

The boy thinks to himself, "Here is a good example for me. First they were very careful, but then they had a great time. It goes to show that you can think before you act, AND enjoy what you do a lot. I'm going to write this down tonight."

The boy's noticing this and trying to remember it is an example of

A. collecting positive models,
or
B. choosing the right place on the hierarchy of difficulty?

Chapter 29: Kindness

512. A person thinks about his goals. He writes about the reasons for pursuing the goal of becoming a very kind person. Here is what he writes: "1. I will make other people happier, and that's good in itself. 2. When I make other people happier, they may be nicer to me. 3. I will be pursuing a goal that many people throughout many centuries have felt good about. 4. I will feel good from knowing I'm a good person. 5. Figuring out how to make people happier is a very challenging task for the mind, an interesting puzzle to work on. 6. Kind people seem to be happier themselves than mean people."

What he is writing is called

A. stimulus control,
or
B. the internal sales pitch?

513. He writes, in the same word-processing file, a list of situations where he would have the opportunity to be kind but be tempted to be unkind. Here are some of the situations he lists:

1. "My little brother has achieved something. Maybe he has done a cartwheel or he's spelled a word or solved a puzzle. I may be tempted to show him up and show that I can do better. But what's kinder is to celebrate what he's done and compliment him.

2. My dad is doing some work, like washing dishes or raking leaves. I'm tempted to just go and play, but it would be kinder to join in and help out with the work.

3. My sister is telling about something that happened to her. I'm tempted to read a book while she's talking or walk away from her, but it would be kinder to listen to her and look for the interesting part of what she's talking about and be enthusiastic about that.

4. There's a kid at school that most other kids are not friendly to. I'm tempted to avoid this kid. But it would be kinder to chat with him and spend some time with him, and see how much of what he says or does I can enjoy.

5. There's a program where I can tutor a younger kid and help him learn how to read. If I sign up for it, I may be tempted to skip a session and play instead of helping the kid I'm working with. Also, I may be tempted to act bored rather than keeping on being enthusiastic and upbeat."

What he is writing is

A. a list of self-discipline choice points,
or
B. self-monitoring?

514. Each day, he spends some time imagining himself responding in a kind way, in the choice points he has listed. For example, he thinks to himself:

"I'm chatting with my dad, and my little brother runs into the room, saying, 'Look what I got! Look what I got!' He holds out a paper from school, where he got 95% correct and an A. I'm tempted to be grumpy with him for interrupting. I'm also tempted to tell him about the time I got 100% correct. But wait, this is a kindness choice point. I want to make him happy, and I want to reinforce his good work. So I say to him, 'All right! Congratulations! I'll bet you worked hard to get ready for that, didn't you!' He smiles and looks proud, and I feel good. I'm glad I can feel good about helping to make him happy."

This is an example of

A. a written plan for how to achieve a goal,
or
B. a fantasy rehearsal?

515. He reads in a book about another way of practicing in his mind. The book says that one of the most important ways to be kind is to cultivate good will toward people – wishing for their happiness and success. He thinks of the people he knows – the people in his family, the people in school, the people in his neighborhood. Then he practices wishing for the best for each one of

them. He thinks of his brother, who is named Tim. He says to himself, "May Tim become the best he can become. May he give and receive compassion and kindness. May he live happily and productively." Then he thinks of his sister, and says to himself the same three sentences about her. He keeps doing this for a few minutes, thinking of most of the people he comes in contact with.

What he is doing is another form of

A. stimulus control,
or
B. fantasy rehearsal?

516. After supper his dad starts washing dishes and cleaning up, and he joins with him and helps him. As he is working, every once in a while his mind flashes on the game he wanted to play instead of working, and he also for a moment thinks about how hard it is to get some food off a pot. But he tries not to pay much attention to these things. Instead he chats with his dad and pays attention to how nice it is to have some time together to chat while working. He finds that he starts to enjoy the task of cleaning up after supper.

He is using

A. external reinforcement for self-discipline triumphs,
or

B. an "advanced self-discipline" technique: selective attention to the pleasant parts of working on a goal?

517. He decides that one act of kindness is just to smile and say hi to people he sees at school. Each time he does this, he tries to think to himself, "I did another little kind act. I made the world better in a small way."

He is using

A. self-reinforcement for bits of progress toward a goal,
or
B. exposure and habituation to increase work capacity?

518. Each night, he writes in the word-processing file for this goal a little diary of some of the kind acts he has done. Here's an example.
"January 4, 2004: This evening I told my sister that when she finished her homework, I had a riddle for her. She was excited to look forward to hearing it. She worked hard to finish. When she did finish, I congratulated her for doing her work, and I told her the riddle. It was the one about the cowboy who rode into town on Friday and rode out two days later, but he still rode out on Friday. How could that be? His horse was named Friday. She enjoyed hearing the riddle, and she ran off to tell my brother. I'm glad I helped her have some fun and reinforced her for finishing her work."

What was he doing?

A. the celebrations exercise,
or
B. routines to keep up momentum?

519. There is a video game in which you play the part of a character, and your character has to kill lots of other characters to win the game. He decides that when he does this game he is practicing not caring about someone else's pain or suffering, in the imaginary situation. He decides that since his goal is to become a really kind person, he will not play this game.

He is

A. avoiding models and fantasy rehearsals that would set back his goal,
or
B. choosing consciously among twelve types of thoughts?

520. He gets some books about kindness. These give lots of examples of kind acts and lots of thoughts about the goal of increasing the amount of kindness in the world. As part of his program he reads a little in one of these books every day.

This technique is

A. the celebrations exercise,
or
B. frequently reading instructions?

521. One day he has helped out with younger kids at a camp all day long. On his way home, he realizes that he is very tired of dealing with kids. He is tired of focusing his attention on deciding how to act. He anticipates that it will be very hard to be kind to his brother and sister. When he gets home, he goes straight to his room and closes the door. He sits with his eyes closed, by himself, and lets his mind drift in any direction it chooses. After doing this for twenty minutes, he feels refreshed and ready to be kind to his brother and sister.

He figured out how to

A. restore his persistence power,
or
B. use external reinforcement?

Chapter 30: Nonviolence and Respectful Talk

522. Someone reads the subject of ethics, searching for ideas about the best activities to do. Among other writings, he reads a quotation from the Buddha that says, "Those who drive out anger and fear do the world's most important work." He thinks very carefully about the effects he has had on people by yelling at them and hitting them. He realizes that he has made people unhappy and has made himself less happy. He decides that learning to be nonviolent and use respectful talk is the goal that he should put as number one on his priority list. He thinks, "This goal has to go higher than learning to skateboard better; this has to go higher than playing video games. This has to be number one."

This is an example of

A. advanced self-discipline,
or
B. careful goal selection?

523. The person writes, in a word-processing file in his "self-discipline" folder, the following:

"How will I know when I have reached this goal? It is not the type that you achieve once and are done with it. You have to keep working on it.

"But I can make up some milestones.

"It will be a milestone if I can accumulate 10 days with nonviolence: that means not hitting or otherwise trying to hurt anybody physically.

"It will be a big milestone if I can accumulate 20 days without trying to hurt anybody AND without yelling at anybody.

"It will be a big milestone if I can accumulate 50 days in which I have been totally nonviolent and have had respectful talk to people almost 100% of the time. To do this I would have to never yell at anybody, and to have all my disagreements with people be fairly polite. I say "almost 100% of the time" because I will allow myself to have a more irritated tone of voice than I want when someone bugs me, and still count this milestone as met."

What is the person doing?

A. writing a very specific definition of what it means to reach the goal,
or
B. doing the celebrations exercise?

524. The person writes, in the same file, the following:

"Reasons for Working on Nonviolence and Respectful Talk:
1. I won't lose friends quickly the way I sometimes have in the past.
2. I won't get fired from jobs for losing my temper.

3. I will break a habit that could lead to me or someone else getting hurt badly or killed.

4. I will break a habit that could lead to my going to prison.

5. I will avoid scaring people and making them feel bad without good reason, and that's necessary if I want to be a good person.

6. I will not give people such a reason to want to get even with me somehow.

7. I will be able to have a much happier family. I will break a habit that could lead me to hurt a wife or child.

8. If I do have kids, they will grow up better off by not being yelled at.

9. If I do have kids, they will not fight and yell at each other so much, because they won't have the model of this behavior.

10. I will not get kicked out of schools.

11. I will have a much greater chance of being successful in my job and making lots more money during my life.

12. If I learn ways of being assertive and negotiating in a polite way for what I want, I will probably get more of what I want than I do now.

13. I will set an example of nonviolence and respectful talk that other people will imitate, and I will make the world a better place that way.

14. I will feel better about myself because I'll know that I'm living according to good principles."

What has the person just written?

A. the celebrations exercise,

or

B. the internal sales pitch?

525. The person continues to write in his file, as follows.

"Plan for Nonviolence and Respectful Talk

1. I will carefully study my book on anger control, nonviolence, and conflict-resolution.

2. I will carefully study the list of 'Situations for Practice in Anger Control' in that book, and I will add to that list by thinking of any situations that have made me very mad.

3. I will use all these situations to practice responses that are examples of nonviolence and respectful talk. I'll practice the thoughts, emotions, and behaviors that are good responses to these situations.

4. I will get to where I can recognize and classify the twelve types of thoughts really well, by doing the exercises I have on this.

5. I will then practice doing the twelve-thought exercise with situations on the list. Then I'll particularly practice coming up with examples of not awfulizing, not blaming, goal-setting, listing options and choosing, and celebrating my own choice.

6. I'll read about ways of relaxing and turning down my excitement, and I'll practice these ways. I'll use temperature biofeedback as I practice.

7. I'll learn a list of options for nonviolent behaviors in response to situations that might make me mad:

negotiating, being assertive, speaking in calm tones, leaving the situation, appealing to the rule of law, kindness, ignoring, and so forth.
8. I'll practice identifying and classifying those behaviors.
9. I'll fantasy rehearse thoughts, emotions, and behaviors for each of the situations on the list, many times.
10. I'll program my mind to celebrate any good examples in real life just after I do them.
11. I'll keep a celebrations diary of the good examples in real life.
12. I'll keep a list of any times that I mess up, and I'll add those situations to my list.
13. I'll rate, every day, how well I did that day, on a scale of 0 to 10.
14. I'll avoid entertainment violence.
15. I'll read from the literature on peace and nonviolence to keep myself motivated for this goal.
16. I'll spend an average of at least half an hour a day working on this goal, and I will do something each day."

What he has just written is an example of a

A. written plan for how to achieve the goal,
or
B. the use of selective attention for "advanced self-discipline?"

526. Suppose that part of his plan was as follows: "I resolve to spend 10 hours a day working on this goal."

For most people, this would be an unrealistically difficult resolution to follow. Many people, having failed to keep it, would then do less work than if they had made a more realistic resolution.

His resolving to average half an hour a day and to do something each day is probably an example of

A. stimulus control,
or
B. a resolution that is probably neither too hard nor too easy to carry out?

527. He thinks about the situations in which he has lost his temper lately. He lists some of them, as follows:
1. "I'm playing a game of chess with someone, and it starts to look as though I'm going to lose.
2. I'm at school, and we get back a test with our scores written on our papers. A classmate sees my score and says, "Ha ha ha, I did better than you," and shows me his paper.
3. I look for a CD to use in the computer, but it is gone. I think that my brother has probably borrowed it without asking me."

What he is doing now is an example of

A. advanced self-discipline,
or
B. listing self-discipline choice points?

528. He thinks about the situation in which a classmate brags about getting a better grade. He thinks about what he'd like to do in that situation, as follows.

"What would I like to do? I could scribble on his paper. But that would be hostile and might lead him to be violent. I could say in a sarcastic voice, 'Well, aren't you so smart.' I could say in a sincere voice, 'Good for you, congratulations,' but that wouldn't feel right, because I'd be reinforcing him for taunting me. I could just ignore him and not say anything. That's the best one so far. Or I could say, 'If you weren't taunting me and trying to put me down, I would feel like saying, "Congratulations."' I like that one the best, because it may give him some helpful information, but it also makes me feel good about myself.

"What do I want to think to myself? I *don't* want to think, 'I can't let him get away with this!' That's the type of thought that gets me in trouble. A better thought is, 'His acting this way is his problem and it's not my job to straighten him out.' I also want to think, 'Hey, here's a good opportunity for me to come through with a self-discipline triumph! Let's see if I can stay cool!'

"How do I want to feel? I don't want to feel intensely angry and excited. I want to be cool and calm. I want to turn down my excitement by relaxing my muscles."

What this person is doing is an example of

A. deciding clearly what to do, think, and feel in the choice point situations, or
B. using routines to keep habits and precedents on his side?

529. After deciding what he wants to do, think, and feel in each of the self-discipline choice points, he spends some time each day going over those patterns in his mind. For example, he imagines the following:

"I'm looking for the CD of the math game, but it isn't where I thought I left it. I'll bet my brother borrowed it without asking me, but I'm not sure of this. It could be that I left it somewhere. Anyway, this isn't the end of the world. In five minutes I can look for it and probably find it. If I can't find it, there are other things I can do now that are almost as fun. I'll relax my muscles and turn down my excitement level. If I find the CD with my brother's stuff, later on I'll ask him to put it back if he borrows it. But I won't get my hopes up too high that he'll always do it.

"Now I'm looking, and it turns out that this time I find it in my stuff. My brother may not have had anything to do with it. I'm really glad I kept cool about this, and thought carefully. I did a great job of anger control!"

This is an example of

A. a fantasy rehearsal,
or
B. self-monitoring?

530. He reads about a way of solving conflicts. In this method, you do seven things. You tell your point of view about the problem, listen to and reflect the other person's point of view, list options, think about the advantages and disadvantages of options, choose an option, and stay polite the whole time.

    He looks at a list of things that people could disagree on. He practices making up conversations where people talk things out in a reasonable way rather than insulting each other and fighting with each other.

He is doing

A. fantasy rehearsals,
or
B. advanced self-discipline?

531. One day at school he is walking down the hall, and he hears someone call out, "Hey, you dumb dork-face!" He gets the urge to turn and see if someone is taunting him. But then he thinks, "If he's taunting someone else, that's none of my business. If he's taunting me, I don't want to reinforce him with my attention. So either way, ignoring him is better." He just walks on.

    One second later he thinks to himself, "Hey! I made a good decision! I did something good for my goal of nonviolence and respectful talk! I'm might not have done that before! Hooray, I'm making progress!"

What he said to himself at the end of this story is an example of

A. self-reinforcement for a bit of progress, also known as celebrating his own choice,
or
B. using "exposure" to increase his work capacity in this goal area?

532. One evening he thinks to himself, "What have I done today that I'm proud of? Oh yeah! In school, my teacher promised me I could use the computer game, and then the fire drill came up and afterwards she said to me, 'I'm sorry, there's not going to be time for you to do the game today.' I said, 'I understand, it's not your fault.' That was an example of kindness. Before I might have gotten mad and called her a name instead. I'm making progress!"

He is doing

A. careful goal selection,
or
B. the celebrations exercise?

533. He gets a piece of paper with a grid drawn on it, with 50 squares. Each day that he does not hit anybody or yell at anybody all day, he writes the date in one of the squares. He wants to see how fast he can fill up the whole grid.

He is using

A. the twelve thought exercise,
or
B. self-monitoring?

534. One day his mom says to him, "Guess what, your granddad is willing to get you the computer game you've been wanting!"

He says, "Great! That's really nice. But could we do something that I read about in a book? Could you get it, and keep it with your own stuff hidden, and I will get it only when I've done 50 days without hitting anybody or yelling at anybody? I've already done it for 35 days."

He is planning to use

A. external reinforcement for his triumphs,
or
B. the internal sales pitch?

535. A teacher at his school is impressed with how he is doing. He sometimes tells his celebrations to her. One evening, he works on fantasy rehearsals and the celebrations exercise and practicing relaxing and reading about peace and nonviolence. At one point he starts to feel tired of doing this. But he turns his attention away from the feelings of being tired. He imagines impressing his teacher even more with what he has been able to do. When he imagines his teacher and other people approving of what he has done, this helps him enjoy the work he is doing. It becomes fun rather than hard boring work.

He has used

A. a written plan,
or
B. selective attention to do advanced self-discipline?

536. At the beginning, he got tired of working after 5 minutes. But as he does it more and more, he gradually gets used to it. As time goes by, he works longer and longer. Sometimes he works for a whole hour or hour and a half, just to give himself the chance to get used to a lot of work. After he does that, his 30 minutes of work doesn't feel like such a big deal.

What is he doing?

A. using exposure and habituation to increase work capacity,
or
B. external reinforcement?

537. A bunch of "tough kids" hang out at a playground he knows. He thinks these kids should be taught a lesson. He thinks they probably aren't nearly as tough as he is. They've just got big mouths, and they deserve to be beaten in a fight. He's pretty sure he could beat each one of them in a fight.

He decides that this playground is a bad place to go if he is not looking for a fight. He decides that there are plenty of other good places for him to hang out. There are other kids for him to be with. He thinks to himself, "Why tempt myself, when nonviolence is such a big goal for me?" So he stays away from that playground.

He is using

A. stimulus control,
or
B. advanced self-discipline?

538. He notices that as the school day goes on and he has to sit in one place for longer and longer, he gets more angry and irritable. He talks with his teacher about this. He gets permission to leave lunch early and go to the gym and run. He runs very hard for ten minutes. He finds that the exercise allows him not to be nearly so irritable afterwards. He is able to use anger control more effectively.

He is using the technique of
A. habituation to running by repeated exposure,
or
B. restoring persistence power by doing the opposite of what used it up?

539. He tries to write some celebrations, every night before he goes to bed. He also imagines his celebrations diary every time he gets together with other kids his age. He tries to get something to go into his celebrations diary whenever someone provokes him. He also starts keeping track of how many days it has been since he hit someone. He feels good as the number gets bigger and bigger.

All these are examples of

A. reading instructions,
or
B. using routines and momentum?

540. Sometimes when he gets an idea for something to do or read, he writes it in his to do book so that he won't forget it. When he does it, he checks it off and feels good about it.

He keeps all the things he writes about this goal it all in one word-processing file called "nonviolence" in his self-discipline folder of the computer. He prints out a copy on paper every so often and keeps it in a file folder in his desk drawer.

He tries to keep things put away so that he will be able to sit down to his desk and work on this goal without being distracted by a bunch of clutter.

All these are

A. external reinforcement,
or
B. organization techniques?

541. On the playground, another kid grabs his hat and runs off with it. He

thinks to himself, "Let me do some not awfulizing. I'll get it back sooner or later. It's not that cold today, so this is not such a big deal. How about some not blaming: I don't want to go over and over in my mind what a horrible person this kid is, even though he can be kind of irritating. But I don't want to get myself all worked up. Listing options? Do I want to encourage him to do this or not? If I don't want to encourage him, I could ignore him. Actually I kind of like games of chase. I think I'd enjoy chasing him, but doing it smiling and laughing rather than mad. If I get mad, I'll ignore him from that moment on. Celebrating my choice: Hooray for me thinking in this way!"

In this example the kid is consciously trying to

A. choose which of the twelve thoughts he uses,
or
B. increase his work capacity?

542. In his reading about peace heroes, the boy reads about how Martin Luther King worked really hard to keep civil rights workers from getting violent, even when violent things were done to them. He also read about how Mohandas Gandhi tried very hard to help people in India work for independence from Britain without violence, even when the people were treated badly. The boy wrote these examples in his file. He also looked for good examples of anger control and nonviolence whenever he read a novel or saw a movie. If he saw one, he would write it.

What he did is an example of

A. listing choice points,
or
B. collecting positive models?

543. He got into the habit of reading books on nonviolence and anger control every day, and working every day on this topic for at least half an hour.

These are the techniques of

A. frequently reading instructions, and time on task,
or
B. self-monitoring, and the internal sales pitch?

Chapter 31: Sleep and Waking

544. A girl is in the habit of going to bed about 2 a.m. On the weekends, she sleeps till about 2 in the afternoon. On weekdays, she is supposed to get up at 6 a.m. so that she can go to school on time. But often she misses school or sleeps late, because it is just too hard for her to get out of bed.

She reads about sleep rhythms. She learns that there is a part of her brain that is like a clock. This clock gets set so that your body expects to fall asleep and wake up at a certain time. If you go to bed and get up later than you are used to, you set your clock later. If you go to bed and get up earlier than you are used to, you set your clock earlier.

She also reads that bright light, food, and exercise in the first part of your day set your clock earlier, and the same things later in your day set the clock later.

She reads that people who try to be awake when their body clock is telling them they should be asleep generally don't think as well or feel as good as those who are awake when the body clock says to be awake.

She does a lot of thinking about how her sleeping and waking problems have made her life worse. She thinks of many times when she has felt really bad when she has tried to get out of bed. She is amazed to read that some people feel refreshed when they get out of bed each morning. She thinks about how her

schoolwork has suffered from her being half asleep during morning classes and from her missing school.

She decides that getting a regular sleep schedule is a very high priority for her.

This is an example of

A. stimulus control,
or
B. careful goal selection?

545. She writes in a file, in her self-discipline folder: "My goal is to reset my body's clock so that I can feel good when I wake up for school. This means regularly sleeping from about 9:30 or 10 pm to 6."

This is an example of

A. writing a specific goal,
or
B. external reinforcement?

546. She writes, in the same file:

"Here are the reasons I want to do this.
1. I will not feel so bad when I try to get up for school.
2. There won't be any conflict between my parents and me about getting up in the morning.
3. I will be able to think better in my morning classes.
4. I will miss less school.

5. I will probably get better grades.
6. Getting better grades may help me be more successful in life.
7. I may be in a better mood almost all the time.
8. If my schedule is regular, it will be easier to make plans.
9. I may have lots more energy to get things done.
10. I read an article saying that regular sleep rhythms help people not to have headaches, so I might have fewer of these.
11. I read an article suggesting that people with certain types of mood problems do much better with a regular rhythm. It may help my mood too."

What she has written is called the

A. internal sales pitch,
or
B. work capacity?

547. She writes in her "sleep" file:
"Here's how I want to accomplish this goal.
"I want to go to bed close to 9:30 or 10 every night and get up close to 6 every morning.
"I will set a "light alarm" by rigging up a timer to turn on lights in my room a little before I get up. I hope to make my body think that dawn is breaking.
"I want to spend fifteen minutes exercising hard each morning, as soon as I get up. I will have a bright light shining on me while I do it. I will then eat breakfast. All these things will help my body know that it's supposed to wake up. I'll exercise in the afternoon, too, so that I'll be sleepier when 9:30 or 10:00 comes around.

"I'll try going to bed at 9:30 or 10:00 each night. If I can get to sleep, fine. If I can't, I'll get up and organize my things or study or do something else that's not very exciting for an hour and then lie down again.

"Going to bed early will be the hardest part. I'll have to let my friends know that I won't be staying up late to chat on the phone or on instant messenger.

"If there's a special event like a concert or a party that will keep me up late, I want to try still getting up at the same time the next morning. On the weekends, I want to get up at the same time. If I'm really sleepy the next day, I want to take a nap from about 2 to 330 or so.

"I want to keep track of how good my mood is each day and how well I do in my school work. I'm betting that I will see an improvement. If I do, I want to celebrate this in my mind really often."

What she has written is a

A. celebrations exercise,
or
B. plan for achieving her goal?

548. She continues to write in her file, the following:

"Here are situations where I'll really have to use self-discipline:
1. It's afternoon or early evening. I need to start my homework if I'm going to be done in time for my early bedtime.
2. It's 9:30 or 10:00. I'm about to go to bed, but a good friend calls me to chat.
3. It's 9:30 or 10:00. It feels good to relax and read, rather than get in bed and turn out the light.
4. It's 6 a.m. Saturday morning, pitch black outside, and all my friends and family are asleep. The light comes on in my room, and I'm tempted to turn it out and go back to bed.
5. It's any other morning, and I also don't feel like getting out of bed!
6. It's 6 a.m. on a school morning. I don't feel like exercising.
7. It's 6 a.m. and the light feels too bright for me; I'm tempted to turn it off."

This list is an example of

A. positive models,
or
B. self-discipline choice points?

549. In thinking over her plans, she thinks this to herself: "Getting up at 6 a.m. on Saturday and Sunday morning is something that right now I just can't see myself doing. It might be the best idea, but I know myself well enough to know I'm going to want to go back to sleep. If I go back to sleep, I may sleep a lot longer. I think it's more realistic to let myself sleep till 7 a.m. on Saturday and Sunday morning. Getting up then will be a big enough accomplishment for now." She revises what she's written, to reflect this change in plan.

This revision in her plans is an example of

A. advanced self-discipline,
or
B. trying to make resolutions that are not overly difficult?

550. For each of the self-discipline choice points that she has listed earlier, she tries to decide what she wants to think to herself. She decides that when she has to wake up, it's important to think, "I want to get any bad feeling of waking up over with quickly. I don't want to drag it out by struggling with whether to wake up or go back to sleep." She decides that when she goes to bed when she has planned to, she wants to reinforce herself by saying, "Hooray for me! I did something good for myself!" She decides that when she exercises and uses the light in the morning, she wants to think to herself, "Some day, if I keep this up, I'm going to wake up refreshed, without feeling that horrible pull to go back to sleep. That will be a really big accomplishment!"

What she is doing is part of the activity that we can call

A. decisions about the choice points,

or
B. stimulus control?

551. After deciding what she wants to do, think, and feel in bunches of self-discipline choice points, she practices them in her imagination. Here's an example of one of them. She speaks it out loud.

"It's early afternoon. I want to socialize with a friend and get my homework done. That way, I won't be feeling that either of these is not done when it's time for me to go to sleep. So I'm inviting my friend over to my house to have a homework party. We get our work done and have some time to go for a walk and chat with each other too, and we are able to have supper together. She goes home, and I do a little more work and I'm done. I'm thinking, 'Hooray, I'm glad that I thought ahead and prepared for having an early bedtime! Now I won't feel distressed over not having work finished or not being with a friend!"

This is an example of

A. self-monitoring,
or
B. a fantasy rehearsal?

552. One morning early in her program of work, she sees the light come on in her room and she knows it is time to get up. She's very tempted to go back to sleep. But she remembers that she wanted to get the sleepy waking over

with quickly. She jumps out of bed and starts running in place and lifting dumbbells.

As she does this, she thinks, "Hooray for me! I am already feeling wide awake! I saved myself a lot of misery by getting up quickly. And also it will be a little bit easier to do tomorrow, because I did it today!"

What technique is she using?

A. avoiding negative models,
or
B. self-reinforcement immediately after a success?

553. One night, she writes in her "sleep" file, another thing she is proud of, as follows:

"I had a free period at school, and I was tempted to goof off. But I thought about the fact that I had a lot of homework to do, and I want to finish it early so I can stick to my pattern of going to bed early. So I worked on my homework all during the free period. As a result, I'm all done now, and I can go to bed on time!"

This is an example of

A. careful goal selection,
or
B. the celebrations exercise?

554. She keeps a chart in the same computer file. Each night when she writes her celebrations, she also writes

what time she got up in the morning and how refreshed and ready to get up she felt. Her chart looks like this:

1/9/2004: Up at 6, refreshed 0 on a scale of 10, felt totally wiped out.
1/10/2004: Up at 6, refreshed 4 on a scale of 10. Had gone to bed at 9:30 the night before after lots of exercise.
1/11/2004: Up at 6, refreshed 3 on scale of 10.
1/12/2004: Up at 8, missed my deadline by 1 hour. Still, lots better than sleeping till noon as per prior habit!
...
1/16/2004: Up at 6. For first time, felt wide awake and ready to go when the time came! Refreshed 8 on scale of 10!

What she is writing is called

A. fantasy rehearsals,
or
B. self-monitoring?

555. She works on the habit of taking a long walk on a treadmill while reading, watching a video, or looking out the window when she gets up early on week end mornings. She turns her attention to how good it feels to be able to read anything she wants. She pays attention to how she is keeping her weight down and keeping in shape. She notices the nice feeling of being alone and having some time to reflect on things. She feels good about how much time there is left in the day to do the things she wants to do.

She also tries to ignore the temptation to go back to bed, and to ignore that other people are enjoying sleeping.

These techniques are examples of

A. using selective attention to do advanced self-discipline,
or
B. using stimulus control to do organization techniques?

556. She notices that when she gets on a steady sleep cycle, the number of headaches she has is far fewer than she had before. She talks with a friend who has lots of headaches, and she tells her about what she has done. The friend does some reading about this, and decides that she wants to do the same thing.

The two friends decide that they will get in touch with each other really often and celebrate their successes with each other and congratulate each other. They will sometimes call each other early on weekend mornings or get together to go for a walk.
The one who is just starting says, "I've been wanting to get some sweat pants. I'll let myself buy them only when I've been up before 6:30 for 10 days in a row." She tells her friend each day how many days she has to go, and they keep track together. When she succeeds, they go together to the store for her to buy her prize.

These are examples of

A. external reinforcement, both social and tangible,
or
B. the internal sales pitch?

557. She gets invited to a sleepover party. She knows that the people there will very likely be up till at least 3 a.m. She considers going to the party and trying to go to sleep early. But then she thinks, "If I'm going to try to sleep early, why try to do it in a place where I'll be constantly tempted not to?" She decides to go to the party until 10 p.m. and then go home and go to sleep.

This is an example of

A. advanced self-discipline,
or
B. stimulus control?

558. A couple of times she remembers something that she needs to do, just before she is about to go to bed. She has to stay up to do it, and this throws off her plan some.

She decides that to keep this from happening in the future, she will write all her plans in one notebook. She will look at this book often, and check off her tasks as she does them. She finds that using this to do list helps her not to stay up late to finish things.

She is using

A. an organization technique,
or
B. an internal sales pitch?

559. She gets a bunch of articles about sleep rhythms. To keep herself motivated, she tries to reread these articles often. There is also a book that tells about general techniques of self-discipline, and she rereads this often, as well.

This is an example of the technique of

A. writing a specific goal,
or
B. frequently reading instructions?

560. Her friend who had headaches keeps in touch with her often. This friend asks her very frequently about what she is doing and how she has done it. The friend tries to use all the ideas that the girl has used. She thinks, "Why reinvent the wheel? If she has figured out some good ideas for how to do this, I can use them, too!" The friend imitates most of the things the girl has done, and ends up reducing her headaches by a good amount, also.

The friend's imitation of the girl is an example of the power of

A. modeling,
or
B. self-reinforcement?

Chapter 32: Thrill-Seeking

561. A boy reads about a trait that people can have, called "thrill-seeking" or "stimulus-seeking." In the book he reads, there is a list of questions, with the title, "Are You a Thrill-Seeker?" Some of the questions are as follows:

1. Do you often get into conflicts with people or get people mad, just to get some excitement going?

2. Would you rather have someone yell at you in anger than have a boring conversation?

3. Are you more easily bored than other people?

4. Do you find it very unpleasant to have to wait for something?

5. Do you prefer taking risks to playing it safe?

6. Would you enjoy parachute jumping, hang gliding, rappelling off cliffs, bungee jumping, mountain climbing, and other exposures to high places?

7. Would you enjoy driving fast, riding roller coasters, speed boat racing, being a test pilot, riding motorcycles, and other exposures to great speed?

8. Do you like action and adventure movies, and dislike love stories?

9. Do you like loud rock or rap music with shocking lyrics?

10. Do you yell at people a lot, and do you often provoke other people to yell?

11. Are you attracted to danger, such as emergency rescues?

12. Does the fantasy of making an authority, such as a parent or teacher or principal, very angry strike you as funny and pleasant rather than scary and unpleasant?

13. When you were a young child, did you tend to climb up anything you could climb, or zoom down anything you could zoom down?

14. Have you been often hurt by risk-taking activities?

15. Do you enjoy violent entertainment?

16. Is it unpleasant for you to sit by yourself and read or write?

17. Is it unpleasant for you to sit by yourself and think?

The general idea of these questions is that a thrill-seeker

A. is attracted to danger,

or

B. avoids danger?

562. As the boy thinks about these questions and the other ideas in the article, he realizes that he has always been a thrill-seeker. He thinks about how he has lost lots of friends by making people mad for the fun of it. He thinks about how he has gotten into lots of trouble at school by stirring up excitement for the fun of it. He thinks about how one time he just missed getting killed when he skateboarded into the street.

He decides that he would like to stop doing stupid things because of his attraction to danger and risk and excitement. He writes in a file on his computer, "The biggest challenge of my life will be to make smart decisions despite the fact that I seem to be built for thrill-seeking."

He is doing some

A. careful goal selection,
or
B. fantasy rehearsal?

563. He continues to read about this problem, and he writes how he intends to deal with it. Part of what he writes is as follows:

"I plan to train myself to decide very carefully whether the possible benefits of a certain action outweigh the risks. I plan to go over lots and lots of situations and possible actions, and practice figuring out what is a smart action and what isn't. I will train myself to think a lot, so as to make up for the fear that I seem to be short on.

"I will keep a log of choice points in my real life that are like the situations I practice with. I will try to be aware whenever a situation comes up where I want a thrill but there is danger. I will try to decide carefully, and I'll write down what happens in my log, no matter which way it comes out. That way I can learn from my successes and from my failures.

"I will also practice handling low stimulation situations like sitting and relaxing or just walking on a treadmill with my eyes closed or sitting and reading or studying. I'll keep a record of how unpleasant these situations are, and I'll try to make them more and more pleasant over time."

These words are an example of a

A. written overall plan,
or
B. stimulus control?

564. He writes, in the same file, the following:

"Here's why I want to learn to handle my thrill-seeking nature better.
1. If I don't, I could get killed or badly hurt.
2. If I don't, I could do something that hurts or kills someone else.
3. I could do things that make lots of people mad, and I could find myself without friends.
4. I could get into trouble with the law.
5. If I learn not to dislike low stimulation so much, I'll enjoy school a lot more.
6. I'll also enjoy other situations that have low stimulation, like having to wait for something.
7. If I learn to handle low stimulation better, I will not be as tempted to use drugs to get kicks and thrills.
8. I will be much more successful in a career if I learn to make decisions

carefully rather than just going for the most excitement."

What he has written is an example of an

A. internal sales pitch,
or
B. external reinforcement?

565. He has a couple of friends who, he decides, are also thrill-seekers. These kids have gotten ideas about ways to get thrills that have gotten all of them into trouble. For example, one of them stole something from a store, just for the thrill of it. The other one tends to get into fights with other kids and tries to get his friends to team up with him.

     The boy makes a very hard decision. Although he likes these kids, he decides that being around them after school hours is not good for him, because these kids tempt him to do thrill-seeking things with them. He decides that he wants to hang out with these kids less and to try to hang out more with other kids who don't tempt him to do bad stuff.

The idea that he is using is

A. organization techniques,
or
B. stimulus control?

566. He has been having trouble with homework. In the room where he does homework, there is a television, a computer that is connected to the Internet, and a video game player. He makes another hard decision. He thinks, "Homework just can't compete with these other things that tempt me when I am in this room. I need to get these things out of here." He moves the more stimulating types of entertainment to other rooms in the house so that he can sit down and do homework without being tempted to distract himself.

The idea he is using is

A. stimulus control,
or
B. self-reinforcement?

567. At first he makes a resolution: "I want to expose myself to low stimulation so that I can get used to it. So I am going to go into this room that doesn't have anything stimulating in it, and work on homework for four hours without stopping." As he thinks more, he realizes that he is bound to fail at this resolution. He thinks, "I have not come close to working that long without more stimulation. Let me start with something easier. I'll start with a goal of working for thirty minutes. After that, I'll take a break and socialize with my family some. That will be a reward for me."

One principle he is using now is

A. advanced self-discipline,
or

B. trying to choose the best place on the hierarchy of difficulty?

568. He writes in his file in his self-discipline folder the following. "Here are some times when it's important for me to make the best choice.
1. I get the urge to ride my bike without a helmet.
2. I'm riding my bike, and I get the urge to do dangerous stunts just for the thrill of them.
3. The same as in 1 and 2, only with a skateboard.
4. I hear some kid say something, and I get the urge to tell him in an angry tone that he's wrong and he doesn't know what he's talking about, just to stir up some excitement.
5. I get the urge to fight with my brother about something little, like who gets to sit in a certain car seat, just to get some excitement going.
6. I get the urge to nag my mom or dad about something until they get impatient and yell at me, just to get some excitement stirred up.
7. My brother is trying to get some work done, and I get the urge to distract him and make him mad at me, just to keep from being bored.
8. There's a rule against having knives at school, and I'm tempted to bring a knife and keep it hidden just for the thrill of trying not to get caught.
9. I get the urge to make a fire where it isn't safe, just for the thrill of watching it burn."

What he is doing is called

A. making an internal sales pitch,
or
B. listing choice points?

569. He thinks to himself, "Let me list the advantages and disadvantages of bringing a knife to school.
    "The advantage is that it would be exciting to try to keep it hidden and keep from getting caught. The danger of getting caught would be exciting to me.
    "One disadvantage is that I couldn't use it for anything like sharpening a pencil, because I would have to keep it hidden. Another disadvantage is that if I did get caught with it, the people at school would punish me, and so would my parents. They would probably take the knife away. There would be some other kids at school who might not want to hang out with me because they would see me as a troublemaker. I would stay in the habit of getting in trouble at school rather than breaking that habit. If I don't break that habit, it's possible I could get kicked out of a school. If I keep the habit of breaking rules for the fun of it, I could get into serious trouble with the law some day, so I might as well start now to try to break that habit.
    "What I want to do is to leave the knife at home and think to myself, 'This will be a chance to practice making a choice that brings lower-stimulation but better results.'"

What is he doing now?

A. deciding clearly what he wants to think and do,
or
B. using advanced self-discipline?

570. He sets aside a little time each day to imagine himself handling each of his choice points the way he has decided is best. One day he imagines getting the urge to set a fire, and he says the following to himself:

"I'm doing my homework. I have some matches, and I'm getting the urge to set some paper on fire in my room. Maybe I can use the big jar to put it out. I'm thinking, what are the advantages and disadvantages? It would be a thrill, and it would be fun, but that's sort of a disadvantage, because I would be keeping myself hooked on thrill-seeking. I could possibly start a fire in the house. I would make some smoke that other people in my family would smell. The smell would bother them, and they would be mad at me for starting a fire. They would be really worried about a fire starting in the house, and that would make them less happy. I think the disadvantages outweigh the advantages. OK, it will take self-discipline, but I'm going to follow through with my choice. I'll do something else instead. I'm supposed to be getting my homework done; I'll just turn my attention back to it. That's what I'm doing, and I feel determined. Now

I'm getting some work done, and I feel really proud that I made a good choice."

What he is doing is a

A. use of stimulus control,
or
B. fantasy rehearsal?

571. One day he does get the urge to set a fire, but he resists it, just as he had practiced in his fantasy. When he does that, he says to himself, "All right! I used self-discipline! I did what I had fantasy rehearsed! Hooray for me!"

What he is saying to himself is an example of

A. choosing the right place on the hierarchy of difficulty,
or
B. self-reinforcement?

572. He sits down in the evening and opens up the file in his "self-discipline" folder on "thrill-seeking." He writes the following:
3-6-2004: "Today at school my teacher brought in a rat for an experiment on learning. When the teacher was out of the room, I had the urge to let the rat out and let it run around on the floor some. This would have caused a lot of excitement. But my teacher had told me just the other day he had begun to trust me more, that I wouldn't do things like that. I decided to keep up my good

reputation. I resisted the urge. Hooray for that decision!"

What he is writing is an example of doing the

A. celebrations exercise,
or
B. choosing the correct point on the hierarchy of difficulty?

573. He keeps a record of every time he makes a bad decision because of thrill-seeking. He rates each of these about how important they are, where 0 means not important at all and 10 means super-important. He tries to make the "bad decision" score as low as he can. He notices what this score is, each day and each week.

This process of measuring how you are doing in accomplishing a goal, and putting it into numbers, is called

A. work capacity,
or
B. self-monitoring?

574. He reads about ways of meditating. He tries a system where he sits silently and closes his eyes. He visualizes people, one by one, and practices wishing that each person will be happy, will be the best that he or she can become, and will live in peace. At first he finds the practice of meditation very unpleasant. He gets the urge to get up and do something thrill-seeking. But the more he makes himself do it, the less unpleasant it becomes. Gradually he learns to meditate for longer and longer periods of time.

The principles that are letting him meditate for a longer and longer time are called

A. exposure and habituation,
or
B. self-monitoring and listing choice points?

575. He gradually practices in the same sort of way, with working at his homework. He thinks of his homework as a way of practicing handling a low-stimulation situation. He keeps track of how long he can work without needing some different type of stimulation. He gradually becomes able to keep working for over an hour at a time without needing a break, whereas at the beginning he hardly ever worked for fifteen minutes without finding some other form of stimulation.

He has used exposure and habituation to improve his

A. internal sales pitch,
or
B. work capacity?

576. He goes to a camp where every morning, everyone takes a long cross-country run. Every afternoon, everyone goes swimming. He notices that he gets

into much less trouble with thrill-seeking when he is physically tired. He tries to keep up the habit of getting lots of exercise when the camp is over.

We can think of his ability to resist unwise thrills as a form of persistence power.

What did physical exercise do to his persistence power in resisting unwise thrills?

A. It used it up, or depleted it,
or
B. It increased it, or restored it?

577. He notices that sometimes he has had blaming thoughts toward other people just to get himself angry for the excitement of it. After reading about types of thoughts, he decides to try consciously choosing the thoughts he says to himself.

One day in school the kid who sits behind him taps out a rhythm with his foot against the leg of the boy's desk. The boy's first impulse is to think to himself, "You little twerp, quit that." But then he thinks, "I don't want to blame this kid and get mad at him. How about some goal-setting instead? I want to have a little fun in a way that won't get me in trouble or lose friends. I'll list some options and choose. I know. I'll move my head a little in rhythm with his tapping, like I'm dancing. I'll make some faces like I'm dancing when I'm doing it. He'll think it's funny. But it

won't be enough that either of us will get in trouble."

The boy does what he decided on, and the other kid laughs very quietly. The boy thinks, "I want to celebrate my own choice. I did something that gave me a little bit of excitement without getting mad at anybody or getting anybody mad at me, or getting in trouble."

This is an example of

A. choosing consciously among the twelve types of thoughts,
or
B. increasing work capacity?

578. The boy reads all he can about the thrill-seeking trait. He keeps looking in the library and on the Internet for more information.

The principle he is following is

A. external reinforcement,
or
B. frequently reading instructions?

579. In his reading, he runs across the stories of several people who had thrill-seeking traits but used those tendencies in good ways. He reads about one of them who got thrills by running for public office. This leader got lots of attention, both support and criticism. He constantly had to figure out how to deal with the people who argued against what he wanted to do. He constantly

had to make high stakes decisions. He very often made speeches in front of huge numbers of people. All this was really exciting to him. He worked hard to get his excitement in ways like this, rather than in ways like using drugs or driving fast cars.

The boy thinks to himself, "Here's an example of a person who did lots of good for the world and seemed to have a great time, even though he was a real thrill-seeker. He probably couldn't have enjoyed his work so much if he hadn't been a thrill-seeker. I want to remember his example, and choose ways of thrill-seeking that help people."

Remembering good examples that you want to imitate is called

A. the internal sales pitch,
or
B. collecting positive models?

580. The boy writes in his "thrill-seeking" file, "Here are ways that I can put in time toward helping myself deal well with my thrill-seeking tendency.
1. I can add to and review my internal sales pitch.
2. I can add to my list of choice points.
3. I can spend time deciding what to do in those choice points.
4. I can do fantasy rehearsals.
5. I can write the celebrations exercise.
6. I can monitor myself and keep written records of how well I'm doing.
7. I can practice meditating.

8. I can practice doing homework without stimulation.
9. I can study the twelve thoughts, and practice choosing the ones I want in the situations that on my list of choice points.
10. I can read about people and keep trying to collect positive models.
11. I can read books and articles about this subject."

With respect to the goal of dealing well with his thrill-seeking trait, the boy has listed ways of putting in

A. time on task,
or
B. advanced self-discipline?

Chapter 33: Weight Control

581. A man reads about the risks of heart disease, strokes, high blood pressure, diabetes, and a type of joint disease. He finds out that the fatter you are, the more likely you are to get these diseases. He reads some research that people who eat less live longer. He looks at himself in the mirror and thinks that he would look better if he weighed less.

He does more reading. He finds out that there are ways of figuring out about how much someone should weigh for his height. He learns that someone his height should weigh between about 165 and 190 pounds. He weighs about 205.

In the past he has tried, without much success, to lose weight. He decides that it will be much more pleasant to succeed at this goal than to fail at it.

He decides, after lots of reading and study, that he would like to take several months to lose to 170 pounds.

What he has done is an example of

A. careful goal selection,
or
B. exposure and habituation to increase work capacity?

582. He does some more reading on about how fast he should expect to reach this goal. He decides to lose about a pound a week.

In a file entitled "weight" in his self-discipline folder, he writes his goal weight for the beginning of each month. It looks like this: "I want to weigh 200 by November, 196 by December, 192 by January ... and 170 by August."

This is an example of

A. describing specifically what it would be like to achieve the goal,
or
B. advanced self-discipline?

583. He writes further in his file:
"Here is why I want to achieve this goal:
1. I will decrease my chances of getting diabetes, which is a very unpleasant and dangerous condition.
2. I will decrease my chances of having a stroke. A stroke could really interfere with the ability of my brain to work well.
3. I will decrease my chances of having to take medicine for high blood pressure. Those medicines can have side effects I don't like.
4. I will decrease the chance of painful joints in my knees and hips and other places.
5. I will have less chance of getting a heart attack, which could kill me.
6. I will in other ways increase my chances of living longer.
7. I will be in better shape and have more energy.

8. I will look better.

9. I will feel great success.

10. I will not feel the discouraging feeling of wanting to lose weight but failing at it.

11. I may be able to help other people to use the successful techniques I've used."

What he has written is called the

A. stimulus control,
or
B. internal sales pitch?

584. A twelve-year-old girl is also interested in losing weight. She writes the following in her "weight" file.
     "Reasons for losing weight:

1. I will look better.

2. People at school will not make fun of me for being overweight.

3. It will be easier for me to make new friends.

4. I will feel proud of my accomplishment."

This is an example of

A. a list of self-discipline choice points,
or
B. another internal sales pitch?

585. The man writes the following in his file:
     "Here is how I intend to lose the weight. I will keep track of what I eat and how many calories I've taken in. I'll write down what I eat and how

many calories it is, before I eat it. I'll eat no more than 1800 calories per day. My diet will mainly be made up of fruits, vegetables, and whole grains. I'll eat a maximum of 100 calories of "junk food" per day. I'll wear a pedometer and try to take 10,000 steps per day. I'll weigh myself every morning and record my weight. I'll try to feel really good about my successes."

This is an example of

A. stimulus control,
or
B. a written plan?

586. The girl writes,
     "I plan to cut out soda altogether from my diet. That will cut out lots of calories per day right there. I want to have a maximum of 300 calories of other junk food per day. I want to stop eating between meals except for certain healthy snacks that I've listed, like apples and carrots. I will eat these whenever I am hungry. I will eat more vegetables and whole grains and fruits. I will switch to nonfat dairy products. I will have some vegetable soup on hand to eat if I am hungry. I will exercise every day, starting at 30 minutes and working up to an hour a day. I'll do this by taking the dog out for a long walk. I'll weigh myself each day. If this plan doesn't work I'll revise it."

     The girl planned to eat apples or carrots or vegetable soup whenever she was hungry. She could have planned, "If I'm hungry, I'll just tough it out."

Her planning not to have to stay hungry lots of the time is an example of

A. trying to make a resolution that is not too hard to follow,
or
B. increasing her work capacity?

587. The man makes another list that looks like this.
1. "I'm busy one morning, and I'm tempted to rush off with a quick breakfast without writing anything.
2. I'm tempted to keep eating without writing anything down, past the point where I can remember what I ate.
3. I'm enjoying eating, and I am tempted to think, "I'll go ahead and eat my daily quota of calories now; I just won't eat anything for the rest of the day," instead of spacing out my eating over the day so that I'm not hungry at any time.
4. I'm getting ready to eat something, but it's work to measure or even estimate how big it is, how much of it I'm eating. So I'm tempted to abandon the idea of figuring out how many calories I take in for that day instead of taking 20 seconds to make my best guess and write it down.
5. I've neglected to write down a little thing that I've eaten. Or I've eaten more than 100 calories of junk food. I'm tempted to think, "Oh, I've broken my rule. I may as well break it altogether

and have a lot more pleasurable food," instead of recovering from the lapse as quickly as possible."

The man has made a list of

A. self-discipline choice points,
or
B. the twelve thoughts?

588. The girl has also listed some choice points. One of them is as follows: "I'm at a friend's house in the afternoon. The friend offers me some potato chips and soda, and is going to have some herself."

She thinks to herself, "Do I want to just say, 'No, thank you,' or do I explain to my friend that I'm trying to lose a little weight? The advantage of explaining is that maybe my friend will support me and help me by not tempting me. Maybe she will even want to do some of the same things. If I just say 'No, thank you,' she might think that I'm not wanting to be too greedy, and that as a good host, she should urge me more strongly to have some. I think I want to explain to her what I'm trying to do."

This is an example of

A. external reinforcement,
or
B. deciding clearly what to do in a choice point?

589. The man has been in the habit of sitting at the breakfast table, reading the newspaper, eating more and more. When he sits at the table reading the newspaper, he finds it very difficult not to keep eating. He breaks his resolutions several times in this situation.

He decides that the situation of sitting at the table reading, with food all around him, is too tempting for him now. He decides that he will eat a quick breakfast and get away from the breakfast room. He decides to take the newspaper and read it while walking on a treadmill. Using this plan, it's much easier for him to follow his resolution.

His getting away from the temptation of food is an example of

A. advanced self-discipline,
or
B. stimulus control?

590. The girl, while riding on a bus, has the following image go through her mind:

"It's later this afternoon. I get home from school and I'm hungry. I'm on my way to get a cup of soup or some fruit but I see some marshmallows and graham crackers and chocolate bars lying on the kitchen counter. It would feel pleasant for a few seconds to load up on them. But then I would blow my momentum. I've been keeping up my routine for a while. I want to stay in it. I can be tough. I know I will not be hungry. I'm feeling determined. I get

the junk food out of sight as quickly as possible, get my cup of vegetable soup, which tastes really good. I turn my attention away from food and toward what I want to do next. I feel great that I was able to triumph in this choice point!"

Is this an example of a

A. fantasy rehearsal,
or
B. self-monitoring?

591. The girl eats meals, and drinks water with them. She imagines herself as very thirsty, in the desert, and she imagines how she would crave water. When she actually drinks the water, she focuses her attention on how clean and cold and pure the water tastes. Especially when she is eating salty food, she sometimes lets herself get very thirsty before taking a big drink of water to quench her thirst. She anticipates the pleasure of the water and she focuses on that pleasure when she drinks it.

Through using her mind like this, after a while she comes to really enjoy drinking water much more than she ever did before when she mainly drank pop.

This is an example of

A. advanced self-discipline through selective attention,
or

B. listing choice points?

592. The girl sometimes is able to exercise for only fifteen minutes or so. On some other days, she is able to take two or three long walks mixed with some running, plus work out with weights, for a total of two hours. She notices that when she has exercised really hard, she sleeps much better at night. She enjoys the tired feeling she has when she goes to bed after a lot of exercise. She is glad that she has noticed this pleasant result, because it helps to motivate her to exercise more.

She is glad that she has noticed

A. an effort-payoff connection,

or

B. a fantasy rehearsal?

593. The man has been in the habit of going out with his family to eat supper. He thinks to himself, "During this time, I have to sit in front of food for half an hour or an hour. It takes me only five to ten minutes to eat the number of calories that I want. The rest of the time, I'm being tempted and expecting myself to resist." He talks this over with his family members. They decide together that they would like to go out together to a gym to play basketball more often, and go out to eat less often.

The principle that the man is using in his thinking about this is called

A. work capacity,

or

B. stimulus control?

594. The man often reads about what scientists have found out about weight control. He reads an article that explains a way of eating less without being as hungry. The article says that if you divide up the food you will eat in a day into 7 or 8 small amounts, and have one of them every couple of hours, you will keep your level of blood sugar from going too low, and won't feel as tempted to overeat. He tries this strategy and finds that it works well for him. He is able to keep his resolutions a much higher fraction of the time when he uses the principle of eating small amounts often.

He got a useful idea by

A. using organization techniques,

or

B. frequently reading instructions?

595. The man finds himself, without thinking, picking up a cookie. But before he eats it, he thinks, "Wait a second. It's not too late. I can put this back and choose not to eat it." And he does so. As soon as he does, he thinks to himself, "Wow! That's the first time I've ever stopped myself in just that way! That really took self-discipline! Maybe my self-discipline is getting better!"

He is using

A. self-reinforcement

or

B. external reinforcement?

596. The girl writes in her "weight" file in her self-discipline folder:

"12/19/2004: Today I was tempted to lie on the couch and watch a video I was assigned to watch for school. But instead I walked and jogged in place and lifted dumbbells while I was watching it. It took some self-discipline to get started, but once I got going, I felt energized."

This is an example of

A. the internal sales pitch,

or

B. the celebrations exercise?

597. The man keeps a chart. Each morning he weighs himself and writes his weight on the chart.

He also keeps track, each day, of how many calories he eats. He writes down each food he eats and the estimated number of calories it contains, in a piece of paper he keeps in his appointment book. Each morning, when he records his weight, he records the number of calories he ate the previous day. He writes the number on the same chart. He puts yesterday's paper in a stack, and gets a new piece of paper to put into his appointment book.

Then he looks at his pedometer. He also records in his chart the number of steps he took the previous day. Then he resets the pedometer.

He frequently studies his chart and looks for patterns. He sees how his weight responds to his daily calorie total and exercise total.

Recording this information and thinking about it is called

A. modeling,

or

B. self-monitoring?

598. The man monitors himself in the same way every morning at the same time. He even goes in the same order, writing down first his weight, then his calorie total, and then his total number of steps.

He is using

A. routines and momentum

or

B. the right place on the hierarchy of difficulty?

599. The girl breaks her resolution by eating a big piece of pie that is more junk food than she resolved to eat in a day. She finds herself starting to think to herself, "I've blown it. I'll never succeed. I might as well just eat another piece of pie." But then she thinks, "Rather than getting down on myself like that, I want to do some goal-setting

and thinking of options. My goal of weight control is still the same as it always was. My goal right now is to get back on track quickly and not let this little slip throw me off the track. What's a good option for helping myself? I want to get away from this food into a place where there is none."

The technique she is using is

A. choosing among the twelve types of thoughts,
or
B. frequently reading instructions?

600. Later that night before she goes to bed, she thinks back over the things she is proud of. She thinks, "Hooray for me! I was tempted to use those few extra calories as an excuse to go on more of an eating binge, but I didn't! I stopped and cut my losses early! That took real self-discipline! I'm proud of myself!"

She is using

A. the celebrations exercise,
or
B. frequently reading instructions?

601. The man keeps a daily to do list. He writes in his to do list, "Organize office while stepping." When he gets to this item on his list, he sorts through mail, puts some papers into a file cabinet, throws some papers away, and puts objects back into their homes. All the time he is doing this, he is gently

running or walking in place. He is increasing the total number of steps that he accumulates on his pedometer.

He's exercising while using

A. organization techniques,
or
B. external reinforcement?

602. The girl wants to buy some pretty clothes. She makes a deal with her mom that she will do this when she has reached her goal weight and stayed there for one month.

This deal is an example of

A. collecting positive models,
or
B. external reinforcement?

603. The girl notices that she finds it harder not to overeat when she feels like a failure. She has been taking a course in dancing that is very hard because it makes her remember very complicated steps. Each time she gets out of it she feels like a failure.

She decides to transfer into a different dance class, where she doesn't have to remember so much but can just dance joyously. In the new class, she feels that she is succeeding. She is also gradually learning steps that will prepare her for more advanced classes if she ever wants to take them. She finds that after these new classes her self-discipline for resisting overeating is greater.

What she did is an example of

A. restoring persistence power by arranging to get more success experiences,
or
B. using stimulus control by avoiding tempting situations?

Chapter 34: Overcoming Addiction

604. A woman got into the habit of smoking when she was a teenager. Now that she is older, she has not broken the addiction. She has tried to quit smoking many times, but she has always returned to the habit.

Then the woman's aunt gets emphysema. The woman sees the constant discomfort her aunt goes through by not being able to get enough air.

The woman also reads about how whenever she smokes inside, she increases the risk that other people have for getting smoking-related illnesses.

She decides to read a book about smoking. Reading the book and thinking a lot convinces her that stopping smoking should be close to her first priority in life.

She has now done some

A. advanced self-discipline,
or
B. careful goal selection?

605. The woman says to herself, "I've made an important decision. I've spent my time well in reading about it, and I've done something really important by deciding that this is high priority for me. This is an important step toward the goal, and I celebrate it."

She is using

A. stimulus control,
or
B. self-reinforcement?

606. At first she thinks, "I will just quit smoking today, and that's it. I'll suffer the withdrawal and get over it." Then she remembers how bad the withdrawal symptoms have been when she has tried to quit before.

She remembers from her reading how people have used nicotine gum to gradually withdraw from nicotine. So she plans: "I will quit smoking today. I will get some nicotine gum and follow the directions for the use of it. That way I can gradually withdraw from nicotine rather than do it all at once."

She is making a plan that she thinks will be easier for her to follow. This is called trying to

A. pick the right place on the hierarchy of difficulty,
or
B. increase her work capacity?

607. She has a whole carton of cigarettes in her house. She tries to decide what to do with them. She considers keeping them, so that in case she fails to quit smoking, she won't have to waste money buying more cigarettes. But then she thinks to herself, "If I own any cigarettes, they will tempt me. I need to make it as

inconvenient to smoke as I can." So she takes the cigarettes she owns and puts them in the garbage.

She is using the principle of

A. the celebrations exercise,
or
B. stimulus control?

608. She takes a piece of paper and writes on it, "The last cigarette smoked was January 28, 2004! My goal is that this will remain true for the rest of my life!" She tapes this paper on the wall above her desk and she resolves to read it every morning.

This is an example of

A. a written goal, and reading those words often,
or
B. collecting positive models and avoiding negative ones?

609. The woman fears that she will gain weight when she stops smoking. She realizes that her plan to stop smoking should include a plan to avoid gaining weight. She writes down, "I enjoy walking. I want to schedule myself at least an hour a day to go for a walk. This will be a way of having some enjoyment, to make up for the enjoyment of smoking. It will also help me keep from gaining weight."

She is

A. writing an overall plan,
or
B. frequently reading instructions?

610. She writes, "Why stop smoking?
1. I will not cough so much.
2. I will be less likely to get emphysema.
3. I'll be less likely to get lung cancer.
4. I'll be less likely to get a heart attack, stroke, heart failure, bladder cancer, and a lot of other bad diseases.
5. My skin will not shrivel up so fast and I'll not look old so soon.
6. I won't poison other people's air.
7. I won't make children who breathe the smoke more likely to get asthma.
8. I'll save over a thousand dollars a year on cigarettes.
9. I will not have the pain of knowing I should do be doing something and I'm not doing it.
10. I will have the happiness of knowing I've done something difficult but very worthwhile.
11. My clothes will not smell like smoke.
12. I won't have the embarrassment of having to go outside to smoke.
13. My breath won't smell like smoke.
14. My house won't smell like smoke.
15. People will admire me more, and not think of me as a cigarette addict."

What she has written is called the

A. celebrations exercise,
or

B. internal sales pitch?

611. She thinks, "When will I be most tempted to smoke?" She writes down the following list:
"1. There's a lot of work I have to do in a very short time. I'm feeling lots of pressure. I'm in the habit of smoking at moments like this.
2. I am at the convenience store, and I pass the shelf of cigarettes where I always used to buy them before.
3. I need to get a little bit of food, and I want to decide whether to go to the healthy foods grocery store, where there are no cigarettes for sale, or the convenience store."
4. I get into an argument with someone close to me, and I'm feeling very stressed about that.
5. Someone criticizes something I've done.
6. I submit a piece of work and it gets rejected.
7. Someone else who smokes comes over to my house, lights up, and offers me a cigarette.
8. I'm just feeling a strong craving for a cigarette, for no particular reason."

She is

A. listing self-discipline choice points,
or
B. keeping routines and momentum?

612. She thinks about the situation when someone criticizes something that she has written. She decides, "When this happens, I want to think to myself, 'This isn't such a big deal. I don't have to be perfect. I want to use their criticism to make my writing better, if I can. If I don't agree with the criticism, I want not to let it bother me.'"

She is

A. deciding clearly what she would like to do in a choice point,
or
B. using organization techniques?

613. In the example we just looked at, she decided that in the situation of being criticized, she wanted to "not awfulize" and to do "goal setting," instead of "getting down on herself" and "blaming someone else."

So she is wanting to

A. use stimulus control,
or
B. choose consciously among twelve types of thoughts?

614. She practices in her imagination what she will do when she gets a strong craving for a cigarette. She thinks in this way: "I'm at home and I've just finished eating, and I get a strong craving for a cigarette. I think to myself, this is a choice point. Let's see if I can triumph. I will feel really good if I can. I can tough out this feeling. I remind myself of all the reasons I want not to smoke – health, smells, looks, other

people, and money. I'm feeling determined. I'm glad there are no cigarettes in the house. I want to do something useful or enjoyable to get my mind off this craving. I'll go ahead and start my walk outside. Now I'm walking, and I realize that I triumphed in that choice point! Hooray for me!"

This is an example of

A. an external reinforcement,
or
B. a fantasy rehearsal?

615. She is a writer for a newspaper. She decides that she will write an article about people who have successfully stopped smoking. She finds several people who have been successful, and she interviews them. She writes a very interesting article about what techniques they used.

She is

A. using self-reinforcement,
or
B. collecting positive models?

616. As she stays off cigarettes, she keeps track of how much money she has saved. When she has saved a total of $500, she allows herself to take a vacation as a reward for staying off cigarettes.

She is using

A. external reinforcement
or
B. stimulus control?

617. Each night she sets aside a little time to celebrate the things that she is most proud of doing that day. She always celebrates in some way her staying off cigarettes one more day. For example, one day she thinks, "Today when everything seemed to go wrong at work I got the urge to run out and buy some cigarettes and smoke one. But I went right away into the thought routine that I had fantasy rehearsed. I gutted it out without smoking. I'm really glad I did that."

What she is doing each night is called

A. daily plans,
or
B. the celebrations exercise?

618. She also sets aside a little time at least once a week to read some from one of a few books that she has about smoking. Reading these books tends to get her psyched up again and motivated to keep her new habit.

She is

A. frequently reading instructions,
or
B. listing choice points?

619. Exercising, reading, doing the celebrations exercise, and doing fantasy

rehearsals all take time. But she thinks to herself, "The goal is super-important. It's worth much more time than I'm spending on it now, if that is what it takes to be successful. The time I'm spending now is a small price to pay for my really important success."

She is reminding herself of the relationship of success in achieving goals to

A. modeling,

or

B. time on task?

Appendix: The Psychological Skills Inventory

This questionnaire will allow you to rate the "psychological skill" strengths and weaknesses of yourself or someone else. It contains a fairly comprehensive list of the skills people need for psychological health. Each item will ask you to rate the degree of skill in a certain area. Please rate each item according to the following scale:

0 = No skill
2 = Very little skill
4 = Some, but not much skill
6 = Pretty much skill, moderate amount of skill
8 = High amount of skill
10 = Very high amount of skill

Please rate all items.

Group 1: Productivity
_____1. Purposefulness. Having a sense of purpose that drives activity
_____2. Persistence. Sustaining attention, concentrating, focusing, staying on task
_____3. Competence-development. Working toward competence in job, academics, recreation, life skills
_____4. Organization. Organizing goals, priorities, time, money, and physical objects; planfulness

Group 2. Joyousness
_____5. Enjoying aloneness. Having a good time by oneself, tolerating not getting someone's attention
_____6. Pleasure from approval. Enjoying approval, compliments, and positive attention from others
_____7. Pleasure from accomplishments. Self-reinforcement for successes.
_____8. Pleasure from your own kindness. Feeling pleasure from doing kind, loving acts for others
_____9. Pleasure from discovery. Enjoying exploration and satisfaction of curiosity
_____10. Pleasure from others' kindness. Feeling gratitude for what others have done
_____11. Pleasure from blessings. Celebrating and feeling the blessings of luck or fate
_____12. Pleasure from affection. Enjoying physical affection without various fears interfering
_____13. Favorable attractions. Having feelings of attraction aroused in ways consonant with happiness.
_____14. Gleefulness. Playing, becoming childlike, experiencing glee, being spontaneous
_____15. Humor. Enjoying funny things, finding and producing comedy in life

Group 3: Kindness
_____16. Kindness. Nurturing someone, being kind and helpful
_____17. Empathy. Recognizing other people's feelings, seeing things from the other's point of view
_____18. Conscience. Feeling appropriate guilt, avoiding harming others

Group 4: Honesty
_____19. Honesty. Being honest and dependable, especially when it's difficult to be so
_____20. Awareness of your own abilities. Being honest and brave in assessing your strengths and weaknesses

Group 5: Fortitude
_____21. Frustration-tolerance. Handling frustration, tolerating adverse circumstances, fortitude
_____22. Handling separation. Tolerating separation from close others, or loss of a relationship
_____23. Handling rejection. Tolerating it when people don't like or accept you, or don't want to be with you
_____24. Handling criticism. Dealing with disapproval, criticism and lack of respect from others
_____25. Handling mistakes and failures. Regretting mistakes without being overly self-punitive
_____26. Magnanimity, non-jealousy. Handling it when someone else gets what you want

_____27. Painful emotion-tolerance. Avoiding "feeling bad about feeling bad."
_____28. Fantasy-tolerance. Tolerating mental images of unwanted behavior, confident that you will not enact them

Group 6: Good decisions

6a: Individual decision-making
_____29. Positive aim. Aiming toward making things better. Seeking reward and not punishment
_____30. Thinking before acting. Thinking, rather than responding impulsively or by reflex, when it's useful to do so
_____31. Fluency. Using words to conceptualize the world: verbal skills
_____32. Awareness of your emotions. Recognizing, and being able to verbalize your own feelings
_____33. Awareness of control. Accurately assessing the degree of control you have over specific events
_____34. Decision-making. Defining a problem, gathering information, generating options, predicting and evaluating consequences, making a choice

6b: Joint decision-making, including conflict resolution
_____35. Toleration. Non-bossiness. Tolerating a wide range of other people's behavior
_____36. Rational approach to joint decisions. Deciding rationally on stance and strategies for joint decisions

_____37. Option-generating. Generating creative options for solutions to problems

_____38. Option-evaluating. Justice skills: Recognizing just solutions to interpersonal problems

_____39. Assertion. Dominance, sticking up for yourself, taking charge, enjoying winning

_____40. Submission: Conciliation, giving in, conceding, admitting one was wrong, being led

_____41. Differential reinforcement. Reinforcing positive behavior and avoiding reinforcing the negative

Group 7: Nonviolence
_____42. Forgiveness and anger control. Forgiving, handling an insult or injury by another

_____43. Nonviolence. Being committed to the principle of nonviolence and working to foster it

Group 8: Respectful talk, not being rude
_____44. Respectful talk, not being rude. Being sensitive to words, vocal tones, and facial expressions that are accusing, punishing, or demeaning, and avoiding them unless there is a very good reason

Group 9: Friendship-Building
_____45. Discernment and Trusting. Accurately appraising others. Not distorting with prejudice, overgeneralization, wish-fulfilling fantasies. Deciding what someone can

be trusted for, and trusting when appropriate

_____46. Self-disclosure. Disclosing and revealing oneself to another when it's safe

_____47. Gratitude. Expressing gratitude, admiration, and other positive feelings toward others

_____48. Social initiations. Starting social interaction; getting social contact going

_____49. Socializing. Engaging well in social conversation or play.

_____50. Listening. Empathizing, encouraging another to talk about his own experience

Group 10: Self discipline
_____51. Self discipline. Delay of gratification, self-control. Denying yourself present pleasure for future gain

Group 11: Loyalty
_____52. Loyalty. Tolerating and enjoying sustained closeness, attachment, and commitment to another

Group 12: Conservation
_____53. Conservation and Thrift. Preserving resources for ourselves and future generations. Forgoing consumption on luxuries, but using resources more wisely. Financial delay of gratification skills

Group 13: Self-care
_____54. Carefulness. Feeling appropriate fear and avoiding unwise risks

_____55. Habits of self-care. Healthy habits regarding drinking, smoking, drug use, exercise, and diet

_____56. Relaxation. Calming yourself, letting the mind drift pleasantly and the body be at ease

_____57. Self-nurture. Delivering assuring or care-taking thoughts to yourself, feeling comforted thereby

Group 14: Compliance

_____58. Compliance. Obeying, submitting to legitimate and reasonable authority

Group 15: Positive fantasy rehearsal

_____59. Imagination and positive fantasy rehearsal. Using fantasy as a tool in rehearsing or evaluating a plan, or adjusting to an event or situation

Group 16: Courage

_____60. Courage. Estimating danger, overcoming fear of non-dangerous situations, handling danger rationally

_____61. Depending. Accepting help, being dependent without shame, asking for help appropriately

_____62. Independent thinking. Making decisions independently, carrying out actions independently

Annotated Bibliography

Chapter 1: The Meaning and Worth of Self-Discipline

Baumeister RF, Heatherton TF (1996), Self-regulation failure: an overview. *Psychological Inquiry* 7: 1-15
This article does a nice job of defining and illustrating self-regulation and its failures. In the language I use in this book, this article has to do with self-discipline and how it is that people give in to temptations.

Freud S (1911), Formulations regarding the two principles in mental functioning. In *Collected Papers, Volume 4*. New York: Basic Books, 1959
This is a good article to show us that the ideas of working toward long-term goals and giving in to temptations are not new. Freud wrote about these ideas, calling them the "reality principle" and the "pleasure principle" respectively.

Logue AW, (1995), *Self-Control: Waiting Until Tomorrow For What You Want Today*. Englewood Cliffs, New Jersey: Prentice-Hall
An excellent and enlightening overview of research on self-control.

Mischel W (1974), Processes in delay of gratification. In L Berkowitz (Ed.), *Adv Exp Soc Psychol* (Vol 7 pp 249-292), New York: Academic Press

Mischel W, Ebbesen EB, Zeiss AR (1972), Cognitive and attentional mechanisms in delay of gratification. *J Pers Soc Psychol* 21: 204-218
Mischel W, Metzner R (1962), Preference for delayed reward as a function of age, intelligence, and length of delay interval. *J Abnorm Soc Psychol* 64: 425-431
Mischel W, Shoda Y, Peake PK (1988), The nature of adolescent competencies predicted by preschool delay of gratification. *J Pers Soc Psychol* 54: 687-696
Mischel W, Shoda Y, Rodriguez ML (1989), Delay of gratification in children. *Science* 244: 933-938
Patterson CJ, Mischel W (1975), Plans to resist distraction. *Dev Psychol* 11: 369-378
Patterson CJ, Mischel W (1976), Effects of temptation-inhibiting and task-facilitating plans on self-control. *J Pers Soc Psychol* 33: 209-217
Rodgriguez ML, Mischel W, Shoda Y (1989), Cognitive person variables in the delay of gratification of older children at risk. *J Pers Soc Psychol* 57: 358-367
These are some of the pioneering articles on delay of gratification published by Walter Mischel and his colleagues.

Schweitzer JB, Sulzer-Azaroff B (1988), Self-control: Teaching tolerance for delay in impulsive children. *J Exp Anal Behav* 50: 173-186

Near the end of chapter 1 I posed the question, what would happen if Mischel's subjects could have been taught delay of gratification skills? The Schweitzer and Sulzer-Azaroff study found that children could be taught to delay gratification, at least in a very specific situation, namely a paradigm like the one Mischel used.

Strayhorn JM (2002), Self-control: theory and research. *J Amer Acad Child Adol Psychiat*, 41, 7-16.

Strayhorn JM (2002), Self-control: toward systematic training programs. *Jl Amer Acad Child Adol Psychiat*, 41, 17-27

These are a couple of articles I wrote. They review the literature on self-discipline and try to emphasize the most important ideas. I especially searched for ideas related to training people in self-control or self-discipline.

Chapter 2: Types of Self-Discipline Choice Points

American Psychiatric Association (1994), *Diagnostic and Statistical Manual of Mental Disorders, Fourth Edition.* Washington, DC, American Psychiatric Association

If you read the official criteria for various disorders, you may be struck, as I was, with how many disorders have as part of their definition impulsivity, the inability to work for long-term goals, and difficulties with delay of gratification.

Baumeister RF, Heatherton TF, Tice DM (1994), *Losing Control: How and Why People Fail at Self-Regulation.* San Diego: Academic Press

A very important work on the subject of self-regulation. This book covers the relationship of self-discipline skills to a wide number of the sorts of problems covered in this chapter.

Black DW, Moyer T (1998), Clinical features and psychiatric comorbidity of subjects with pathological gambling behavior. *Psychiatr Serv* 49:1434-1439

This article gives evidence that the people who have pathological gambling problems tend to have other self-control problems as well, particularly substance abuse.

Gottfredson MR, Hirschi T (1990), *A General Theory of Crime.* Stanford, CA: Stanford University Press

This book argues that a high fraction of problems of criminal behavior are traceable to self-control problems.

Jessor R, Donovan JE, Costa FM (1991), *Beyond Adolescence: Problem Behavior and Young Adult Behavior.* New York: Cambridge University Press

Jessor and colleagues' research gave us evidence that people with one sort of self-discipline problem tended to have other ones as well; the problems are correlated.

Chapter 3: Attitudes Toward People With Self-Discipline Problems

Baumrind D (1967), Child care practices anteceding three patterns of preschool behavior. *Genet Psychol Monogr* 75: 43-88
This study concludes that a harsh and punitive style of parenting doesn't lead to optimum self-control.

Skinner BF (1953), *Science and Human Behavior*. New York: Macmillan
Skinner was a very articulate spokesman for the idea that influencing behavior by shaping and positive reinforcement is greatly to be preferred to influence by punishment. Shaming and blaming are forms of punishment to which Skinner's arguments apply.

Chapter 4: What's the Point of Self-Discipline? Choosing Goals

Bandura A (1996), Failures in self-regulation: Energy depletion or selective disengagement? *Psychol Inquiry* 7: 20-24
Bandura discussed the usefulness of breaking long-term, or distal goals, into smaller steps, or proximal goals.
Piaget J (1962), Will and action. *Bull Menninger Clin* 26: 144
Piaget argued that the strength of motivation toward a goal was the central determinant of will power or self-control.

Shapiro D (1996), The "self-control" muddle. *Psychol Inquiry* 7: 76-79
Shapiro also argues that strongly held goals are central to self-control.

Chapter 5: The Internal Sales Pitch

Miller WR, Rollnick S (2002), *Motivational Interviewing*. New York: The Guilford Press.
Motivational interviewing is certainly more than getting someone to make an internal sales pitch list. But the philosophy of this technique is very much in keeping with that of the internal sales pitch: it encourages the seeker of self-discipline to take an active role in finding the reasons for change that are motivating to him or her.

Chapter 6: Plans for Goals: Overall Plans and Daily Plans

Lakein, A (1973), *How To Get Control of Your Time and Your Life*. New York: The New American Library (Signet).
Lakein's book is in my opinion the classic self-help guide to time management. One of the best aspects of this book is his directions and examples of how to form goals and translate them into daily to do list items.

Chapter 7: Finding the Right Place on the Hierarchy of Difficulty

Csikszentmihalyi M (1990*), Flow: The Psychology of Optimal Experience.* New York: Harper Perennial
One of the major points of this mind-expanding book is that optimal experience, happiness, and a feeling of "flow" are very closely associated with striving in activities that are at the correct level of challenge for your current level of skills.

Chapter 8: Anticipating and Listing Self-Discipline Choice Points

Chapter 9: Fantasy Rehearsal

Berthoz A (1996), The role of inhibition in the hierarchical gating of executed and imagined movements. *Brain Res Cognitive Brain Res* 3: 101-113
Kazdin AE (1982), The separate and combined effects of covert and overt rehearsal in developing assertive behavior. *Behav Res Ther* 20: 17-25
Suinn, RM (1972) Behavior rehearsal training for ski racers. *Behavior Therapy* 3, 519-520.
Wieselberg N, Dyckman JM, Abramowitz SI(1979), The desensitization derby: in vivo down the backstretch, imaginal at the wire? *J Clin Psychol* 35: 647-650
The above are four of many studies that contribute to the conclusion that fantasy rehearsal works similarly to the way real-life rehearsal does. The Suinn (1972) study is the experiment with ski racers I mentioned in the text. I also

referred to the Berthoz (1996) study, in mentioning the similarity of brain activity with imagined movements and movements actually carried out.

Chapter 10: Self-Reinforcement of Steps Toward Goals, or Internal Shaping
Ducharme JM, Atkinson L, Poulton L (2000), Success-based, noncoercive treatment of oppositional behavior in children from violent homes. *J Amer Acad Child Adolesc Psychiatry* 39: 995-1004
This is one of several studies by Ducharme and colleagues which demonstrate the effectiveness of shaping in overcoming some tough problems.

Chapter 11: The Celebrations Exercise
Strayhorn JM (2001), *Exercises For Psychological Skills.* Wexford, PA: Psychological Skills Press
The celebrations exercise, and several others mentioned in this book, are some of over fifty exercises I described in this compendium of ways to practice psychological skills.

Chapter 12: External Reinforcement
Eisenberger R Cameron J (1996), Detrimental effects of reward: Reality or myth? *Am Psychol* 51: 1153-1166
This is a very important article, countering the idea that extrinsic rewards take away one's intrinsic motivation for a task. The take-home

message is that external reinforcement usually makes something more fun, not less.

Kazdin AE (1982b), The token economy: A decade later. *J Appl Behav Anal* 15:431-435
An insightful article about the token economy, one form of external reinforcement.

Chapter 13: Self-Monitoring

Baker RC, Kirschenbaum DS (1998), Weight control during the holidays: highly consistent self-monitoring as a potentially useful coping mechanism. *Health Psychol* 17: 367-370
Boutelle KN, Kirschenbaum DS(1998), Further support for consistent self-monitoring as a vital component of successful weight control. *Obesity Res* 6: 219-224
These studies demonstrate the usefulness of self-monitoring. The context is that very difficult self-discipline arena, weight control.

Chapter 14: More on Advanced Self-Discipline

Solomon RL (1980), The opponent-process theory of acquired motivation: The costs of pleasure and the benefits of pain. *Am Psychol* 35: 691-712
"Acquired motivation" is the process by which you come to enjoy doing something that at first you didn't enjoy. Solomon's theory speaks of habituation

to the aversive elements of the situation, as well as other mechanisms.

Chapter 15: More on Work Capacity

Eisenberger R (1992), Learned industriousness. *Psychol Rev* 99 248-267
Eisenberger R, Masterson FA, Lowman K (1982), Effects of previous delay of reward, generalized effort, and deprivation on impulsiveness. *Learning and Motivation* 13: 378-389

Eisenberger R, Adornetto M (1986), Generalized self-control of delay and effort. *J Pers Soc Psychol* 51: 1020-1031
Eisenberger R, Mitchell M, Masterson FA (1985), Effort training increases generalized self-control. *J Pers Soc Psychol* 49: 1294-1301
Eisenberger R, Weier F, Masterson FA, Theis LY (1989), Fixed-ratio schedules increase generalized self-control: preference for large rewards despite high effort or punishment. *J Exp Psychol: Anim Behav Process* 15: 383-392

The works of Eisenberger and colleagues contain very important findings about the increase of work capacity through practice.

Muraven M, Baumeister RF, Tice DM (1999), Longitudinal improvement of self-regulation through practice: Building self-control strength through

repeated exercise. *J Soc Psychol* 139: 446-457
An important article, giving evidence that repeated practice of self-control tends to increase it.

Seligman MEP (1975), *Helplessness. On Depression, Development, and Death*. San Francisco: WH Freeman and Company
Seligman's ground-breaking research established that helplessness, where effort has no connection to rewards, tends to cause depression. Conversely, what I call here the effort-payoff connection, otherwise known as contingent reinforcement, is a very powerful antidepressant and producer of happiness.

Chapter 16: Using Stimulus Control

Miltenberger RG (1997) *Behavior Modification: Principles and Procedures*. Pacific Grove, CA: Brooks/Cole Publishing Company.
This text reviews research literature in applied behavior analysis. Miltenberger uses the term "antecedent manipulations" or "antecedent control" to refer to efforts to arrange stimulus situations for best results. See especially Chapter 14, "Antecedent Control Procedures," and Chapter 19, "Antecedent Manipulations to Decrease Problem Behaviors."

Chapter 17: Momentum Effects: Getting on a Roll

Baumeister RF, Heatherton TF, Tice DM (1994), *Losing Control: How and Why People Fail At Self-Regulation*. San Diego: Academic Press
Baumeister and colleagues' book has an excellent discussion of momentum effects.

Marlatt GA (1985), Relapse prevention: Theoretical rationale and overview of the model. In: *Relapse Prevention*, Marlatt GA, Gordon JR, eds. New York: Guilford, pp 3-70
Marlatt reports and examines the research on the momentum in self-regulatory efforts.

Chapter 18: Organization Skills for Self-Discipline

Winston, S (1978). *Getting Organized: The Easy Way To Put Your Life In Order*. New York: Warner Books.
Winston, S (1983), *The Organized Executive: New Ways To Manage Time, Paper, and People*. New York: Warner Books.
These books are classics in the field of organization skills. I would only quibble with the word *easy* in one of the subtitles!

Chapter 19: Self-Talk and the Twelve Types of Thoughts

Beck AT (1976) *Cognitive Therapy and the Emotional Disorders*. Madison, CT: International Universities Press.
This is one of the earliest books on cognitive therapy by one of its founders.

Burns DD (1980) *Feeling Good: The New Mood Therapy*. New York: Penguin.
A very useful self-help book on taking control of your own self-talk to overcome depression.

Dush DM, Hirt ML, Schroeder HE (1989), Self-statement modification in the treatment of child behavior disorders: a meta-analysis. *Psychol Bull* 106: 97-106
The bottom line of this meta-analysis is that self-statement modification works, even though the average "time on task" the participants spent in these studies seems to me to be so small that I would not have expected much effect.

Meichenbaum, D (1977), *Cognitive-Behavior Modification: An Integrative Approach*. New York: Plenum Press
A pioneering work on the modification of self-talk and cognitive therapy.

Strayhorn JM (2001), *Programmed Readings For Psychological Skills*. Wexford, PA: Psychological Skills Press.
The categorization of thoughts into the twelve categories described in this chapter is original with me. In the 1970's I wrote The Journey Exercise, which is now published as part of Programmed Readings for Psychological Skills. This is a story which gives practice in classifying thoughts into these categories.

Chapter 20: Modeling

Bandura A, Mischel W (1965), Modification of self-imposed delay of reward through exposure to live and symbolic models. *J Pers Soc Psychol* 2: 698-705
This is the study, mentioned in this book, where modeling was shown to influence children's willingness to choose larger delayed rewards over smaller immediate rewards.

Gandhi MK (1948) *Autobiography: The Story of My Experiments with Truth*. Translated by Muhadev Desai. New York: Dover Publications, 1983.
Gandhi is perhaps the greatest "peace hero" of recent times. I quoted from this book to illustrate how children may be influenced, for better or for worse, by works of fiction. Gandhi felt that he was very much influenced for the better by some fictional works that moved him greatly during his childhood.

Mazur JE (1998) *Learning and Behavior. Fourth edition*. Upper Saddle River, New Jersey: Prentice-Hall.
Mazur's text on learning theory and behavior modification has an excellent chapter entitled "Learning by Observation."

Meltzoff AN, Moore MK (1977) Imitation of facial and manual gestures by human neonates. *Science*, 198, 75-78.
Meltzoff AN, Moore MK (1989) Imitation in newborn infants: Exploring the range of gestures imitated and the underlying mechanisms. *Developmental Psychology* 25, 954-962.
I mentioned the Meltzoff and Moore studies in the chapter on modeling. These studies show us that we human beings don't just learn to imitate – we seem to be born with an innate urge to imitate.

Stumphauzer JS (1972), Increased delay of gratification in young prison inmates through imitation of high-delay peer models. *J Pers Soc Psychol* 21: 10-17
A study finding that modeling is helpful in teaching delay of gratification behavior.

Chapter 21: Reading the Instructions

Ackerson J, Scogin F, McKendree-Smith N, Lyman RD (1998), Cognitive bibliotherapy for mild and moderate adolescent depressive symptomatology. *J Consult Clin Psychol* 66:685-690
Reading instructions on how not to be depressed seemed to work for the adolescents in this study.

Apodaca TR, Miller WR (2003) A meta-analysis of the effectiveness of bibliotherapy for alcohol problems. J Clin Psychol 59:289-304
While reading instructions did not perform miracles for problem drinkers, there was considerable evidence for its helping with this problem.

Chapter 22: Time on Task

Berliner DC (1990), What's all the fuss about instructional time? In Berliner, D.C., *The Nature of Time in Schools: Theoretical Concepts, Practitioner Perceptions*. New York and London: Teachers College Press.
Discusses, in a sophisticated way, the relationship of time on task to academic achievement.

Bloom BS (1985), *Developing Talent in Young People*. New York: Ballentine Books
A study, mentioned in this chapter, of talented achievers. One of the findings was that the achievers had all worked for many, many hours at their skills.

Lovaas OI (1987), Behavioral treatment and normal educational and intellectual functioning in young autistic children. *J Consult Clin Psychol*, 55, 3-9.
McEachin JJ, Smith T, Lovaas OI (1993), Long-term outcomes for children with autism who received early intensive behavioral treatment. *Am J Mental Retardation*, 97, 359-372.
Sallows GO, Graupner TD (1999), Replicating Lovaas' treatment and findings: preliminary results. Presented

at the annual meeting of the Autism Society of America, Kansas City, Missouri, July 1999.
The work of Ivar Lovaas with autistic children was mentioned in this chapter. These articles report empirical tests of his method. I regard these studies as heroic efforts in the application of "time on task" to the training of children.

Scheerens J, Bosker R (1997), *The Foundations of Educational Effectiveness*. New York: Elsevier. These authors rank ordered nine school variables with respect to how effectively they promoted academic success. Time on task was first on the list.

Chapter 23: Ways to Get Back Your Persistence Power

Muraven M, Tice DM, Baumeister RF (1998), Self-control as a limited resource: regulatory depletion patterns. *J Pers Soc Psychol* 74: 774-789
A very important study, contributing evidence that self-control in the short run can be depleted by certain tasks, in ways that carry over to different self-control tasks.

Strayhorn JM, Bickel DD (2002), Reduction in children's symptoms of attention deficit hyperactivity disorder and oppositional defiant disorder during individual tutoring as compared with

classroom instruction. *Psychological Reports* 91, 69-80.
Much of what I say in Chapter 23 on the power of success experiences in increasing persistence power is based on watching what children do when individual tutoring allows them to experience success a high enough fraction of the time. The above study had to do with this phenomenon.

Chapter 25: Preparing for a Test

Rowntree D (1983) *Learn How to Study: A Programmed Introduction to Better Study Techniques*. New York: Charles Scribner's Sons.
This text teaches the SQ3R technique: survey, question, read, recall, review. The principle of asking questions, answering them, and checking your answers is similar to what I recommend in this chapter.

Chapter 26: Doing Written Assignments

Proffitt E (1992) *The Organized Writer: A Brief Rhetoric*. Mountain View, California: Mayfield Publishing Company.
The GIOW format for stages of writing (generation, inclusion, ordering, and wording) is original with me. The author of this book gives similar advice about writing, with respect to one crucial point: you should separate writing tasks into stages and not try to do everything at once.

Chapter 27: Improving Concentration

Fontani G, Lodi L (2002) Reactivity and event-related potentials in attentional tests: effect of training. *Percept Mot Skills* 94:817-833

Giaquinto S, Fraioli L (2003) Enhancement of the somatosensory N140 component during attentional training after stroke. *Clin Neurophysiol* 114:329-335

These are examples of articles describing programs in which people are trained in the art of paying attention or selective attention, through repetitive practice and feedback with an attention-demanding task.

Chapter 28: Thinking Before Acting

Barkley RA (1997a), *ADHD and the Nature of Self-Control*. New York: Guilford Press
Barkley RA (1997b), Behavioral inhibition, sustained attention, and executive functions: constructing a unifying theory of ADHD. *Psychol Bull*, 121: 65-94
These works by Barkley point out that the problems of Attention Deficit Hyperactivity Disorder, such as trouble concentrating, certain interpersonal difficulties, and insufficient thinking before acting, may all usefully viewed as varieties of self-control problems.

Chapter 30: Nonviolence and Respectful Talk
Meichenbaum D (2001) *Treatment of Individuals with Anger-Control Problems and Aggressive Behaviors: A Clinical Handbook*. Clearwater, FL: Institute Press.
This book is a great resource on anger management and the promotion of nonviolence.

Chapter 31: Sleep and Waking

Wolfson AR, Carskadon MA (2003) Understanding adolescents' sleep patterns and school performance: a critical appraisal. *Sleep Med Rev* 7:491-506
Erratic sleep schedules and later bedtimes and waking times in students from middle school through college are associated with poorer academic performance.

Watanabe T, Kajimura N, Kato M, Sekimoto M, Nakajima T, Hori T, Takahashi K (2003), Sleep and circadian rhythm disturbances in patients with delayed sleep phase syndrome. *Sleep* 26:657-661
This article explains some of the disturbances with delayed sleep phase syndrome, the problem associated with going to bed and getting up late.

Chapter 32: Thrill-Seeking

Kosten TA, Ball SA, Rounsaville BJ (1994) A sibling study of sensation seeking and opiate addiction. *J Nerv Ment Dis* 182:284-289

Mawson AR, Jacobs KW, Winchester Y, Biundo JJ (1988) Sensation-seeking and traumatic spinal cord injury: case-control study. *Arch Phys Med Rehabil* 69:1039-1043

Mawson AR, Biundo JJ, Clemmer DI, Jacobs KW, Ktsanes VK, Rice JC Biundo JJ Jr (1996) Sensation-seeking, criminality, and spinal cord injury: a case- control study. *Am J Epidemiol* 144:463-472

Patkar AA, Murray HW, Mannelli P, Gottheil E, Weinstein SP, Vergare MJ (2004), Pre-treatment measures of impulsivity, aggression and sensation seeking are associated with treatment outcome for African-American cocaine-dependent patients. *J Addict Dis* 23:109-122

Joireman J, Anderson J, Strathman A (2003), The aggression paradox: understanding links among aggression, sensation seeking, and the consideration of future consequences. *J Pers Soc Psychol* 84:1287-1302

These articles help us understand the challenges that sensation-seekers (a.k.a. thrill-seekers or stimulus-seekers) have in life. Those of us with this trait have to work harder to avoid drug abuse, aggression, and severe injury.

Chapter 33: Weight Control

Kirschenbaum, D (2000), *The Nine Truths About Weight Loss: The No-Tricks, No-Nonsense Plan for Lifelong Weight Control*. New York: Henry Holt and Company.
This is one of the most "evidence-based" works on weight control that is available. You'll notice his title doesn't include the word *easy*!

Chapter 34: Overcoming Addiction

Bishop FM (2001) *Managing Addictions: Cognitive, Emotive, and Behavioral Techniques*. Lanham, MD: Rowman and Littlefield.
Ellis A, Velten E (1992) *When AA Doesn't Work For You: Rational Steps to Quitting Alcohol*. Fort Lee, NJ: Barricade Books.

Both of these books present cognitive-behavioral approaches to overcoming addiction. Ellis is one of the founders of cognitive therapy.

Appendix 1: The Psychological Skills Inventory

Strayhorn JM (1988), *The Competent Child: An Approach to Psychotherapy and Preventive Mental Health*. New York: Guilford Press

In this book I advanced the theory of the psychological skills axis, a fairly comprehensive list of the psychological skills one needs for mental health. Self-discipline is a very important one of them.

Index

CPSIA information can be obtained at www.ICGtesting.com
Printed in the USA
LVOW121400040612

284578LV00005B/116/A